P.H. Sable

"JENNIE may be the finest British product ever seen in this country!"
—*Variety*

The Inimitable
JENNIE

At nineteen, she dismayed English society by marrying the son of the Duke of Marlborough; at forty-six, she outraged them by marrying a guards officer twenty years her junior.

Vivacious, beautiful, mother of Winston Churchill, the man who led England in its finest hour, she combined American daring with an emancipated European love-style, dazzling and daunting the whole of British aristocracy with an insatiable zest for living and an unquenchable thirst for romance that has marked her forever as one of the most fascinating women in history!

D1306928

JENNIE
Lady Randolph Churchill

A Portrait with Letters

Peregrine Churchill
and
Julian Mitchell

BALLANTINE BOOKS • NEW YORK

Copyright © 1974 by Thames Television Limited

All rights reserved.

Library of Congress Catalog Card Number: 74-14403

SBN 345-25019-2-195

This edition published by arrangement with
St. Martin's Press, Inc.

First Printing: January, 1976

Printed in the United States of America

BALLANTINE BOOKS
A Division of Random House, Inc.
201 East 50th Street, New York, N.Y. 10022
Simultaneously published by
Ballantine Books of Canada, Ltd., Toronto, Canada

CONTENTS

PREFACE

It is hard to believe, in the age of the telephone, how many hours a day an Edwardian society lady spent scribbling notes and letters. First there was the family: husband away shooting or fishing, perhaps, sons at school, daughters being 'finished', mother and father in the country, brothers and sisters married and scattered, in-laws, cousins—all of whom had to be kept informed of what one was doing and where one was dining. Then there were close friends in England, and distant ones in India or South Africa or America, who required regular bulletins from the home country.

There might be one special friend, too, rather closer than close. On top of all that, there was the whole demanding business of issuing and answering invitations and writing thank-you letters, without which the social round could not be kept going. Finally, and very much last, there were tradesmen to be dealt with, and their tiresome bills. One lady's lifetime correspondence would fill a house.

Jennie Jerome, Lady Randolph Churchill, did not keep absolutely everything, but she kept a great deal. She once wrote what a great boon a tell-tale scrap of paper could be for a playwright, novelist or historian, and as a playwright herself, perhaps she had future dramatists in mind as she carefully put away her private correspondence. One of these is extremely grateful that she did, for it is on the papers she left at her death that Julian Mitchell has based his seven scripts for the Thames Television series, *Jennie: Lady Randolph Churchill*. The letters to be found there are a family chronicle in themselves, recording how domestic dramas and public events affected both Jennie and her husband Lord Randolph, and revealing the gradual development of their sons Winston and Jack.

Among Jennie's papers, for instance, are all the letters Randolph ever wrote her, and nearly all hers to him. She kept every ink-blot from her sons, too. And though her second marriage to George Cornwallis-West ended in the divorce court, she never destroyed his love-letters. Then there is a long correspondence from the Prince of Wales, later Edward VII: there are several files about *The Anglo-Saxon Review,* the short-lived literary magazine which Jennie edited: there are some most revealing letters from her mother-in-law, the Duchess of Marlborough. But there are gaps, too, and significant ones. For instance, one of the greatest loves of Jennie's life was the Austrian diplomat Count Kinsky, but only one letter and one telegram from him are to be found among her papers, and those from long after their affair was over. There is nothing whatever about Jennie's not very successful play, *His Borrowed Plumes,* perhaps because George Cornwallis-West went off with the leading lady. And Jennie kept surprisingly few letters from her parents and sisters.

Some of the missing letters may turn up in time, but it has been the material actually available which has dictated the form of this book. It is not a full biography of Jennie: instead, we have tried to draw a portrait with letters, selecting particular moments in her life, and using the documents to throw new light upon them. Jennie's papers contain far more letters than we could possibly hope to publish, and many of them are naturally of little interest to a modern reader. Furthermore, a good many have already been published in the excellent life of Sir Winston Churchill, begun by his son Randolph, and now being completed by Martin Gilbert. We have not felt we need reprint more than a few of these: our subject is Jennie, not her famous son, and we have played down his role in this book deliberately. For the same reason, we have not tried to give more than the outline of Lord Randolph Churchill's political career, a subject of enormous and enduring interest in itself, but going well beyond the scope of an intimate portrait. Nonetheless we believe we have answered some previously puzzling questions and corrected a good many errors, some of them damaging, about Jennie's life. We hope we have shown her as she really was.

We have silently corrected spelling errors, removed insignificant repetitions, expanded obscure contractions, capitalized words according to modern convention, and have sometimes added the punctuation to avoid obscurity. Something very characteristic would be lost from Jennie's letters if we put commas and full stops instead of her almost invariable dashes. French phrases have been left as written: the less obvious ones have been translated in notes at the end of each chapter. The source of each letter or quotation can be found in the references at the end of the book.

We are most grateful to all those who have given us permission to quote from letters in which they hold copyright: the Duke of Marlborough (the Duke and Duchess of Marlborough and the Marquess of Blandford), Lady Mary Grosvenor (Shelagh, Duchess of Westminster), Mr. J. H. Pless (Daisy, Princess of Pless), John Farquharson Ltd (Henry James), Baroness Spencer-Churchill (Clementine Churchill), Mrs. Bryda Hill-Murray (Montagu Porch), the Earl of Rosebery), Mr Seymour Leslie (Leonie Leslie), the Hon. Mark Bonham Carter (Lady Violet Bonham Carter), Viscount Scarsdale (Lord and Lady Curzon), Mrs E. J. Spurrier (Lady Warwick), Prince F. U. Kinsky (Count Kinsky), Lady Leslie (Shane Leslie), Miss E. M. Watson (George Cornwallis-West). In some cases it has been impossible to trace the holders of copyright. Will any copyright holders who have not been acknowledged, please accept the authors' apologies? Copyright in the papers of Lord and Lady Randolph Churchill, Major John Churchill and Lady Gwendeline Churchill belongs to Mr Peregrine Churchill. The Chartwell Trust, the Duke of Marlborough, Miss Anita Leslie and Mr. Seymour Leslie have kindly allowed us to quote from letters in their possession.

We are also grateful to the following publishers for permission to quote from the works mentioned: William Heinemann Ltd (*Winston S. Churchill* by Randolph S. Churchill and Martin Gilbert), Hutchinson & Co. Ltd (*The Fabulous Leonard Jerome, Jennie* and *Edwardians in Love,* all by Anita Leslie), John Murray Ltd (*Parliamentary Reminiscences* by Lord George Hamilton, *From My Private Diary* by Daisy, Princess of Pless, and *The Jerome Connexion* by Seymour Leslie), the Hamlyn Publishing Group Ltd (*Lord Randolph Churchill* and *My Early Life* by Winston S. Churchill), and the Bodley Head Ltd (*Edwardian Hey-Days* by George Cornwallis-West). All these books have proved extremely useful, as has *Perfect Darling* by Eileen Quelch, Jennie's own books, *The Reminiscences of Lady Randolph Churchill* and *Small Talks on Big Subjects,* and her contributions to *The Anglo-Saxon Review,* were also invaluable.

We are indebted to many people for their help, especially Lady Betty Cartwright, Mrs Peregrine Churchill, Mr Martin Gilbert, Mr David Green, Mr John Hambley, Dr M. A. Hoskin, Miss Anita Leslie, Mr Seymour Leslie, Miss Eileen Quelch, Miss Angela Raspin, Mr Richard Rowson, Professor Peter Stansky, Miss Elizabeth Thomas and Miss Alison Wade, who helped most of all.

INTRODUCTION

Jennie Jerome, christened Jeanette, was born on January 9th, 1854 in Brooklyn, New York. In 1874 she married Lord Randolph Spencer Churchill, the younger son of the Duke of Marlborough. Their eldest son became Sir Winston Churchill.

Randolph came from the old world, Jennie from the new. The Spencers and Churchills had played leading parts in the history of the British Isles over the course of four centuries. The Jeromes had emigrated from England to America in the early eighteenth century, and had, until Jennie's father's generation, made no mark on history at all. Yet it was the combination of these extremely different families which produced the greatest British statesman of the twentieth century.

The Spencers first came to notice under the Tudors when they were successful sheep-farmers; later they achieved fame when they married into the Sydneys, a more ancient family of soldiers and statesmen. The Churchills were solid West Country folk, rather close to the earth. A link with Sir Francis Drake's family produced John Churchill, the brilliant general whom Queen Anne created first Duke of Marlborough in 1702. The Spencers and Churchills came together through the marriage of the first Duke's daughter to Charles Spencer, Earl of Sunderland. The Duke having no surviving male issue, his titles descended through this female line. The surname Spencer-Churchill was not in fact adopted till 1817.

For a hundred years and more after the death of John Churchill, the Dukes of Malborough were distinguished mainly for their colossal extravagance. Though the ducal income was vast, they spent it and more. It was not until Randolph's father that a Marlborough again became a national figure of any importance. John Winston, the seventh Duke, was serious and puritanical: he took a passionate interest in Church reform. He was married to Frances Anne Emily Vane, daughter of the Marquess of Londonderry. His mother-in-law was a great political hostess and close friend of Disraeli, and with his wife's encouragement the Duke soon became a political figure in his own right. In 1867 he became Lord President of the Council, and a Cabinet Minister. Thus Randolph grew up in an atmosphere which was as political as it was aristocratic.

Jennie's background was neither. Her father, Leonard Jerome, was born in 1818, one of the large family of a farmer in Syracuse, in upper New York State. The Jeromes were not rich, though they were prosperous. It was Leonard's elder brothers who unselfishly paid for his education at Princeton, and even so there was not enough money for him to complete his degree there. He worked first in his uncle's law office in Palmyra, then bought the local newspaper at Rochester with his younger brother. In 1847 he married Clarissa, or Clara, Hall, one of three orphaned heiresses. Clara's great-grandmother was reputed to be an Iroquois squaw. True or not, the Hall sisters were dark and appeared more Red Indian as they grew old, and Clara was known as 'Sitting Bull' by her impertinent sons-in-law. The Jeromes soon moved to New York, where Leonard rapidly made a fortune on the stock exchange.

The marriage was a triumph—and later a failure—of opposites. Leonard liked racing and yachting, patronized the opera, and had a weakness for female opera singers. He had been passionately fond of music since his boyhood. Clara was rather puritanical, and practically tone-deaf. Her ambitions were social.

Their first daughter, also called Clara, was born in 1851. Shortly after her birth the family went to Europe for nearly two years, for Leonard had been appointed American Consul in Trieste. Europe, Mrs. Jerome decided, was where she really wanted to live. But Leonard lost his first fortune and had to make another before they could leave New York again. It did not take him long. In 1858, when Jennie was four, the Jeromes went to live in Paris, where their last daughter, Leonie, was born in 1859. (A fourth girl died in childhood.) The family returned to America in 1860, to a splendid mansion which Leonard built in Madison Square: for the opening ball there were fountains of champagne and eau de Cologne: he liked things to be on a lavish scale. But after the Civil War, when he plunged again into a hurly-burly life of business, sport, and special performances by favoured singers in his private theatre. Mrs. Jerome decided she could live a more dignified life in Europe. Although there was nothing the matter with her at all, she announced that her health made it imperative for her to live in Paris; besides, Paris was the only possible place to educate one's daughters. In 1868 she settled there with Clara, Jennie and Leonie: Leonard paid regular visits, but his home remained New York.

Paris was everything Mrs Jerome desired. The Emperor Napoleon III and the Empress Eugénie accepted Americans with none of the haughtiness of other European monarchs, and wealth was a sufficient passport to social success. Mrs. Jerome took on a new lease of life: she wrote her name with French accents, Jérôme, and Jennie became Jeannette, with two Ns. Mrs Jerome even began to take an interest in music, and could be heard to hum the simpler leitmotivs of Wagner.

Jennie was fourteen now, and must have peeped with longing from behind the schoolroom door when Princes and Princesses paid their calls, and listened with impatience and envy to her sister Clara's thrilling descriptions of life at the Imperial court. But she must have missed her father, too, for she was his favourite. She loved to ride, like him, and she shared his passion for music: she could play the piano to concert standard. She had a natural eye for the fine arts: in later life she could never resist acquiring things of beauty whether she could afford them or not. But in spite of the close bond between father and daughter,

Jennie's ambitions were Parisian ones. In only another year or two she would make her début at that glittering Imperial court.

But, alas, in 1870 came the Franco-Prussian war, with Paris besieged by the Germans. The Jeromes were among the last to flee. Mrs Jerome, hobbling with a sprained ankle, just got her daughters on to the last train to Deauville. Leonard, who was taking part in the first international Atlantic yacht-race, hurried to the rescue, and installed his family in London. But London was not a success. English society was as cold as the climate, and the news from France grew worse and worse. When the Jeromes returned to Paris it was to a very mournful city. The Emperor was deposed, the Tuileries Palace was in ruins. There was no court, no society, nowhere for an ambitious American girl to make her début. All the Jeromes had to look forward to was their annual visit to England, and Cowes regatta. Usually Leonard came too, but in 1873 he was busy in New York, having just lost his fortune again. So he was not there when Jennie was presented to the Prince and Princess of Wales. It wasn't the same as an Imperial presentation, of course, but it was the best she could hope for.

1

COURTSHIP

Cowes, in the Isle of Wight, was in 1873, as it is now, the yacht-racing centre of the world. Led by the Prince of Wales, who took a keen part in the racing itself, fashionable British society came down to the little seaside village to relax after the rigours of the London season. Queen Victoria lived close by at Osborne, the house she had built with her husband, Prince Albert, but the chill formality which her name implied did not extend beyond the walls of her estate. Cowes itself was a delightful place to gossip and flirt and watch the boats and go on picnics. Everyone knew everyone else, and there were no glorified villas or piers or bands or nigger minstrels, and there weren't, Jennie wrote later, too many yachts for too few moorings. It was all very casual and charming. At Cowes the Prince and Princess of Wales could stroll about without ceremony and enjoy themselves like ordinary mortals.

Albert Edward, Prince of Wales, was thirty-two in 1873, and his reputation for fast living was already well established. He was a welcome and regular visitor in the less respectable parts of Paris, and although in that case completely innocent, he had already been summoned to give evidence in a divorce court. He led a thoroughly frivolous life, eating too much, gambling, shooting, fishing, racing, making love—while he waited, and waited, to inherit his kingdom. Excluded from all political life, he needed constant diversion to prevent him becoming bored, and though Princess Alexandra did her best, she was quite unable to keep

1

him amused by herself. Inevitably he became surrounded by people with tastes and morals similar to his own: his friends were known as the Marlborough House Set, after the Prince's London home on the Mall. Marlborough House was no longer anything to do with the Duke of Marlborough, but among the leaders of the Set were his sons—George Charles, Marquess of Blandford and Lord Randolph Churchill. Blandford, as even his family called him, was twenty-nine and unsatisfactorily married. Randolph was twenty-four, and his life had so far been singularly carefree. He had gone to Eton and Oxford, he had been taken on a grand tour of Europe, he had applied himself to nothing except his pack of hounds, the Blenheim Harriers. He was somewhat moody, and had rather poppy eyes, and as he strolled about Cowes that August he had with him a little pugdog called Puggles.

Now they had been presented to the Prince of Wales, Jennie and Clara Jerome were invited to all the fashionable goings-on. Jennie at nineteen was far more beautiful than her elder sister; she was dark, with shining eyes. But the blonde Clara was far more knowing about society: she had spent a weekend with the Emperor Napoleon III at Compiègne. For both girls Cowes was a delight. Their mother's social circle in Paris was dull and snobbish and frowsty: Cowes was all light and air, the sun sparkling on the water, the boom of the starting-gun, dancing. Jennie was an excellent dancer.

That year Cowes received a visit from the future Czar Alexander III of Russia, whose sister Marie had just become engaged to the Prince of Wales's brother, the Duke of Edinburgh. The Czarevitch was a huge man, and his wife was tiny, so they must have made an extraordinary couple when they danced. But they did dance, indeed a special ball was given in their honour on board HMS *Ariadne,* guardship to the regatta, on August 12th. It was an afternoon dance, from 3.30 to 7.30, and the harbour must have been filled with boats carrying the elegant and fashionable across the dancing waves to the flag-bedecked warship.

Jennie had been looking forward to the ball with great excitement—she had never been to such a grand and glittering social occasion, graced not only by the Russian royalties, but by the Prince and Princess of Wales, too. She kept the invitation all her life. But under the words 'To meet', setting him above the Royal and Imperial Highnesses, Jennie later wrote the one word 'Randolph'. For it was on the *Ariadne* that August afternoon that Lord Randolph Churchill was introduced to Miss Jennie Jerome by their mutual friend Mr Frank Bertie, Randolph quickly found himself at a disadvantage: waltzing, he was obliged to confess, made him dizzy. So after a formal quadrille, they sat and talked. It was love at first sight. Before the ball was over, Jennie persuaded her mother to ask Randolph and another friend, Colonel Edgcumbe, back to dinner that night. They were only too delighted to accept. 'We spent a very pleasant evening', Jennie wrote years later, 'my sister and I playing duets at the piano and chatting merrily.' There must have been more to the merriment than music and chat. After dinner, Randolph, immensely struck, told Colonel Edgcumbe half-seriously that he meant to try and marry 'the dark one.' After he'd gone, Jennie asked Clara what she thought of him: he did not, it seems, come up to Clara's exacting Parisian standards. Jennie interrupted her, and told her to say no more: she had a presentiment she would marry him. Clara laughed—it was absurd!

Next day Randolph and Jennie met again 'by accident' and had a walk. The Isle of Wight is very beautiful in summer, but they cannot have spent much time discussing the scenery. On the Friday Randolph came to dinner again. It was a perfect night. The harbour glimered with reflected lights from the yachts. It was only natural to want to go out into the garden and stand beneath the stars. So Randolph and Jennie went. And Randolph asked her to marry him. And Jennie said yes.

Though swept away by their mutual love, Jennie and Randolph had not altogether lost their senses. They knew very well that there would be aghastness and horror and hands raised in outrage by all those who had forgotten what it was to be young and in love. Mrs Jerome, for instance, would certainly not understand the suddenness of it. So they decided not to tell her. Randolph was supposed to leave Cowes on the Saturday morning, but of course he postponed his departure. The first note he ever wrote to Jennie was carefully unimpassioned, so that Mrs Jerome would not become suspicious:

Marine Hotel
Dear Miss Jeannette   Saturday
I missed my boat & have not been able to go; so shall not start till early Monday morning Thankyou so very much for the photograph which is much better than the others; shall hope to see you after church tomorrow. You see I keep turning up like a bad shilling

Yrs vy sincerely
Randolph S. Churchill

The letter is in an uncharacteristically neat hand, but for all its artificiality there is something endearingly arrogant—perhaps essentially Churchillian—in the way Randolph ennobled the common penny to a shilling. He valued himself highly.

The weekend was idyllically happy, as the lovers exchanged vows and tokens under the unsuspecting eyes of Jennie's mother. But after he had left on Sunday night, Jennie broke the news to Mrs Jerome. Her reaction was just what they had expected: they were both quite mad, she thought, and she refused to hear of anything so precipitate. Jennie scribbled a first quick note to Randolph that same evening:

I cannot bear to have you leave Cowes—dearest without a last good-bye—I have told Mama who

although she likes you *very* much won't hear of it
But I am sure we shall easily get her on our side
later on—when we see you in London or perhaps
here—God bless you darling—

yours
Jeannette

Sunday night
Don't smoke too much——

Randolph received the note next morning:

Steamboat
7.15 a.m.

A thousand thanks dearest Jeannette for your darling
little note which cheered me up wonderfully. I only
got it just as I was getting on board. It is a wet
misty morning & I feel wretched. I cannot think
your mother will really not hear of our engagement
only I am sure she thinks we have known each other
for too short a time. You and I do not think so,
but it is natural your mother shld. Oh dear how I
hope I may be able to get back to Cowes, but I
hardly think I shall be. Write me some more of
those charming notes of yours to Blenheim. They
will be the only gleams of sunshine I shall get for
some time. I will CERTAINLY meet you in London.
What a happy evening we had last night, in fact
all yesterday was too happy for me. I have got your
photographs & your dear little pin, to look at, they
will keep you every minute, in my memory Do not
you be unhappy at all or low, you have no need
to be so dearest. We shall assuredly meet again before long, till which happy period may you be pro-
tected from every kind of wrong annoyance or harm.
Think of me sometimes & have confidence &
patience.

Goodbye dearest
Love to Clara
Yrs ever devotedly & lovingly
Randolph

And off he steamed into the morning mist, on his way back to the mainland. Between a Tuesday afternoon and a Friday night a great Anglo-American alliance had been arranged, with consequences which no one that August morning could possibly have dreamed.

Mrs Jerome remained, for the moment, firm against the engagement, and forbade Jennie to write. But Randolph could scarcely keep pen from paper once he was back home at Blenheim, the enormous palace given to the first Duke by Queen Anne:

Blenheim
My own darling Jeannette   Tuesday

I cannot let another day pass without writing to you. I do not think I ever had such a day as yesterday; such a melancholy journey away from you. & then to have to listen to the twaddle & gossip of my mother & sisters when my heart & thoughts were elsewhere. It is so curious that my rooms & my things & my occupations here which I used to take interest in are quite hateful to me now, all I can do is to keep reading your letter & looking at your photographs & thinking thinking till I get quite stupid. I do not think dearest you have any idea of how much I love you, or what sacrifices I wld not make to call you my own. My whole life & energies shld be devoted to making you happy & protecting you from harm or wrong, Life shld be to you like one long summer day. Oh dear how few & short were the days we had together, so happy tho; I hope you are passing the time pleasantly. I told my mother everything. Of course she was vy much surprised & cld not understand anything taking place so rapidly. I am going to write to my father in a day or two & when I get his answer I shall then write to your mother & tell her exactly what my position & prospects & means are. The two former are good enough but the latter I must tell you are by no means grand. For myself I am careless, & wld face if necessary even starvation if I had you, but love is selfish as well as blind, I cld not ask you to give up any one of those luxuries & comforts to which you have been all along accustomed; Dearest if you only knew how unhappy & wretched I am away from you. I cannot imagine now however I got myself away from Cowes. Those too few hours we spent together will tell either one way or the other on the future happiness or misery of my whole life. I enclose you a little photograph I had done about 3 years ago at Isch.[1]* It is not a vy good one but you may like to have it. Dearest Jeannette please do not forget me, I know how much you are *entourée* [2] & admired and feel quite mad sometimes to think that I am not by your side. Goodbye darling.

Believe me ever
Yrs most devotely & lovingly
Randolph

Randolph's father and brother were both away in Scotland, and with only two of his six sisters married, he may well have felt oppressed by feminine gossip. But it was not twaddle that he would have got from his mother on breaking his unexpected news. The Duchess of Marlborough was a formidable character, who was most ambitious for her youngers son, Blandford having proved nothing but trouble since his schooldays. Though he was highly intelligent and took a great interest in scientific inventions, Blandford was also wilful and wayward, violent in temper, and unfaithful to his wife. His parents had abandoned all hope of his ever having a serious political career. Instead they looked to Randolph.

At the gates of Blenheim Palace stands the small Oxfordshire town of Woodstock. In 1873 Woodstock, although it had only eleven hundred and one registered voters, was still a parliamentary constituency. For generations it had been completely under the control of the Dukes of Marlborough. Randolph's father had himself held the seat, before he inherited his title,

* See notes at end of chapter.

and when he resigned he handed it over to his brother. Political contrariness ran in the family, however, and the Duke and Lord Alfred Churchill quarrelled over Free Trade: after a still more bitter dispute over Church Rates, a subject on which the Duke held very strong opinions, Lord Alfred had been obliged to resign. For the time being, Blandford being considered unsuitable, and in any case unwilling, the seat was occupied by the Duke's nominee, a Mr Barnett, a banker who was squire of nearby Glympton Park. It was the Duke and Duchess's ambition that Randolph should take over at the next election, which was expected to be soon. Randolph had not yet begun to think for himself, and there was no political disagreement between him and his parents. He rightly, however, anticipated strong parental opposition to his proposed marriage. When he wrote to his father, therefore, the letter was carefully phrased:

I must not any longer keep you in ignorance of a very important step I have taken—one which will undoubtedly influence very strongly all my future life.

I met, soon after my arrival at Cowes, a Miss Jeannette Jerome, the daughter of an American lady who has lived for some years in Paris and whose husband lives in New York. I passed most of my time at Cowes in her (Jeannette's) society, and before leaving asked her if she loved me well enough to marry me; and she told me she did. I do not think that if I were to write pages I could give you any idea of the strength of my feelings and affections and love for her; all I can say is that I love her better than life itself, and that my one hope and dream now is that matters may be so arranged that soon I may be united to her by ties that nothing but death itself could have the power to sever.

I know, of course, that you will be very much surprised, and find it difficult to understand how an attachment so strong could have arisen in so short a space of time; and really I feel it quite impossible for me to give any explanation of it that could appear reasonable to anyone practical and dispassionate. I must, however, ask you to believe it as you could the truest and most real statement that could possibly be made to you, and to believe also that upon a subject so important, and I may say so solemn, I could not write one word that was in the smallest degree exaggerated, or that might not be taken at its fullest meaning.

I hope you won't feel any annoyance with me for not having consulted you before saying anything to her. I really meant to have done so; but on the night before I was leaving Cowes (Friday) my feelings of sorrow at parting from her were more than I could restrain, and I told her all. I did not say anything to her mother, but I believe that she did after I was gone; for she wrote to me just as I was starting (I did not, after all, leave Cowes till the Monday), and she said in her letter that her mother could not hear of it. That I am at a loss to understand.

I told Mama when I got here and should have written at once to tell you; but I was so wretched and miserable at leaving thus, I was quite incapable of writing quietly.

I now write to tell you of it all, and to ask you whether you will be able to increase my allowance to some extent to put me in the position to ask Mrs Jerome to let me become her daughter's future husband. I enclose you her photograph, and will only say about her that she is as nice, as lovable, and amiable and charming in every way as she is beautiful, and that by her education and bringing-up she is in every way qualified to fill any position.

She has an elder sister, and one younger, who is not yet out. Mr Jerome is a gentleman who is obliged to live in New York to look after his business. I do not know what it is. He is reputed to be very well off, and his daughters, I believe, have very good fortunes, but I do not know anything for certain. He generally comes over for three or four months every year. Mrs Jerome has lived in Paris for several years and has educated her daughters there. They go out in Society there and are very well known.

I have told you all I know about them at present. You have always been very good to me, and done as much and more for me always than I had any right to expect; and with any arrangement that you may at any time make for me I shall be perfectly contented and happy. I see before me now a very happy future, almost in one's grasp. In the last year or so I feel I have lost a great deal of what energy and ambition I possessed, and an idle and comparatively useless life has at times appeared to me to be the pleasantest; but if I were married to her whom I have told you about, if I had a companion, such as she would be, I feel sure, to take an interest in one's prospects and career, and to encourage me to exertions and to doing something towards making a name for myself, I think I might become, with the help of Providence, all and perhaps more than you had ever wished and hoped for me. On the other hand, if anything should occur to prevent my fondest hopes and wishes being realized (a possibility which I dare not and cannot bring myself to think of), how dreary and uninteresting would life become to me! No one goes through what I have lately gone through without its leaving a strong impress and bias on their character and future. Time might, of course, partially efface the impression and recollection of feelings so strong as those I have tried to describe to you, but in the interval the best years of one's life would be going, and one's energies and hopes would become blunted and deadened.

I will not allude to her. I believe and am convinced that she loves me as fully, and as strongly if possible, as I do her; and when two people feel towards each other what we do, it becomes, I know, a great responsibility for anyone to assist in either bringing about or thwarting a union so closely desired by each.

Good-bye. I have written to you all I have done, all I feel, and all I know.

Anxiously wishing for an answer from you,

I remain

Ever your most affectionate son,

Randolph

Randolph's skill in drafting an awkward political letter had been remarked on by one of his Oxford tutors: 'He made up his own mind; having well reflected, he chose his ground of attack, and then took every pains about the form of expression.' Now he chose to attack his parents where they were weakest; in their love and ambition for him. There was really only one way in which Randolph's phrases about 'an idle and comparatively useless life' and his 'energies and hopes' becoming 'blunted and deadened' could be taken. If the Duke and Duchess refused to let him marry Jennie, then he wouldn't stand for Woodstock at the next election. He did not tell Jennie exactly what tactics he was adopting:

I cannot keep myself from writing any longer to you dearest, although I have not had any answer to either of my two letters. I suppose your mother does not allow you to write to me Perhaps you have not got either of my letters, but still I write on the chance, as I am so dreadfully afraid that perhaps you may think I am forgetting you. I can assure you dearest Jeannette you have not been out of my thoughts hardly for one minute since I left you Monday. I have written to my father everything, how much I love you how much I long & pray & how much I wld sacrifice if it were necessary to be married to you and to live ever after with you never to be parted till death. I shall [not] get an answer till Monday & whichever way it lies I shall go to Cowes soon after & tell your mother everything. I am afraid she does not like me vy much from what I have heard. & yet I feel I cld be so fond of her *really*. She was so kind to me at Cowes, & so good-natured that I wld do anything, she wished if she only wld not oppose us. Dearest if you are as fond of me as I am of you as I like to think you are nothing human cld keep us long apart. This last week has seemed an eternity to me; Oh, I wld give my soul for another of those days we had together not long ago. I daresay the people you see are only too ready to abuse me. God knows they cannot say with truth any real bad of me; only I get so mad and distracted when I think that perhaps you might listen to anybody except me. *Les absents ont toujours tort*,[3] they say. Oh if I cld only get one line from you to reassure me, but I dare not ask you to do anything that your mother wld disapprove of or has perhaps forbidden you to do. If she has kept my letters from you even I cannot blame her. I can only wish & long that she knew me better and trusted me more. I do not mind her seeing everything I write as long as you see it too. Sometimes I doubt so I cannot help it whether you really like me as you said at Cowes you did. If you do I cannot fear for the future tho' difficulties may lie in our way only to be surmounted by patience. But remember dearest

There is a love beyond all that the poets have told
When two that are bound by one heavenly tie
with hearts never changing & brows never cold
love on through all ills & love on till they die
One hour of a passion so sacred is worth
Whole ages of heartless & wandering bliss
& oh if there be an elysium on earth
it is this it is this.[4]

Goodbye dearest Jeannette. My first and only love Hoping & praying that you may get this & longing I can not tell you how much to see you

Believe me ever to be

Yrs devotedly & lovingly
Randolph S Churchill

While the Duke took his time to reply, Blandford, to whom Randolph had also written, soon gave vent to his feelings. He was unhappily married, and placed his own example before his brother as one to be avoided at all costs. He wrote at length, and in very peculiar though vigorous prose: [5]

Arisaig, Aug. 25/73, N.B.

My Dear Old Chap

I got your letter on Saturday when I arrived but as there is only a post twice a week I could not write before today. I may say that I am not in the least surprised at the contents of your letter as I know you so well that I can easily judge of the effect that impressions such as you describe have on you. You will say when you read this that you expected as much from me. This will be partly because you know my general opinions & partly because you realy feel dowbtful of yourself & your hasty judgement I feel that what I am about to say is like words scattered to the raging gale however! I resemble Samson who tried to slay 1,000ds of men with the jaw bone of an ass (if we are to believe history) only that he succeeded, & that I shall not. I am going to place before you argument & persuasion the two weakest weapons we have in our mental armoury arraid againts your combined infatuations! Had you written to me on half a sheet of note paper I should have understood your story as well as if I had been with you & seen you myself wading through that slough of despond which every one in the world is perpetually tumbling into, & from which some get out (perhaps somewhat mudied & begrimed) but where others stick & held fast hopelessly. With a rashness that, I even I, was never capable of you run *tête basse* [6] into the wildest superlative of conceivable folly. This is my Vienna Philosopher, making laws for the nation & following them are widely different are they not? I hold up my hands in silent dismay. You go from impression to impression. Good! *'Mais la suite de cela?'* [7] Listen you will either live to see my predictions fulfilled to the letter *viz,* that before a

year you will be painfully aware of your grievous &
immutable folly, or you will some day extole my
wisdom to the sky's & be careful to avoid like com-
binations in future. I can say no more without only
repeating myself. You are my only brother & what
you do affects me far more than anything that can
befall to any one else. You know however the
weight of your own actions, & with open eyes, not
blindfolded, you may chose to throw yourself head-
long from a rock, & we can none of us help you or
prevent you. It shall not be though without heartfelt
counsel from me. It is no use my imploring you,
because that adds nothing to the argument. If you are
not quite mad & have yet a glimmering of rational
ideas about you, Consider once more! Risk anything!
'Même une bassess' [8] but dont marry. [TEAR] nothing
teach a man but [TEAR] experience! Has Destiny
[TEAR] powerful a force over him. [TEAR] no one can
deliver him [TEAR]—gnash!! I fear it! I myself am a
specimen of the latter class, & I would therefore
place before you my own example as one to be
avoided. Had you been five & thirty or forty I
should have pitied you but at five & twenty, with life
before instead of behind you, I tell you that you are
mad simply mad. I dont care if *la demoiselle* was
the incarnation of all moral excellencies & physical
beauties on Gods earth, my opinion is the same.
Had you told me that it was a married woman you
wanted to go off with, I should say if you cant live
happy without her go! Fate calls you. Had it been
a woman for whom you were ruining yourself, I
should say Fatality. But my friend *Le marriage!* It is
a delusion & a snare, like all the rest, only with this
disagreeable addition that it is irrevocable.

Will no one believe me!

Have you any solid end in view in this affair No!

Do you marry for a fortune No!

Do you marry to get children No!

Do you marry because you have loved a woman
for years No!

Do you marry because you feel you are getting old & played out No!

You realy only want to marry because you are in love with an *idea, 'une phantasie de six jours au bains de mêr'.*[9]

Damnation! here you are a sensible man no longer a child, positively triffling in this manner & here am I a born ·ass, trying to argue the matter seriously with you. My dear Randolph for God's sake listen to me, (though of course you wont) you are bored *desoeuvré*[10] in fact, *'vous êtes a la recherche des emotions, et vous avez touche mal,' tres mal!*[11]

'God help your judgement' would say the sectarian, 'use your undeniably good wits' is my advice & the inevitable deduction that you will arrive at as you calm down is that you are a D—d fool. Excuse my plain speaking old Chap, but seriously I do pity you more than I can say *'ce sont de ces choses qui font veillir les jeunes têtes.'*[12] You know what I have often told you but so it must be, I have given you my opinion once for all, as you ask me, & I do most sincerely hope & trust that this my answer may assist in persuading you of your intense misjudgement in this affair Remember old Chap that there is only you & I, & that when you do marry, it is everything for both of us that we should all live together, not in the *decousu*[13] sort of fashion of so many people we know, everything I have is at your service for God's sake dont go & set up a separate existence otherwise, I shall go & camp out abroad for good when England becomes intolerable. I come south the middle of Septer. & will meet you at Blenheim or in London I am going abroad for 3 weeks DO COME. I will listen to all your most *exalté* notions most peacebly so long as you dont set them into operation, & be ever your most affect bro (Damnably anoyed)

Bla (PAGE TORN)

P.S. Love to my mother (PAGE TORN)

Though this letter reveals Blandford's genuine affection for his brother, it made Randolph very angry. But it did not stop him going back to Cowes for two blissful days with Jennie. Mrs Jerome had written to Leonard, and refused to countenance any official engagement till definite permission had been given by both fathers. But she did not frown on the lovers, indeed she seems to have been perfectly happy to let the romance blossom.

The Prince of Wales was still at Cowes, and Randolph took the opportunity to present Jennie to him as the girl he was hoping to marry. The prince liked her at once, and encouraged the lovers to resist all parental doubts and hesitations. But, alas, Randolph could not stay at Cowes. When he got back to Blenheim he wrote:

Blenheim

Dearest Jeannette   Saturday

I have made up & forwarded to you a few photographs of my father & mother & three of my sisters. I also send one of myself for your sister which I promised her. I daresay you will give it to her. It was dreadful work for me having to leave you, but still not quite so bad as the first time, I feel more hopeful of everything coming right now, and I know for certain now that you do really love me; I wish I was great & very rich in order to be more worthy of you dearest, I cannot help always feeling how much too good you are for me. I hope & trust and pray every day that nothing may ever come between us. If anything ever did I shld not care how soon I died as the world can never contain any attraction for me, if you were kept away from me. I really am afraid I did not half thank your mother for having let us be so much together for those two days, I really am so grateful to her. But I was so *boulversé* [14] at having to go away that I cld hardly say anything. I do not think I half said Goodbye to you even. I hope some day dearest we may never have to say goodbye to each other. Sometimes I get worrying and rather low thinking what your father will say. I hope he wont be very long answering & God grant that he may take the views I shld wish him to.

I go to London on Tuesday to get a locket to put your little bit of hair & your photograph in, & also to go and get photographed myself & try if I can get one done that you will like better than the one you have got. On Monday I am going out to kill some partridges as it is the first of September. I have got some shooting of my own that I rent, & if I can get a good bag I shall venture to send some to Rosetta.[15]

Today I have been driving with my mother. She was rather cross at my not coming back on Thursday but I managed to pacify her. The Prince seems to have spoken on all sides of how much he liked his visit on Thursday afternoon, & how glad he was to have made your acquaintance. My own darling do not be angry with me if I do not write every day or think I am forgetting you. I do not want to make your mother cross by writing too often. Send me back the photographs in a few days dearest if you do not mind as I have taken them out of my book. Remember me most kindly to your sister and that God may ever bless & protect you & soon bring us inseparably together is the constant prayer of

Yrs devotedly for ever
Randolph S. Churchill

Jennie replied at once, on paper headed with her name alone:

Monday

The photographs are charming—& you see dear I have taken long to send them back—I was more happy than I can say this morning when I received yr letter but dear Randolph I am very angry at yr not telling me the truth I know you are going to

London to meet the Standishes [16]—& go to the
Play with them—why not say so?—Do you suppose
I care? I would never doubt or distrust yr love—if
you went with fifty Standishes *Cher ami je suis
tellement triste ce matin—encore un petit mot
demain n'est ce pas? Seulement pr me réconforter* [17]—
The Prince talks to me constantly of you—I am afraid
this will be left—

ever yours
Jeannette

By now Randolph must have received his father's
measured response to the idea of an engagement to
an unknown American girl. It was discouraging. The
letter began:

It is not likely that at present you can look at
anything but from your own point of view but
persons from the outside cannot but be struck with
the unwisdom of your proceedings, and the un-
controlled state of your feelings, which completely
paralyses your judgement; never was there such an
illustration of [the] adage *'love is blind'* for you seem
blind to all consequences in order that you may
pursue your passion. . . .

The Duke had made preliminary enquiries about
Leonard Jerome, who sounded 'a sporting, and I should
think vulgar kind of man'. Worse, he was 'of the class
of speculators' and had already been bankrupt once.
It would be a connection 'which no man in his senses
could think respectable'. 'I am deeply sorry', wrote
the Duke, 'that your feelings are so much engaged;
and only for your own sake wish most heartily that you
had checked the current before it became so over-
powering.'

Randolph remained unperturbed. He went up to
London as he said he would, though whether he went
to the theatre with the Standishes or not he somehow
forgot to say:

Thursday 4
Blenheim

Dearest Jeannette,

I had hoped so to have had a line from you ere this. Do try & persuade your Mother to let you write darling I am sure there is no harm in it and your letters are perfectly SAFE with me. Just a short line every now & then, it is such a comfort to me and I do so love your little notes. I came back from London yesterday. I had a long talk with the Prince on Tuesday afternoon; he spoke much of you & your sister, & said the Princess liked you both so vy much. He said I was a very lucky fellow in which I quite agree with him. For when I am alone here I keep wondering often why you shld like me, as you do, I know; I suppose it is partly because you feel I am so very fond of you & wld do anything or sacrifice anything for you I am sure you must be very dull now at Cowes as most of your friends have I suppose left now. I shall hope to be able to run down the end of next week, only you MUST write & tell me whether your mother will mind, & what she says of me & whether you think of me sometimes. I keep counting the days till yr father's answer can arrive, I get so low & nervous about it sometimes, I feel it depends so much on how your mother has written to him. I went & got photographed the other day in London & shall send you the proofs when they come. I have got your photograph & your little curl in a locket now & am always looking at it. My father comes home tomorrow from the North. Of course we shall have a lot of talk about you my darling, tho I have written to him volumes. I shall write to you again soon. . . .

The Duke's return meant a stiffish interview. Randolph's threats about not standing for Parliament seem to have been ignored, and he was forbidden to return to Cowes. The Duke's orders had to be obeyed: Randolph had no income except what his father gave him.

He was not downcast, though. He was too much in love for that:

I am afraid there is no chance of my being able to go to Cowes again dearest. I wrote to your mother yesterday & told her that my father did not wish me to do anything more till your father's answer had arrived. I do not want to cross him just now when there is no absolute necessity for it, tho I wld have given much to have seen you again even if it had only been for an hour or so. I suppose your mother will not let you write to me or else I feel sure you wld have done so. It is very hard I think on both of us, but we must look forward my love to a better time not very far distant I trust. It is very wretched for me here time drags itself along like lead & I am getting quite to hate this place. Another fortnight I suppose at least, to wait before your father's answer comes. I am sure that in these last three weeks I seem to have lived a lifetime. *'Ce sont de ces choses qui font veillir les jeunes têtes'.* Dearest I wonder whether you really love me. God knows I do not want to pain you by expressing the least distrust of you, but by love I do not mean the cold ordinary attachment that the world is accustomed to call by that name, but something far higher far deeper seated far more enduring which we often read about, & which does sometimes exist, tho very rarely. A love that is ready to go through any trials to surmount any difficulties to wait if necessary almost a lifetime that looks only to one end & to one goal, that is resolved to look at no other & to be content with no other. Have you that my darling? I feel that I shld be the most conceited emptyheaded creature on this earth if I were to make sure that a love such as I have tried to describe to you cld have sprung up so rapidly in so brief an acquaintance for one so ordinary & commonplace as myself, & yet I like to think it & to dream about it. I know beyond any doubt that it does exist on my side & I cannot help thinking that it must be mutual. God what a cheerless void what an utter blank my existence wld become if the stake that I am playing for shld be lost to me if the dice on which I have set all my hopes of present & future happiness shld turn up adverse. But I cannot think it nor do I allow myself often to dwell on what is to me so melancholy so utterly despairing a view. No I rather fix my thoughts on a happy & bright future shared with you & I incessantly dream & picture to myself the pleasures of an existence which wld be almost divine, the pleasures of having at last found the object to which one can devote what energies and abilities one may possess the pleasures of having an inseparable companion whom it wld be one's highest idea of duty to protect & shield from every harm & worry & on whom one wld continually & untiringly endeavour to heap every source of happiness that this world can afford. Is this only a dream? I cannot think so or at any rate it is a dream which I pray may soon be converted into a reality. Many wld tell you that feelings such as I feebly attempt to describe to you are quite out of date in this practical 19th century, that a love such as this is an anachronism & that what I have written is only the effusions of a too ardent imagination or perhaps the ravings of a lunatic.

God knows with me they are neither one nor the other, but simply the sincere & real description of a true pure love, which I own unhappily for the world is not common, but is not on that account less admirable or less possible. Feelings such as these are not as many wld say from their very strength short-lived, on the contrary they may perhaps from their very strength physically destroy yet they are as enduring as life & I believe fully, last & receive their reward, beyond the grave. The realization of all this will I hope be not long delayed; it is however the one object left to me in this world I have voluntarily with open eyes made it so and it is far from probable that I shall lightly resign the chances of winning so charming so attractive a prize. I wld not weary you dearest by writing more at length on a subject with which I cld fill volumes, I hope I may not have done so already, I feel however that I am writing to one who if unhappily for me cannot reciprocate can at any rate appreciate at its full value a love so deep so great & so true. I asked your mother to let you write to me a few lines from time to time, but if she wld not do so to write herself just to say how you all were & what you were doing. Any news of you the smallest & from whatever quarter, Is longed for by

yr own true & for ever devoted
Randolph S. Churchill

Blenheim
Sunday, Sept. 7th
The Pug I regret to say is still in small health. Like his master ever since he left you, he is down on his luck.

The sincerity of this was unmistakeable, but even Randolph felt he had been a little too gloomy. 'A one-sided correspondence is very disheartening I assure you,' he wrote three days later. 'I hope you did not mind my stupid letter of last Sunday but I happened to be particularly in low spirits & I cld not help pouring out all my feelings for you.' Jennie, one can safely assure, did not mind at all. But she was unable to write and say so. Mrs. Jerome was no more encouraging than the Duke: perhaps she was determined not to be outdone in correctness by the English aristocracy. At any rate, when she wrote to Randolph, she probably meant her letter to be shown to his father:

Rosetta Cottage
Sept. 9th
Dear Lord Randolph
I am very much touched by your kind letter I must acknowledge you have quite won my heart by your

frank & honourable manner since our acquaintance and though you may never be more to us we shall always think of you with the kindest remembrance

I hope you will listen to your Fathers advice He can only have your happiness at heart. As a good son your first duty is to him.

I shall probably receive my husband's answer to my letter the first of next month. I will send it to you immediately. We leave Cowes on Monday the 13th.[18] We stop one day in London en route for Paris It is so cold here we are anxious to get away

With kindest regards from us all, believe me dear Lord Randolph

Ever your sincere friend
Clara H. Jérôme

While waiting impatiently to see Jennie on her way through London, Randolph's temper was not improved by a new communication from his brother, this time in verse. Though its tone is conciliatory—perhaps in response to Randolph's fury at his original letter—Blandford's message is the same. Nor is his poetry any less peculiar than his prose:

AN ELEGY ON MARRIAGE

1

Undine rising out of the waves 1st Act.

T'was yours & not anothers hand that built
    the funeral pile near which you tarry
the daggers plunged unto its bleeding hilt
Thy fate is sealed if thou doest marry.

2

Le Cigne qui chante son dernier chadson! 19

Advice & preaching are an idle strain
For madness hath thy mind o'er-took
Delusions snare entraps thy fevered brain
Thy senses hast thou quite forsook

3

Remorse shall seize up thy stuborn soul
when tinseled charms begin to pall
Thy part is strife, & pitious grief thy
whole
If thou doest thus in weakness fall

4

Does marriage then a lovely sea of calm
appear to thy deluded eyes
Times future gifts of Love wilt thou
embalm
& all freedom of thy will likewise.

5

Despise them not, those strong mysterious
ties
by which the soul is oft-times bound;
Heed not this shaddow that before thee
flies,
True love is free as air arround.

6

See thus no future, though still distant
light
Some Star, which in thy path may rise
& so with dazzling Rays shall dim thy
sight,
and lead thee captive as its prize

7

I know a youth who scarce a year ago
rushed, into the wedded lock
who all his worldly goods would now
forgoe
to take his feet from out the stocks

8

The married tie was made for those, my
    friend!
who revel in lifes worldly good
or would long years of wicked evil mind
& so when old they don the hood*

* Quand
le Diable
se fait
vieux, il
se fait
heremit.20

9

I see thee grumbling oer thy household
    books,
& adding up thy nurses wage.
Ha! Ha! these trifles must thy spirit
    brook!
when thou art married, my young Sage!

* If 'rusks'
and 'sucks'
are objected
to, Read!
'See thou to
the cutting
of its tusks.'

10

Perambulators & the babies rusks
Shall be among thy chiefest cares
See thou to the bottle that it sucks
Revolt? thy spirit will not dare.*

11

And when thy better half shall wine &
    fret
because thou dinest not at home
Perchance the scene shall turn into a pet
Then! wilt thou at thy fortunes moan!

12

Now, think of me in time to come my
    boy!
All this & more shall thee befall
If, thou doest sell, for this thy pretty toy
thyself, thy Friends, & e'en thy very all.

Dedication

13

Thus pause my brother while there's time
& think not that I wish thy harm
to thee, I dedicated this humble rime
in fond advice & counsel calm.

14

Forgive me then if in my fleeting speech
aught could to thy mind offend
Let loving thoughts still bind us each to
  each
& let nothing our friendship rend

15

So go you forth on your appointed way
& treat my poor advice with slight
Still will I for a golden future pray,
'May I be wrong', & 'You be right'!
              Affectionately addressed
              to his brother by the Author
              Bd.
              Sept 7/73

This remarkable effusion did little to calm Randolph's indignation. He had shown Blandford's original
letter to his father; now he sent it to the Prince of
Wales. The Prince criticized both style and composition, and said it was one of the most extraordinary
productions he'd ever read. For his encouragement of
Randolph he was roundly abused by Blandford, who
accused him of not acting the part of a friend. The
Prince was no doubt more amused than cross, and suggested that Blandford must have been writing to him at
a late hour in the evening—that is, probably drunk. He
took the line that Blandford meant well, and that Randolph shouldn't quarrel with him. He then passed the
offending letter to Francis Knollys, his Private Secre-

tary. Randolph had written to him, too: Knollys was so close a friend that he was to be his best man. He gave the same advice as the Prince:

Abergeldie[21]

My dear Randolph   Friday

I was very glad to get a letter from you although sorry to hear that you think your affairs are not going on well. As however you say the Duke is kind to you I am sure he will do what he can for you. At the same time I quite understand how unhappy you must feel until your suspense is over & how much you must be looking forward to the day when it will be all over—I cannot help feeling sorry also for Miss Jerome.

The Prince has shown me Blandford's letter to you —I think you are perhaps right not to answer him, but to wait to say anything until you see him—He is I am sure fond of you & what he writes proceeds from what he considers are good motives however mistaken you yourself may consider them to be, & were you to reply to his letter just now you might be tempted to say something which would perhaps create a life long breach between you & him. Pray forgive me my dear Randolph for writing all this to you.

I hope you will let me hear from you as soon as you have anything fresh to tell me, & believe me

yrs most sincerely
Francis Knollys

Have you asked H. Lennox[22] to Blenheim.

Meanwhile the Prince replied to Blandford and sent a copy to Randolph, which pleased him so much he wrote and asked permission to show it to the Duke and Duchess. Knollys wrote again:

Private   Abergeldie Castle,
Aberdeenshire
19 Sept. 1873

My dear Randolph

The Prince of Wales is very glad to hear that you like his letter to Blandford, & as you are so anxious to show it to the Duke & the Duchess he has no objection to your doing so under of course the understanding that they do not refer to it in any way to Blandford or to any one else. His Royal Highness at first thought of sending to you Blandford's letter to him as well, to enable your Father & mother to judge more properly of his answer, but upon consideration he thinks it would perhaps be hardly fair of him to do this, but you can repeat to them the purport of its contents

I am very sorry that matters do not improve, but we must hope for a favourable report from Sir E. Thornton.[23]

Pray let me hear what it is when it arrives & when you have time to write to me

I quite understand how low you must feel under all this suspense but I trust it will soon be removed.

Ever my dear Randolph

Yours sincerely
Francis Knollys

Meanwhile Jennie and Randolph met briefly in London on Monday September 15th. Randolph then went back to Blenheim to address an agricultural dinner at Woodstock, while the Jeromes went on to Paris. He had reason, he thought, to be cheerful, though Jennie had seemed depressed:

Blenheim
Wednesday

I could not write to you yesterday dearest Jeannette as all my time was taken up with that tiresome agricultural dinner I am happy to say I have got that off my mind now. I think it went off very well upon the whole, but I am sure if I had not had the excessive pleasure & happiness of seeing you again in London I shld never have had the spirits to go to it. We have had a few people staying here this week Lady Wilton [24] by herself & Walter Harbord,[25] both of whom I think you know. & the two county members; a very

stupid party Next week thank goodness I shall be
quite alone, as my father & mother are going away for
two or three days. I never liked being alone before
but now I long to be alone if I cannot be with you.
I can think of you all day long & have not anything
else to take away my attention. Dearest I hope you
are in better spirits than when I left you. You appeared so dreadfully low that I tried to be in as good
spirits as possible to try & cheer you up. But it made
me vy uphappy my darling after I left you to think
that I am the cause of making you who ought to be
so lighthearted at all worried or annoyed. I hope you
keep my poor little bracelet always on your arm.
I look upon that as binding you to me irrevocably,
& dearest as I have told you often if you and I keep
firm & really mean what we have said seriously &
solemnly to each other nothing human can keep us
apart. I assure you my own love those few short hours
we had together in London seem to have given me
new life & fresh hope. And now we have persuaded
your mother to allow you to write to me, & I hope
you will write as often as you can. I shld advise you
to tell her whenever you write & if she thinks you are
writing too often, why then you must give in a little
dearest, & not be cross with her who is so good &
kind to you & indeed to me too. There is only one
thing I must press you to do as strongly as I can,
which is to use all your influence & powers of persuasion which are vy great, together with me to oppose any unnecessary delay. No good can come of it,
we cannot be fonder of each other than we are now
& there is no reason why we shld lose any portion of
our life together, which can only be too happy & like
everything else in this world too brief. I feel dearest
very strongly about this so really must beg and entreat of your father to hasten as much as possible his
journey to Europe. I mean dearest if you are willing
& I know you are to do all that is possible for us to
be married in December. There is no legitimate cause
or good reason against it, & there are many reasons

why it shld be so. Dearest think over all this & write & tell me yr opinion. I never have stood yet any delay in anything I wished vy much for & I never will if I can help it I have always thought that if things are to be the sooner they do take place the better & I will not suffer if I can help it any foolish reasons or empty prejudices to keep me long from one whom I love so dearly & so fondly & whom I cannot exist without. I am going to write to your father & tell him this & I hope you will do so too darling. Our love and affection for each other as I told you in one of my letters has been no ordinary commonplace everyday sort of attachment, there have been all along & are still circumstances connected with it, that I regret to say unless we are both vy firm under the consequences of it doubtful & uncertain & the only one thing certain about it all is that if we are married we shall both be vy vy happy & if we are not (which is a contingency I will not contemplate) well at any rate I for my part, shall be intolerably miserable & unhappy for ever. Dearest I shall hope to get a letter from you in a day or two. I hope you have arrived safely at Paris. & I hope you will amuse yourself there & keep up yr spirits, Darling Jeannette I cannot write more at present, but will write again to-morrow Remember me most kindly to your mother & sister, & tell Clara that I hope when we meet next she wont scold me so much Goodbye & God bless you my love

Yr own devoted & affectionate
Randolph S. Churchill

NOTES

1. In Austria, where Randolph was photographed while on his Grand Tour after leaving Oxford.

2. Surrounded.

3. The absent are always wrong.

4. Randolph is quoting, not entirely accurately, from the then popular *Lalla Rookh*, by Thomas Moore. This verse

comes from 'The Light of the Harem', a tale about how a wife wins back the love of her husband: not perhaps a very well-omened choice.

5. Bandford's spelling is so idiosyncratic that it has not been corrected. Nor has his French, which is highly personal.

6. Blindly ahead.

7. But how will it end?

8. Even a dirty trick.

9. A six days' seaside fantasy.

10. At a loose end.

11. You are in search of sensations, and you have found bad ones. Very bad!

12. These are the things which make young heads old.

13. Disorganized.

14. Upset.

15. The Villa Rosetta was the small house in which the Jeromes were staying at Cowes.

16. Henry Standish, an American who lived in Paris and at the Château de Montjoye, and his French wife, daughter of Comte Amédée des Cars.

17. Dear friend I am so sad this morning—another little word tomorrow, please? Just to comfort me.

18. In fact the 15th.

19. The swan who sings his last song!

20. When the Devil becomes old, he becomes a hermit.

21. The Prince's estate near Balmoral in Scotland.

22. Lord Henry Charles George Lennox, 1821-86, son of the 5th Duke of Richmond and Lennox, MP for Chichester 1846-85, First Commissioner of Works, 1874-6. Close friend of Disraeli.

23. British envoy in Washington, being consulted by the Duke about Leonard Jerome.

24. Isabella, second wife of the second Earl of Wilton.

25. Walter Harbord (1834-1913) was a brother of Lord Suffield and an officer in the army.

2

AMOR VINCIT
OMNIA

Now that Mrs Jerome had raised her ban on Jennie's letter-writing, Randolph must have been avidly awaiting his first proper letter from his fiancée. But when it came it was a bombshell:

Tuesday Sept. 16th
London

My dear Randolph

I have persuaded Mama to allow me to write these few lines—as they will probably be the last—do not be angry dear—but I have not been able to sleep all night—thinking of all you said—& the more I think the more convinced I am that you are changed—since Cowes—In what way I am at loss to tell but I feel it—& the feeling is sufficient. Sometimes I almost wish I had listened a little more to Mama's advice— from the beginning she asked me not to think of it —& begged me to forget you—as it would only worry & trouble me in the end—not that I mind that—you know I would go through a great deal & sacrifice a great deal for yr sake—if I thought you *really* did care for me—But the truth is Randolph—you are heartily sick & tired of all the ennui it causes you, is it not so? I am sure you think you are bound to me in some way—& that it would be impossible to break off now—even should you desire. Believe me—I con- sider you as free—as if nothing had ever passed be-

tween us—& as I told you last night if yr father or
mother object in the least to our marriage—why cross
them? Is it not much wiser to end it all before it is
too late?—I suppose of course we should both feel
rather badly at first—but with time everything passes
—& you might marry some English girl & be much
happier than if you married me—I cannot tell you
how deeply hurt I felt at the insinuation you gave me
—as to yr having heard something against my father
—I was unable to answer you or defend him—as you
did not choose to confide in me—All I can say is that
I love, admire & respect my father more than any
man living—& I do not think it possible for him to
have an enemy—for a more generous, kind hearted
man never lived—the only thing I have ever heard
people reproach him for is his decidedly *English* taste
for horse racing & gambling—Dearest I have no doubt
this letter will pain you—& make me appear in quite
a new light—& perhaps not a very flattering one—
but I cannot help it—*Je suis ainsi faite!* [1] —& if I have
a bad nature it is difficult to change. My pride always
did get the better of me & it certainly has in this
occasion—I had hoped to leave England without a
doubt that it would all come right—& without a
thought of anything else but you—Oh dear why is
it?? You told Clara you felt as if a great load had
been taken off yr mind—I think it has fallen upon me
—I have just been reading the Court Journal—& I
am ashamed to say that after flying into a most violent
passion—I have been crying over those slandering
stupid lines, written by a crazy old man—& not worth
being even noticed—I wonder if you are very angry
with this letter?—or will you not care? Forgive me—
I really *cannot* break quite yet—for I feel that I love
you more than anything or person on earth—& that
I am ready to do or say anything you like as long
as you leave my family alone and not abuse it—

Ever yrs
Jeannette Jérôme

If you write please send me those papers with yr
speeches. I still take a slight interest in yr affairs!—
6 Rue Presbourg

This dramatic and painful letter is the first in which
Jennie shows some of that American vigour which was
to enchant, and in some cases dismay, English society
for almost fifty years. All her life she was someone who
went directly to the point: if her pride was hurt, she
didn't hesitate to show it. What happened, obviously,
is that Randolph let fall some critical remark about
Leonard Jerome—something he'd heard from one of
his father's investigators, perhaps. But Jennie would not
tolerate any slighting remarks about her father, even
from the man she loved. She clearly doesn't really want
to break with Randolph: offering him his freedom with
one hand, she takes it back with the other. But she
does want him to know there are some things she won't
stand for.

The paragraph in *The Court Journal* over which she
raged, then wept, must rather have clouded the London meeting in any case. Publicity at such a delicate
stage of marital negotiations was dreaded by everyone,
and Mrs Jerome must have been furious to read under
'Approaching Marriages in High Life':

Miss Jerome, one of the prettiest young ladies that
ever hailed from New York and landed at Cowes, is
about to marry Lord R. Churchill, the third son [2] of
the Duke of Marlborough. The young lady, who has
resided for some time in Paris, will receive a splendid
dower on her marriage. Mr Jerome is one of the
most inveterate of American yachtsmen.

Steps were rapidly taken about this paragraph. The
next week's issue of *The Court Journal* was obliged to
state: 'There is no truth in the report of a marriage
between Lord Randolph Churchill and Miss Jerome.'
It looks from her remarks about 'a crazy old man' as
if the indiscretion was Jennie's: she certainly seems to

have known the author. But Randolph, of course, was concerned with a far more important matter. If Jennie's letter showed some of her true character, so did his reply show some of his. They were an excellent match, these two: they struck sparks from one another:

Blenheim
Thursday 18th Sept.

I have just this minute received your letter & cannot rest a moment without telling you what I think of it. This is the first letter I have ever had from you and it certainly is an encouraging one. I can assure you that if I am to receive many like it, I can only say that at any rate I was a good deal happier when the letter writing was only on my side, & when I cld leave your answers to my foolish imagination. I am more pained & hurt than you can imagine, & if that was your object in writing you may congratulate yourself on having fully attained it You are the only person on Earth that has the power to say or do anything to wound my feelings & to vex & worry me for long & certainly you know how to use your power. What in the name of heaven do you mean by saying that I was changed in London from what I was at Cowes. The fact of the matter is (& it is always the way with women when they want to quarrel they take great care to shift the blame off their shoulders) it is you who are changed & who must be changed, if you can write me a letter like your last. How mistaken I was in you & how little you have understood me I thought when I saw you in London blind fool that I was that you loved me as truly as you said you did, & you thought or at any rate persuaded yourself to think, that my feelings for you were less strong. How can you be so cruel so heartless I really may almost say so wicked as to write to me that your impression is that I am heartily sick of the whole affair & only wish myself well out of it. These are your very words & I can hardly bring myself to rewrite them And then

in the end of your letter to tell me that you loved
me still, why it is the heighth of mockery & nonsense
to write in so contradictory a manner. No woman cld
ever write so to a man she really loved. I suppose
you think that the affair has gone quite far enough
that it amused you for the moment at Cowes, but
that you never meant to be led into a serious engagement. Well I tell you that if it is so you have treated
me TOO badly. If words mean anything, I consider
that we are bound to each other That if you cast me
off tho from your beauty & attractions you will have
always admirers at your feet, but you will have trifled
with & spurned, the truest & most honest love &
devotion that man is capable of feeling. I tell you
I have placed all my hopes of future happiness in
this world on you I have voluntarily staked what one
may call one's moral fortune on this game, & that
if I lose it, well then I am indeed lost. I have never
loved before but I have loved & do love you as even
you will never be loved again;

> Who that knows what love is here
> all its falsehood all its pain
> Wld for half Elysium's sphere
> care to dream that dream again?

> Who that in the desert heat
> Sees the waters fade away
> Wld not rather *die* than meet
> Streams again so false as they!

I thought, nay was confident that you returned my
love & with that confidence was prepared to make any
sacrifice & to clear away all obstacles that might
separate us. It might have taken time, but at any rate
I shld have been cheered with that idea, & led on
by the thought of how great a treasure wld reward
one's toil. Is that confidence to be taken away from
me? Am I to lose that hope. By your letter you have
rudely shaken the one, & you have cast great fears

into my mind as regards the other. How can you thus deliberately & coolly write of breaking off a solemn & serious engagement for I will not look at it in any other light. Not that for a moment I wld force you even if I had the power to marry me against your will & inclinations, but have I been really so terribly mistaken? Oh No it cannot be, God cld not allow such utter misery to fall on any one Come write once more & tell me you do not mean what you wrote, that it was only joking that you wrote it, & that you regret having written so unkindly. Tell me my dearest that I am not hopelessly & utterly ruined & left alone. Tell me that I have not wasted all my affection on one who cld not feel it, that I have not so deeply loved where there is & where there can be no return. How can you say that I have abused your family, when you know that I am incapable of doing such a thing? I tell you that as to your mother & sister I am prepared to love them & to be as fond of them as if they were mine, & as to your father I do not know him, but it is quite sufficient to me that he is your father ever to be treated by me with greatest respect & affection. Oh my darling Jeannette pardon me if I have written crossly, but your letter quite took my breath away, & has left me perfectly distracted with grief & worry. I cannot write again to you till I have heard from you that I may, & it will be with the greatest anxiety that I shall wait for & no little fear that I shall open your answer if you care to write one. But I do entreat & implore you to have confidence in me if you really love me & never again to write so cruel & so painful a letter

> Yr as ever devoted
> but despairing
> Randolph S. Churchill

A good quarrel was probably just what Jennie and Randolph needed to establish their love for each other. Jennie seems to have got Randolph's letter the same day. She replied at once:

Paris
Sept. 18th

This must be—& shall be the last misunderstanding between us—my own darling Randolph unless you wish to make it—If my letter pained you & gave you any anxiety—it has caused me a thousand times more —The moment it had gone—I repented & if I could have got it then—you wld never have received it— And yet in [a] way I do not feel sorry—for it has given me a fresh proof of yr love—& has made me discover the strength and depth of mine—I did not know how much I loved you—until I left England & felt that I was leaving all I love most on earth behind me—perhaps for ever—Darling I love yr angry cross letter—it has done me more good—than twenty tender ones—In fact dearest I have been so unhappy, & miserable since Tuesday I was certain it cld not last—Things look brighter now & they *must* come right it is a great comfort to be sure of ourselves. I could leave Father Mother—& the whole world for you—if it were necessary—Now Randolph that I have made this confession you must answer all my questions—& be perfectly frank & confiding in me. I want you to tell me everything—what the 'circumstances are which are doubtful & uncertain' & if there is any particular reason besides the one you gave me —for wishing our marriage to be in December—As I wish this letter to please you—I shall not say what I think it is—you might be angry—But I agree with you—I hate long engagements & if our parents give their consent—I dont see why it should not be in December—When are you coming? I pray & hope it will be soon—if you know how I long to see you it seems an age since Monday—what will it be— before October?—We did not go to Lord George's [3] to tea—nor to the Play—altho' he had got us the Garners [4] box.

The weather here is quite heavenly—Altho' our apartment commands a charming view & has a dear little garden Mama finds it so big & cold—She has

decided to change—We are going back to the Bd
Haussmann 146—but you must still address yr letters here—for we shall not be settled before a week
—A propos why do you ask me not to write too
often Does one letter a week bore you? Shall I make
it two? Clara has just given me a very pretty photo:
frame with yr favorite monogram—I shall put yr
photo: in it I have it in my room where I can see it
the first thing in the morning & the last thing at night
I have not taken off the bracelet yet I shall not until
you come—I do not mind being fettered to you by
such a beautiful chain—Please write to me as often
as possible yr letters are my only pleasure—I wish
I could get ten a day!—*Au revoir, mon seul ami,*

> Ever yours
> Jeannette Jérôme

Randolph and Jennie were both young and of high
mettle, and as those who disapproved of their engagement doubtless told them, they hardly knew each other
yet. After this little flurry they knew each other better. From it, they emerged strengthened against their
opponents. Not that they weren't both a little ashamed
of themselves. Even before he received Jennie's letter,
Randolph was writing to apologize for the sternness of
his own:

> Blenheim
> Friday 19th Sept.

My dearest Jeannette I cannot even if I wld let a day
pass without writing to you. The more I read your
letter over, altho it makes me vy low & wretched still
I cannot bring myself to think that you really doubt
me; I feel sure that you really love me, & dearest
love & confidence are identical & synonymous. Forgive me my darling if my letter was rather cross yesterday or annoyed you at all. I was so taken aback
by yours & wrote on the spur of the moment which
one shld never do. I cannot think what shld have
made you write to me so. I shall be awfully miserable
& wretched till you write to me again & it is indeed

you who have made me so. You know dearest you told me in London that you were angry because you thought I had a great deal of worry & you had none, & that you wld like to share it with me. Well my love it is not the right way to go to work to add to mine. Dearest I love you better than anything on earth & shall *never* love another. Whenever you feel doubts of me, & of course I know that sometimes many horrid thoughts will force themselves unbidden on one's mind when anyone you are vy fond of is away, just read over my letters to you, & I am sure you will feel convinced that no gentleman cld write as I have done to you, without feeling from his heart every word he said. How cld you so calmly write & recommend me to marry some English girl. You have no idea how you pain me when I think you capable of imagining even for a moment that I shld ever look at or speak to again any other girl after you. I mean to marry you my darling & nobody else & I do not intend that anything shall keep us long apart. However dear I have said enough about that letter & shall never refer to it again. I shld like to send it back to you as I cannot help always reading & looking at anything that reminds me of you, & yet it does vex me terribly. I can now assure you dearest that my father & mother will not oppose my marrying you; they will very probably try to insist on some delay in order that their incredulous minds may be fully persuaded that I am as fond of you & that I love you as dearly as I have continually dinned into their heads ever since I saw you that I do. But it wont be for very long. I know them so well, they always pretend to be very stern at first about everything, but they can never hold out long as they are really very kindhearted & vy fond of me (strange to say). And I assure you that when you do marry me they will be as fond of you as of their own daughters & will be vy proud of you indeed & you will never for a moment regret having come into my family. Now dearest I shld not write this to you if I was not certain of it.

I had at first I tell you candidly great doubts as to whether they wld consent, & that was what worried me so & made me so wretched, & that was why I tried to persuade you that perhaps we might have to do without their consent. You see dearest, they do not know you & they think I am very young, & being very practical unsentimental sort of people they will not yet quite believe in so strong an attachment having arisen in so short a time But I am happy to say that since yesterday all my doubts as to their consent have disappeared, & tho they may still try to make difficulties in order to satisfy themselves they are doing their duty. Still ultimately & before very long too it will all come right. Of that I am now confident. I was not quite so before, & perhaps that was what made me appear to you a little changed, when I saw you in London. For it cld but make me a little wretched, when I saw how nice how good you were & what an angel you were to care about me, to think that perhaps my own father & mother wld be the people to step between me and my only chance of happiness, & I felt & they knew that I shld never never speak to them again if they did, & that convinced them of the reality of what I told them & when once they come to know you they will understand why. However as I told you I know it will all come right now although there may still be little 'tracasserie's [5] difficulties & annoyances. But dearest what do you and I care if there are? 'The course of true love never did run quite smooth.' When people just have an ordinary liking for each other as happens in 999 cases out of a 1000, they always seem to marry without the least bother but when as in our case it is no ordinary liking or inclination but a strong deep enduring & I think I may say mutual love, then there seems to be always some malignant power at work to keep those two apart. But my darling true love must always win the day, & when God has made two people for each other, as I am sure he has you & I, intending that we shall lead a happy life on this earth together, never is anything permitted to come permanently between them. Dearest I cld write to you for ever, if I was not afraid of wearying you with such long letters. You MUST now write me an answer not only to my letter of yesterday but to this one. Things are now coming to a crisis; your father's formal answer will soon be arriving & I must then finally speak out all my mind to my father & get a formal answer from him, & I must feel convinced & certain & sure of your sympathy approval & consent, so my darling I not only implore and entreat but I call upon you most solemnly & seriously to write to me words of affection and encouragement such as you know so well how to write. I know you well enough to feel certain that you never wld have spoken to me & talked to me as you have done without feeling every thing you said or without being prepared to abide by it all. Talk of my giving you up!! Why as long as I feel sure of your affection as I do now, thank God, you might just as well expect the earth to stop still from ever moving or the sun to cease to shine. I shall expect a letter from you about Wednesday next, & mind dearest it is this one I want answered, & if you have answered yesterdays you must write another in answer to this. I enclose you two of the small photographs perhaps you may like them better than the others. I will send you the papers tomorrow in which will be the account of our dinner. & now dearest darling Jeannette Goodbye & God bless you & keep you ever true to me; I have written perhaps at too great length, but you have not your equal on this earth, & never will have & there is nothing I will not do say or write to win you & to call you my own.

Ys lovingly & ever devoted
Randolph S. Churchill

It is a magnificent letter, wonderfully written, with touches of the humour which was to make him such a popular political figure, and a sense of confidence in himself, his love, his future, that recent events hardly bore out. It is also very revealing of his relations with his parents: everything he says of them is true: they *were* very fond of him, they *would* make difficulties in order to satisfy themselves they were doing their duty, their sternness *would* give way to acquiescence. He knew them, perhaps, better than they knew him. But for all the confidence the letter exudes, Randolph had had his qualms, as he admitted in his next letter, written after he had received Jennie's one making it all up:

> Blenheim
> Saturday 20th
> Evening

You dear little darling Jeannette Your kind loving reassuring little letter just arrived as I had finished my letter of this morning. I did not expect to hear from you in any case till Monday or Tuesday, so you may fancy how delighted I was. But I assure you when I first got it I was so nervous & frightened I did not dare open it for some minutes. And then oh how glad & relieved I was. I feel quite happy again now & I have been so wretched. However it is all passed. You need not think I shld ever quarrel with you or be angry really. You might treat me as badly as you liked, (I know you never wld) & I shld never do anything but love you all the more. I am very glad you have got back safe to Paris after all we are not much farther apart than we were before, & now dearest I do beg & entreat of you to be careful about riding that horse before it has been properly exercised. I know what those nasty hot fiery brutes are after a long rest. I shall be so nervous & worried about you unless you promise me to be careful. How nice & good of Clara to give you that photograph frame it must be awfully nice to have a sister like her. You quite misunderstand me when I wrote to you not to write too much. I was only afraid perhaps you might make your mother angry & she might forbid you to write at all. Dearest I do implore you to write as much as ever you can to me. Your letters, (like your last) give me new life. You will have got my letter of yesterday by this time. I think perhaps you will like one of the photographs I sent you better for your bracelet than the one I put in. You must tell me all you do at Paris, I have literally nothing in the way of news to write to you from here. I am all alone now here with my two sisters in this enormous house but I had rather be here than anywhere else except with you I have been asked to go to one or two places, but I hate the idea of parties now. I potter about all day thinking of you. The pleasantest time is taken up writing to you & I always make that last as long as possible. The pug has been very ill with distemper, I hope he is getting over it now, He is fed on nothing but beeftea The poor thing had a fit yesterday but I do not think he has got it badly. If he is all right I shall bring him to Paris with me and ask you to take care of him, I am sure he will be happier with you. The man who is taking care of him has just come in to say he has had two more fits, & I feel rather alarmed & have sent for the doctor from Oxford. I am sure you will be sorry for the poor pug. Tell Clara about him. Dearest I cannot write more now as it is just dinner time, thankyou a million times for your letter I feel quite a different being to what I did this morning. Please remember me to your mother & Clara & with a thousand kisses to yourself. Believe me my darling Jeannette

yr most loving & devoted
Randolph S. Churchill

One of the troubles with correspondence is that it is very difficult for the writers to co-ordinate their moods. As one's spirit climbs, the other's sinks. Now Randolph was happy, Jennie was glum:

Friday evening
I have just received yr letter my dear Randolph & I feel so happy that you are in better spirits if you

knew the influence yr letters have over mine perhaps you wld write differently—If I get a gloomy, melancholy letter from you in the morning I am unfit for anything the rest of the day—All I can do is to wander about & wait impatiently for the next mail— My darling if things are as you say—I do not see any cause to be either low or in the least cross—I am sure everything will come right with time. Of course what does worry & torment us—is being apart from each other—but parents forget those things— & we must make the best of it—What I am afraid of is that if we do not see each other for a year—& are not allowed to write—it must necessarily fall through—Do not be angry dearest Randolph but you know few people stand the test—even if they write to each other & see each other occasionally. Oh my darling I wish things might be arranged that is, our engagement settled—as for the date of our marriage that is quite secondary & may remain for a long time yet *dans les nuages* [6]—without its worrying us much for the present—You see dearest I know Mama well enough to know that she will not allow you to come to see us here—under these circumstances—Unfortunately people have associated our names together —& she wld think it very compromising for me to have you seen with us & yet to deny that there is anything in it—as we have done so far—In fact I am more than blue tonight altho' I pretended in the beginning of this letter to be cheery—I do not care what anyone says or does—or what happens! if I can only see you again if only for a day—It is really cruel of you to remain at that Blenheim! Forgive me—I know you wld come if you cld & I am sure you wish it as much as I do—I am ashamed of this letter—instead of giving you advice—& trying to console you—I do nothing but complain—You must try & pacify yr father & after you receive my mother's letter—try & get his consent to our engagement—& then I shld certainly wait until *after* the election to say anything more—Now darling I must say goodbye

—it is very late—& I hope you will forgive this very untidy letter—How did you hurt yr finger—do take care—Don't smoke so much & write *every day*—it is my only pleasure—Ever yrs

Jeannette Jerome [7]

Randolph did write every day, and his spirits remained high:

Blenheim
Monday

Your two darling letters arrived this morning my own dearest Jeannette I was so happy to see yr handwriting again it is the next best thing to seeing you. Well my dearest as you will have seen from my letter of Friday which when you wrote you had not received, we have no cause now to despond or be in bad spirits, everything goes on as favourably as we cld expect, & my father does not wish for a moment to prevent my seeing you as often as I can, & has promised to give his consent to our marriage when he is sure we are fond of each other. As to the year I have every right to say that I do not think they will insist on it, & I enclose you a letter I received from my eldest sister Cornelia [8] who is of the same opinion. It may comfort you. I assure you my dearest I only require to be with you now to be as happy as a lark. I am only waiting to hear from Mdme Jerome to fly over to Paris. As you in the beginning of yr letter freely scolded me, I am going to do the same to you. & I want to know how you can write such a sentence as the following 'What I am afraid of is that if we do not see each other for a year. and are not allowed to write it must NECESSARILY!!!!! fall through'. & then you add 'don't be angry'. My dearest the idea is too absurd to be angry about, as I know you are only joking, but all I wld say is that I think jokes of that sort vy bad ones. What a word 'necessarily'. What in heaven's name can you mean? It nearly made me ill. Why my own darling do you

mean to confess that you cld not keep true to me for
a year even if we did not see each other; you cannot
mean that, or else you cannot care about me vy much.
Or do you mean that you doubt my keeping true to
you. I swear by everything that ten centuries wld
made no difference to me, & I thought you felt it &
knew it. I do not think you have any idea how those
little sentences of yrs which you write quickly & care-
lessly sometimes give me pain, or I am sure you wld
not write them. Thank God there is now no necessity
in our being separated at all, or any reason why there
shld be any concealment about our marriage and I
am sure yr mother will see it in the same light. The
clouds have all cleared away & the sky is bluer than
I have ever known it since I first saw you at Cowes.
It is exactly six weeks to-morrow since I first saw you
on board the *Ariadne*. I am sure I seem to have lived
6 years. Oh how I do bless that day, in spite of all
the worry & bother that has come since. For it has
been bad for me at times my love, more so I think
than you can fancy. I am so glad yr father has written kindly about me, it is entirely owing to you &
your dear mother writing as you have done. Well
I am sure you will never regret it. I have not had
any further conversation with my father since I wrote
to you as I think it is best to leave things for the
present as they are. Our early golden dreams of being
married in December wont quite become realities but
still it wont be very long to wait & I shall be able
to see you from time to time & write as often as I
like & in fact we can be regularly engaged and all the
world may know it. That is dearest if you like. Well
it is a great deal better than I expected at one time,
& I feel a great deal happier. What has kept me up
all along has been the conviction I had that you
darling loved me, & feeling that, I cld have gone
through anything.

I have just come back from shooting with my
father. They all go away to-morrow & I shall go to
London. I cannot stay in this big house quite alone

as even my sisters will be gone. Henry Lennox tells me he will be going through Paris sometime next week & that you promised to give him a dinner. He had a long conversation with my mother about you and me & he told me she spoke very nicely & kindly about us. He is a good friend of yours I think, much better than that old fool G.P. I am very glad to hear you do not ride or go out into the world. I am sorry to say dear that I am afraid I smoke more than ever, & that it will require all yr influence and authority to make me give it up at all. Oh dear how I do long to be with you I hope I shall hear from you again to-morrow in answer to my letter of Friday & I hope you will write in better spirits. I wonder what made you feel so '*blue*'. I like yr good advice & yr scolding & yr cheery letters, so much better than your last; they do me so much good & make me feel quite a different creature It is curious what an effect books have on me. I have two old favourites & when I feel very cross & angry I read Gibbon, whose profound philosophy & easy tho majestic writing soon quiets me down & after an hour I feel at peace with all the world; when I feel vy low & desponding I read Horace; whose thorough epicurianism & quiet maxims & beautiful verse, is most tranquillising. Of late I have had to have frequent recourse to my two friends, & they have never failed to have their usual effect. I strongly recommend you to read some great works or histories, they pass the time & prevent you from worrying, or thinking too much about the future. I wonder whether you will understand all this, or only think me rather odd. Novels and even travels are rather unsatisfactory & do one no good except to create an unhealthy excitement which is bad for any-one. There are three new elections to come off owing to death vacancies, & if they go against the government, as they very probably will do we are sure to have a dissolution, & then I shall become member for Woodstock. But after all, a public life has not great charms for me, as I am naturally very quiet & hate bother & publicity, which after all is full of vanity & vexation of spirit. Still it will have greater attractions for me if I think it will please you, & that you take an interest in it, & will encourage me & keep me up to the mark. I hope your mother wont delay writing to me, as I cannot keep away from you much longer I hope Clara is quite well & comforts you & sticks up for me, when you abuse me to her, or doubt me. Please give her my love & remember me vy kindly to yr mother. Dearest Jeannette Goodbye.

Ever yrs devotedly
Randolph S. Churchill

Years later, Winston was to find much solace in Gibbon, too. Jennie found hers in playing the piano, and the Jeromes' Paris apartment must have rung with some very passionate playing that September, as she waited for her father's letter. Randolph's mercurial ups and downs alarmed her considerably, and she felt he did not always tell her the whole truth about things when he ought to. She wrote and told him so:

Paris Sept. 22

I am afraid I shall not be allowed to write again in a long time my dearest Randolph as Mama seemed quite annoyed this morning when I asked if I might— I suppose you expected a cross letter like yrs *méchant*! & that is the reason you wished me to answer the last one—Your letters astonish me dearest—I am afraid you are too confident of success—too easily moved by a word—One moment you are in the depths of despair—thinking that if you marry me it must be without yr father's consent & the next seeing every thing *couleur de rose* & writing to me that there will be no opposition—Now darling you must not be angry I assure you I am not blaming you in the least —for I am that way myself—but you must not try & cheer me with hopes which are not to become realities—I have been reading a letter you wrote me in Cowes—saying the same thing & after all you confess that the last time I saw you in London you had great doubts 'as to whether yr father & mother would consent or not'—What has made them disappear??—is it quite true that they *have* disappeared or is it only to cheer me that you say so—& to make me think you are not worried & troubled as I know you are—Dearest that is bad policy—for if I am to share all yr troubles for the rest of my life—I had better be a little initiated beforehand—Not that I think we shall have many—on the contrary—when two people love each other as we do—nothing can annoy them much the most matter of fact stupid, dull life on Earth can be made happy by love—And I see no reason why ours should be an exception—After all then—I was right as to yr being changed in London—why not have told me dear?—you must have a very poor opinion of my affection for you—if you think anything your father & mother can say—can change it in the least—Of course they can prevent our marriage —but that is all—& whether I marry you or not I shall always think of you as the only man I could have married & the only man I ever really loved— I hope & pray dear Randolph you will come soon— Paris wld be charming with you—Tomorrow we go to 146 Bd Haussmann do not forget to address yr letters there—I shall be very glad to begin my music & studies I think any town a bore unless one is well occupied—I rather like those last photographs *les 6 boutons sont resplendissants!* [9] Clara sends her best love—

> Ever Yours—
> Jeannette Jerome

How is Puggles?—I found yr paper very interesting— but what a bore such a dinner must be!—

In response, Randolph told Jennie exactly what he had in mind:

> Blenheim
> Tuesday 23rd

Dearest, I got your letter out shooting today. My sister Annie [10] brought it out with my luncheon. I can-

not tell you what pleasure & happiness yr letters give
me they make me feel quite a different being, so you
really must not threaten me with a long silence never
mind if yr mother is a little cross, but DO keep on
writing as OFTEN as you can if you at all care to
prevent my being worried & '*triste*'. I have often told
you that all my bother & worry & sadness is chiefly
owing to being away from you, & so if I hear from
you from time to time I am much happier. You certainly my dearest Jeannette have great powers of per-
ception, & I cannot but own, that there is a good deal
of truth in what you say about my being one moment
vy despairing & another moment vy sanguine; I can't
help it, I was made so. & you say you are a little bit
the same. My father has been away for a few days
& yesterday I got a '*piece*' from him on the subject
of his consent. After a good deal of unnecessary
rigmarole & verbosity he says. 'The great question is
still unsolved; whether you & the young lady who has
gained your affections, are or can be after a few days
acquaintance, sufficiently aware of your own minds
to venture upon a step which is to bind you together
for life. To marry in haste & repent at leisure is a
trite saying but not less trite than true; What I have
now to say is that if I am to believe that yr happiness
is really bound up in yr marriage with Miss Jerome
you must really shew me proof of it by bringing it to
the test of time; I will say no more to you on this
subject for the present but if this time next year you
come & tell me you are both of the same mind we
will receive Miss Jerome as a daughter & I need not
say in the affection you cld desire for your wife.' Now
my darling these are his words but I do not mind telling you that it is all humbug, (at least if I know him
at all) about waiting a year. I cld & wld wait a
good deal more than a year for you, & I am sure you
wld do the same for me, but I do not mean to, &
it is not the least necessary & no good can come of it.
Tho' we have only known each other a short time, I
know we both know our own minds well enough. &

I wrote a vy long & diplomatic letter to my father yesterday, doing what I have never done before, contradicting him and arguing with him & I hope persuading him that he is got a vy wrong & foolish idea into his head. You see my darling I have to a great extent got him in my power & I will tell you why. Both he & my mother have set their heart on my being member for Woodstock. It is a family borough & for years & years a member of the family has sat for it. The present member is a stranger [11] tho a conservative, & is so unpopular that he is almost sure to be beaten if he were to stand, & the fact of a radical sitting for Woodstock is an idea perfectly insupportable to my family. It is for this that they have kept me idle ever since I left Oxford; waiting for a dissolution. Well as I told you the other day a dissolution is sure to come almost before the end of the year. Well I have two courses open to me, either to refuse to stand altogether, unless they consent to my being married to you immediately afterwards or else, & this is still more Machiavellian and deep, to stand, but at the last moment, threaten to withdraw & leave the radical to walk over. This may all appear vy strange to you but you have no idea how much they think of this borough & how much they have set their hearts on it & I am so certain of the success of one or other of these plans that that is why (having obtained their conditional consent) I am in comparatively good spirits as to my being able to obviate any long delay. All tricks are fair in love as well as in war & if I am crossed, I can plot & intrigue like a second Machiavelli. However I really do not think any of this will be necessary. I hope to be able to write to you in a day or two that my letter to my father yesterday, which I wish you cld have seen as it was a sort of 'ultimatum' has had the effect of considerably modifying his resolutions. Now please dont you go and tell yr mother about this idea of a year's delay as I think it is an idea which has already got much too much into her head as it is, & I do not mean to stand it if

I can help it, which I know I can, if I am quite sure of yr entire approval & concurrence. Now my dearest you know really everything I really must make one remark on yr letter & scold you a little & that is upon the apparently calm way in which you continually envisage the fact of our not being married after all. Now my darling this does really rather annoy me I have never suffered such a thought to enter into my head for a moment since I have been quite sure & confident of your dear love & I really must most solemnly protest against yr ever thinking such a thing again. I have told you times & times, yet you will not seem to trust me, that nothing whatever, no circumstances & no people shall ever keep you from me, & that sooner or later if we both live, we will [marry]. I am sure you will not mind my remarking upon this. Dearest you must write vy soon. As soon as I have got one letter from you I never am happy till I get another, & you do write so charmingly & so lovingly you dear that it wld have been better never to have begun than to stop. I know you cant refuse what I beg of you so shall confidently expect letters from you. I have been out shooting today, & it has been terribly hot & *je suis ereinté*.[12] The poor dear pug is in a most critical state. He has frequent fits, & never seems to know me or anyone now. However I have still some hopes of his recovery tho vy slight. I am sure Clara will be sorry about this, she always used to tell me she liked the pug better than his master. Please give her my love, she says I never send her a message but the fact is you dont give them. I shall certainly go to Paris when I hear from yr mother. It wont be long now, your father's final answer must come vy soon. Do tell me what you have already heard from him, as I know you must have heard. The fact is you tell me nothing really altho you are always accusing me of not telling you things & I do tell you everything. Dearest I am afraid my letters are far from amusing & will not give you a very high idea of my abilities, but my life here is a perfect blank as far as excitement or amusement of any sort goes. I hope you really will work hard at your music when anyone plays as beautifully as you do it is well worth working at it. Please do not ride that vicious horse. I have formed the worst opinion of him. Remember me vy kindly to your mother & tell her from me she is not to be cross with you for writing, but only with me for I have told you to. Dearest you may really cheer up & be in good spirits now, as things are looking much brighter, & I begin to see my way quite clear.

With fondest love to you

Yrs ever devotedly
Randolph S. Churchill

Emotional blackmail is permitted within one's own family, perhaps, but even so, Randolph's plan was Machiavellian indeed. His lack of scruple as to the means by which he attained his ends was to prove disastrous within eighteen months. Jennie, however, was shocked less by the unscrupulousness itself than by Randolph's rashness in exposing it to prying eyes:

September 26th
Randolph my dear I think I shall have to put a black faveur on the last letter of yours to mark it from the others—you are really very wicked to *write* such things about your father & mother—it is bad enough to say them—but write them is really dreadful— After all dearest—it is not so very long to wait— & you must have a little patience—I am also angry with you dear for saying you would like 'a peaceful happy life with no particular occupation' indeed I cannot believe you would be contented to sit and fold yr hands for the rest of yr life. I shld like you to be as ambitious as you are clever—& I am certain you would accomplish great things—We might have a nice little home of our own as you say—whatever yr family is to you I know mine will always be kind & loving to both of us—I received two letters from my

father yesterday—I wish you were here to read them —I cannot tell you how kind they are—of course he thinks it all rather sudden & *surtout* rather hurried he is afraid I do not realize how important such a step is etc—but on the whole I can see he gives his consent & I am sure will do everything he can for us— he says he wld have preferred an American for me —but that there is not much difference *au fond* between English & Americans. He adds—'I am as confident that all you say of him is true as though I knew him myself.' You see dear, Papa & I are the greatest friends as I have told you—& he has always done everything on Earth he can to please—Mama also received a letter from him, a very long & serious one full of stupid affairs—& I believe she will write to you in a day or two. I hope you have not quarreled with yr father & that you will come to us very soon —I am getting *so* tired waiting. *Croyez vous que vous êtes le seul?* [13] People are so curious & annoy me so with questions that I have quite retired from the world —I have quite a hermit's life & remain all day in my little salon—only emerging for a walk before dinner I have not been able to ride yet—*malheuresement*— as I have for the present no available chaperon—I am afraid I shall have to wait until Papa comes. . . .

Leonard Jerome's letters were written on different dates, though they arrived in Paris on the same day. In the first he was alarmed:

My dear Jennie,
    You quite startle me. I shall feel very anxious about you till I hear more. If it has come to that—that *he* only 'waits to consult his family' you must be pretty far gone. You must like him well enough to accept for yourself which for you is a great deal. I fear if anything goes wrong you will make a dreadful shipwreck of your affections. I always thought if you ever did fall in love it would be a dangerous affair. You were never born to love lightly. It must be *way*

down or nothing. Something like your mother. Not so Clara—happily not so. . . .

He went on to say he wouldn't object as long his wife didn't—'Provided always he is not a Frenchman or any other of those continental cusses,' a remark which goes some way to explaining why he preferred to live alone in New York rather than with his family in Paris. His next letter was written when he had more details. 'I must say I have been very happy all day,' he wrote. 'I have thought of nothing else.' He promised to give her £2000 a year, and went on:

> I cannot imagine any engagement that would please me more. I am as confident that all you say of him is true as though I knew him. Young, ambitious, uncorrupted. And best of all you think and I believe he loves you. He must. You are no heiress and it must have taken heaps of love to overcome an Englishman's prejudice against 'those horrid Americans'. I like it in every way. He is English. You will live in England. I shall see much of him and you. And my dear Jennie the very best of it is—*a love match.* Like your mother & me. Did you ever know a couple to get on better than we do? There is nothing that compensates for love rank wealth all the honours that all the world can heap upon you are nothing compared with genuine love . . .

Mrs Jerome wrote to Randolph, announcing Leonard's formal consent. But she had serious doubts about the Duke's attitude, in spite of what Randolph had told her:

> Septer 29, 1873
> 146 Bd Haussmann
>
> My dear Ld. Randolph
> I have just received a letter from my husband which I do not send you as there are many things in it which would not interest you. Of course dear Ld.

Randolph he knows nothing about you except what I have written which I need not say was most favourable. Taking for granted that what I said must be true & listening to his daughters earnest appeal who thinks all her happiness in life depends on her marrying you, he gives his formal consent. I must however say that my husband has not the slightest idea of any opposition from your Father as I wrote him very particularly what you told me at Cowes that there would be none. I can only repeat that both Mr Jérôme and myself have too high an opinion of our daughter too much love ever to permit her to marry any Man without the cordial consent of his family.

My husband also writes. 'If the settlement of £2,000 a year & the assurance of one third of all my fortune later is satisfactory this can all be easily arranged.'

If yr Father gives his consent I shall wish you to see more of each other before taking such an important step & if there is any engagement at all it must be a long one.

Pray believe dear Ld. Randolph in my sincere affection for you.

Clara H. Jérôme

Randolph replied to this effusively, thanking Mrs Jerome for having spoken well of him, admitting that his father felt as she did that a long engagement was desirable, and saying how very much he loved Jennie. Jennie's next letter must have reached him the following day:

Monday evening

My darling I can only write a line otherwise this letter will not go tonight as it is late—But I must tell you how happy I feel now that things are coming right—& that I may see you soon—I hope you will never know what a worthless & idle life I have been leading since we came here—& all owing to you *Monsieur!* Really I have not had the heart to do [the] slightest thing—I have felt so anxious about it all indeed I have grown quite thin & I am afraid you will think me so ugly when you come—you wont care for me any more I was glad to see by yr Friday letter that you had not quarrelled with yr father, as I was afraid you wld—I think him quite in the right—& understand perfectly that he thinks as he does—altho' I think it rather tedious—I am not astonished as I expected it if not from yr father—from my mother—who does nothing but sermonize me on the subject—Dearest you must not come to Paris—until you have written to Mama— I know she wrote you yesterday & you must answer before coming—for it is in vain that I have told her all you said & even read her yr letters she does not seem to be quite convinced—& I think it will need all yr eloquence to persuade her to allow you to come—I am afraid she does not quite believe all you say yr father said—I am sure you wont mind my speaking frankly—you must try & get yr father to write—or let Mama know in some way what his decision is—on receiving yr letter this evening I went & had a long talk with her—which resulted in my feeling *fameusement* again—She says she cannot have you come here & be seen with us until things are entirely settled & the engagement an understood thing in both our families & by everyone—darling I hope you are not angry at my telling you this—you know how difficult it is to manage parents indeed I am tired of trying to do it—I shall expect a letter on Wednesday in answer to this—why did you not write Saturday? I cannot do without one *everyday* you have spoilt me too much to stop now—I am *so sorry* about poor dear Puggy—I had hoped we wld have him in our little house—when we are married—it wld remind us of Cowes, Rosetta, & those happy days—How short & few they were—If we love each other so much now—fancy what it will be later! I have a great quantity of photos: taken all sizes & poses—I think I shall wait until you come (which I hope will be next week) to give them to

you—I really must stop—good night my own darling
Randolph—

Ever yours
Jeannette Jerome

Randolph was furious at the suggestion that he was
not telling the truth, and at once wrote and told Mrs
Jerome so, and announced his imminent arrival in Paris.
Jennie was aghast—not at his arrival, but at his letter.
Many of the confusions of the engagement might never
have arisen if people had not replied so swiftly to their
letters. This was a case in point. Another misunderstanding now was more than Jennie could bear to
contemplate:

Friday morning

How could you write such a letter to Mama my darling
stupid Randolph? Did you not see that when I wrote
that wretched letter—neither Mama or I had received
either of yours—& I wrote mine on the spur of the
moment ('a thing one ought never do') after a discussion with her which made me feel very cross—altho'
she did not say half I wrote—but in my stupid anger I
wrote whatever came in my head—that she did not
believe you—words she *never did say*—I did not
know I had written them myself—I shall explain it all
to you when you come—& darling for Heaven sake
don't spoil this meeting by misunderstandings & quarrels—I have been so longing for it—& looking forward
to it—I cld not be so cruelly disappointed—You wld
have a perfect right to be furious & feel very much
injured if things were as you thought them—but they
are not—Pray believe what I say that it is all my fault
& I beg you to forgive me if you love me & not be
angry & come to me as soon as you arrive—We shall
expect you to dinner—& I shall be quite greying with
disappointment if you do not come—oh my darling
don't ever write such a letter again—when shall we

have finished with all these misunderstandings & distrusts?—

> Ever yrs most lovingly
> Jeannette

I am so very sorry Mr Livingstone & another American gentleman are dining with us—I hope it won't annoy you Mama asked them long ago—
DO COME[14]

Randolph came—to the Hotel France et de Bath, in the Rue St Honoré. Misunderstandings seem to have melted away. Even Leonard, weeks behind the events in New York, had his last scruples removed and announced 'Between you & I and the post—and your mother etc. *I am delighted* more than I can tell It is magnificent. The greatest match any American has made since the Dutchess of Leeds.' And so it was— though Leonard would have to learn to spell Duchess. (The Duchess of Leeds, who died one week before Jennie's wedding to Randolph, was the daughter of a Baltimore merchant, Richard Caton.) Bliss seems to have become general. Jennie and Randolph dawdled about Paris, pretending to look at furniture for the 'parrot's perch' they planned to live in, but no doubt much more interested in each other. The wedding, it had been agreed, must wait on the election. Meanwhile Randolph could visit Paris as often as he wished, though he must nurse his constituency as well.

He was planning to come over for Jennie's birthday, on January 9th 1874, but his mother's sister, Lady Portarlington, was taken mortally ill in Ireland, and the Duchess insisted that the family, including Randolph, should attend the death-bed. Jennie and the Duchess had not yet met, and it boded little good for relations between them that the Duchess's first letter to her future daughter-in-law should have indicated quite so plainly her authority over Randolph. On matters of duty, the Duchess rarely had doubts:

Emo Park
Portarlington
Jan. 7

Dear Miss Jerome

Although in great anxiety & affliction I write a line for dear Randolph to enclose as I feel grieved for his disappointment in not being able to start so as to spend your birthday with you. He was on the point of starting when my poor sister had a relapse to the state of fearful gasping for breath which is so anxious & so painful. It was almost impossible for him to go while she was in such a state for if the worst had happened he would have blamed himself & I feel sure you would not have wished it. I therefore urged him to remain & I telegraphed myself to you. He felt much the disappointment not only to himself but to you. I hope he will be rewarded for his self denial in a few days.

I am sorry my first communication with you should be of such a sad nature but the Duke & I hope please God to make your acquaintance under happier Circumstances ere long.

I remain dear Miss Jerome

Yrs Sincerely
F. Marlborough

The hope was not immediately realized. Lady Portarlington kept gasping for some time, then had to be decently buried before Randolph could get away. And when he did, he was half-way to France when he heard that Gladstone had dissolved Parliament and there was to be a General Election. Randolph went straight to Woodstock where 'the stranger' obligingly made way for him (not that he had much choice). Then he threw himself vigorously into the election.

Randolph was inexperienced (he hid the notes for a speech in his hat, much to the merriment of his audience), but he fought the campaign with enthusiasm, knowing that his victory would remove all obstacles to an early marriage. And in fact he won by 165 votes, then sped to Paris, where he was shortly followed by the Duke and Duchess, come to inspect their future daughter-in-law. Their conclusion was apparently satisfactory, though they did not find themselves able to attend the wedding, fixed for April the 15th. This was not the snub it would be today; the cult of weddings had not yet begun. But it was a snub of a sort, and the Duchess found herself unable to spare Randolph's sister Rosamond for the occasion, either. Anglo-American relations were not helped by the negotiations for Jennie's wedding settlement, which dragged on for several weeks. It was agreed by everyone except Leonard Jerome himself that he had behaved disgracefully, mainly, perhaps, because he though it quite wrong that an English husband should have control of an American wife's money. The Duke was extremely sensitive on such points. All was settled in time, however, and Randolph arrived again in Paris in early April. Jennie wrote to him just before he left:

> . . . I think it will be very nice to give Clara & Leonie a locket—but why not get them here? Mme Henry has charming things—much nicer than in London—besides dont you think it wld be better to get them together?—*Pourtant que ce soit comme vs le desirez cher ami—vs étes le maître*[15]—You really must let me ride I am so strong now I assure you I have grown quite fat,—& it will be so charming to go out in the morning—I wont marry you if you dont let (me) do *exactly* as I like—*il faut vs preparer a une vie de sacrifices*[16] with me my dear. . . .

Women are supposed to be contrary, but to say almost in the same breath that Randolph was master, and that she wouldn't marry him unless he let her do exactly as she liked, was going too far. In his reply Randolph ignored the provocation and told her about a dinner party he'd been to with the Prince of Wales. 'I am so glad to hear you have got so strong again', he added, '& that I shant find you such a little bag of bones as I left you.' He ended with an order, perhaps hoping to go on the way he was starting: 'Don't forget to order my apartment at the hotel d'Albe. I shall be furious if I don't find one quite ready.'

The wedding took place in the chapel of the British Embassy on April 15th. Jennie wore white satin with a long train and flounces of Alençon lace. Blandford was there, and three of Randolph's sisters and an aunt. The best man was Francis Knollys. For her going away the bride wore a dark blue dress with white stripes, and a white hat with a white feather. The dress was one of the twenty-five with which Lady Randolph Churchill began her married life.

NOTES

1. That is how I am made!
2. Strictly speaking this was true: a brother between Blandford and Randolph had died in infancy.
3. If this is the same as 'that old fool G.P.' of Randolph's letter of September 22nd, it may perhaps have been Admiral Lord George Paulet (1807-79), ADC to the Queen, CB, and officier de la Légion d'Honneur.
4. William Garner was an extremely rich American cotton manufacturer. He and his wife were drowned in 1876, leaving three daughters: Florence married Sir William Gordon-Cumming in 1891, the moment after his disgrace for cheating at cards in the Tranby Croft affair: Edith became Countess Leon Von Moltke Huitfeldt: and Marcelite the wife of the Marquis de Breteuil.
5. Vexations.
6. Unsettled.
7. Perhaps as a mark of Anglophilia, Jennie now dropped the French accents from her surname.
8. Lady Cornelia Henrietta Maria (1847-1927), married to Sir Ivor Bertie Guest, 2nd Bart, created first Baron Wimborne in 1880.
9. The six buttons are dazzling!
10. Lady Anne Emily, Randolph's third sister (1854-1928), married James Innes-Kerr, Marquess of Bowmont and later

7th Duke of Roxburghe in June 1874, after a much shorter engagement than Randolph's to Jennie.

11. Barnett was hardly a stranger. Glympton Park, where he lived, is precisely four miles from Blenheim Palace.

12. I am exhausted.

13. Do you think you are the only one?

14. Underlined five times.

15. However it shall be as you wish dear friend—you are the master.

16. You must prepare yourself for a life of sacrifices.

3

CHURCHILL
QUARRELS

Blenheim Palace has been the home of the Dukes of
Marlborough since 1715. The Royal Manor of Woodstock was granted by Queen Anne to the first Duke,
and ever since, on the anniversary of the battle of
Blenheim, his heirs have presented to hers a standard
of France, in commemoration of the great victory which
finally checked the pretensions of the Bourbons and the
power of France.

The history of Woodstock begins with the history of
Britain. A Roman road, still visible, paved with cobble-
stones, passes through the park. In Saxon times the
Kingdoms of Wessex and Mercia met nearby. The
country was heavily wooded, and there was probably a
royal hunting lodge in the valley of the little river
Glyme, where the forest began. The neighbouring kings
could meet there to discuss their affairs.

A visitors book of the Royal Manor would contain
all the great names of the succeeding thousand years of
British history. Alfred the Great and Ethelred the Un-
ready hunted the forest. The first great quarrel between
Henry II and Thomas à Becket occurred here. Henry I
had enclosed the park in a continuous wall, still standing, some twelve miles in circumference. Inside it he
kept lions, bears and camels, and other wild animals
from the east: there was no such extensive menagerie
in the whole of Europe until modern times. Henry II
also used the Manor to support a mistress: the fair

Rosamond lived in a 'bower' here, till Queen Eleanor found out. Legend says that Eleanor poisoned the well, and Rosamond went to an early grave in nearby God-stow Nunnery. The Latin inscription on her tomb puns on her name and implies 'The rose was fair but not pure', but pure water now bubbles out of Rosamond's well, and is piped across the valley to play in the fountains around the palace.

Richard Coeur de Lion, King John and the Black Prince were all born at Woodstock. Chaucer lived in the village, and his son became a ranger in the park. Queen Elizabeth I, as a young princess, was imprisoned in the gatehouse of the Manor by her sister Bloody Mary. James I hunted the deer ever year: there is a tradition that his son Charles I was himself hunted through the park by Oliver Cromwell and the Round-heads. But after the Restoration in 1660, the Royal Manor fell into disuse until it was granted to John Churchill, first Duke of Marlborough.

Marlborough had returned from his victories on the continent in triumph, but criticism and frustration met him at home, and complex political intrigue soon lost him royal favour. He turned therefore to planning the construction of his great palace in the old royal park. Blenheim was to be his silent answer to his critics, his monument, and his epitaph. For his architect he chose John Vanbrugh, an old comrade in arms, Flemish by descent (the Flemish were one of the peoples liberated by Marlborough's victories), Vanbrugh was a soldier by profession, but also a playwright of distinction. The dramatic scale of the site suited him, and the grandeur of the building he conceived was symbolic of the mo-mentous events it commemorated. The Duke wanted an English Versailles, combining the arts of England and Europe. Vanbrugh created a setting whose theatri-cal impact is strikingly revealed as one passes the en-trance gatehouse of the park and first sees the lake in the valley, the bridge, and then on the slope of the hill, silhouetted against the sky, the encircling arms of the palace, with its fantastic roofline. (The impact would be still more striking if Capability Brown had not later flooded the valley far more than Vanbrugh designed.)

Inside, the palace was a treasure-house. The Duke had been presented with gifts from all over Europe, and was in any case a great collector of works of art. Splendid tapestries celebrating his victories were specially woven at Brussels, famous pictures were acquired, statues were bought or seized as spoils of war; among the gifts was a scale model of Berrini's famous fountain in the Piazza Navona in Rome. There were silks, marbles, gems, Sèvres china, gold plate, Boulle furniture, Vandyke portaits, to say nothing of the diamond-studded sword presented to Marlborough by the Emperor. To all this splendour his descendants added: if they squandered their money, they often squandered it well. The fourth Duke, for instance, was a connoisseur, and collected the celebrated Marlborough gems. The Sunderland Library was one of the finest in the world. There were magnificent collections, too, of Limoges enamels, Oriental china and eighteenth-century French furniture. Blenheim Palace was altogether magnificent, inside and out.

Randolph brought Jennie to Blenheim on a beautiful spring day in May 1874. Some of the Duke's tenants (who were, of course, also Randolph's constituents) met them at the station, took the horses out of the carriage, and dragged them through the town to the palace. As they entered the park, Randolph turned to Jennie with pardonable pride and said 'This is the finest view in England.' She was deeply impressed, and when they reached the palace itself, awed. But life inside the treasure-house struck her as very strange, stiff and formal. Everything went on with the regularity of clockwork, and there was very little to do. Jennie practised her piano, read and painted, till she began to imagine herself back in the schoolroom. Everyone read the newspapers avidly, and the conversation was largely political. There were afternoon calls to be paid, social and charitable, otherwise there was only the garden to walk in. Dinner was a solemn full-dress affair. After-

wards everyone sat in the Vandyke room: the only
excitement was a mild game of whist, played strictly for
love, not money. People grew so bored that they sometimes surreptitiously advanced the clock so they could
go to bed: no one dared suggest moving till eleven had
struck. Then everyone would rise, fetch his candle, kiss
the Duke and Duchess good night, and depart, with
great relief, to his own room. Jennie was used to a
considerably gayer life than that, and was not amused
by the Duchess's instruction in the correct ways of
behaviour for an aristocrat's wife. If Blenheim was like
a schoolroom, there was no question as to who was the
mistress. The Duke was kind, but the Duchess, Jennie
wrote, 'ruled Blenheim and nearly all those in it with a
firm hand'. *Nearly* all, yes. The household trembled at
the rustle of her silk dress, but not Jennie. Her American pride rebelled. Though she acknowledged that the
Duchess was a very remarkable and intelligent woman,
she never got on with her, and there was continual
sniping and criticism between the two.

Though Jennie and Randolph had their own house in
London, they spent a good deal of time at Blenheim.
Jennie could not go out much in the social world, for
she was immediately pregnant. And it was at Blenheim,
during one of her many visits, that her first child was
born on November 30th, 1874, six weeks premature.
Winston caught everyone by surprise. The Duchess
reported to Mrs. Jerome in Paris that 'we had neither
cradle nor baby linen nor anything ready'. Randolph
sent a full account:

I have just time to write a line, to send by the London
Dr to tell you that all has up to now thank God gone
off very well with my darling Jennie. She had a fall
on Tuesday walking with the shooters, & a rather
imprudent & rough drive in a pony carriage brought
on the pains on Saturday night. We tried to stop them,
but it was no use. They went on all Sunday. Of course
the Oxford physician cld not come. We telegraphed
for the London man Dr Hope but he did not arrive

till this morning. The country Dr is however a clever man, & the baby was safely born at 1:30 this morning after about 8 hrs labour. She suffered a good deal poor darling, but was vy plucky & had no chloroform. The boy is wonderfully pretty so everybody says dark eyes and hair & vy healthy considering its prematureness. My mother and Clementine[1] have been everything to Jennie, & she cld not be more comfortable. We have just got a most excellent nurse & wet nurse coming down this afternoon, & please God all will go vy well with both. I telegraphed to Mr. Jerome; I thought he wld like to hear. I am sure you will be delighted at this good news and dear Clara also. I will write again tonight. Love to Clara.

> Yrs affty
> Randolph S.C.

I hope the baby things will come with all speed. We have to borrow some from the Woodstock Solicitor's wife.

While it would be idle to pretend that Jennie was a doting mother, it would be quite wrong to suggest that she did not love her children. Both her letters and Randolph's are full of references to Winston as a baby, and though no woman of her position spent very much time with her children, Jennie spent quite as much as most. In an aristocratic household a wife was expected to produce her babies, then hand them over to wet nurses,[2] nannies and nursemaids, till they were old enough to go to school. The nursery was an establishment within an establishment, with its own specially cooked meals served by its own staff, and its own hierarchical structure. Meanwhile the father and mother got on with their own lives, looking in occasionally to make sure all was well. Jennie's relations with her two sons were usually very good, but it was not a system which led to invariable accord between parents and children, as was amply demonstrated in the family into which she had married.

Blandford, as we have seen, was a man whose experience of marriage was so bitter that he seriously upset his brother by the way he inveighed against it. His wife was called Bertha. She was a daughter of the Duke of Abercorn, and much given to practical jokes. It was the great age of such jokes, but hers were of the simplest: inkpots on doors and the substitution of soap for cheese. But she was amiable, and did not seem to notice that Blandford was, at this time, in love with someone else. He had also warmed to Jennie, and came to like her so much that he gave her a ring to demonstrate his affection: perhaps she had expressed sympathy for him in his plight. While Randolph and Jennie were staying at Blenheim in October 1875, Jennie showed this ring to the Duchess and Randolph's sister Rosamond. There was immediate trouble. Next morning Randolph wrote to his brother:

My dear Blandford

My mother & Rosamond who appeared strangely annoyed last night about the ring you gave Jennie inform me this morning that it was one of Bertha's rings. I dont believe this for a moment, but as they have permitted themselves several vicious looks and insinuations concerning it, please write me a line to say that they are mistaken. Jennie wishes me to thank you for it immensely. If by any chance the ring ever did belong to Bertha, you wont mind I am sure if Jennie asks you not to press it on her. She knows quite well that you like her very much without any rings, tho' it was most kind of you to wish her to have it. I am sure you will understand this.
Sunday 31st

Ever yr. affly
Randolph S. Churchill

Since his parents found ceaseless fault with him, Blandford was no doubt delighted to have an excuse to find fault now with his mother. His response to Randolph's letter was to send it straight to the Duchess with the following note:

My Dear Mama   36 Piccadilly
    Well acquainted as I am with the intense jealousy that you often display in your actions & the mischief which you so often make in speach I should not have thought you would have allowed yourself to be so far carried away, as to descend to untruth to substantiate an assertion or give color to a fact. I am therefore compelled to write to you to inform you that if in future you condescend to make such statements as the enclosed letter contains you need not expect to hear very often from
                    Your very affec son
                    Blandford

The Duchess received the two letters as she was just setting off from Blenheim to go to London. She was dreadfully upset, and passed them straight to the Duke. As soon as they arrived in London, the Duke wrote to Randolph in indignation so high that it affected his spelling:

                    London
Randolph   Nov. 4
    Your mother has received today the enclosed correspondence.
    I have only three words to say to you upon it.
    1st you have grossly misrepresented facts to Blandford.
    2nd you have while being received with kindness, yourself, wife, and child dishonorably and treacherously abused the confidence, which you yourself pretended you shared with yr mother abt Blandford while you were well aware that she never entertained any motives but those of the truest affection for you both.
    3rd you have thus induced your brother to pen to his mother an unparalelled letter, which I do not trust myself to characterize in words You are the best

interpreter of these things and their natural results and I leave you to form yr own conclusions; further communications upon the subject are needless I am yrs

Marlborough

Randolph replied the same day:

Dearest Papa

I most respectfully remark with regard to yr letter of this afternoon that I think you have formed a hasty judgement of the enclosed correspondence. I venture to think that expressions such as 'dishonourable' 'treacherous' 'liar', are hardly applicable to me. As long as these expressions remain in force further communications between us, are not only as you remark useless but impossible.

Yr affte son
Randolph

It took no time at all for the Spencer-Churchills to put each other into the most terrible rages, rages which seem literally to have 'blinded'. For instance, the Duke did not call Randolph a 'liar', he said he had grossly misrepresented facts to Blandford, which is not at all the same thing.

Doubtless appalled by the violence of the storm which had broken about her innocent finger, Jennie wrote next day to the Duchess:

Almond's Private Hotel,
6 & 7, Clifford St,
Bond St. W.
Friday

Dearest Duchess

I feel I cannot let you go away without saying at least how deeply I regret this unfortunate quarrel of which I am most unhappy at being the unintentional cause—I am sure that at present a discussion on the subject would be more than useless. But I must say that as much as Randolph is to blame in having used expressions in his letter to Blandford that no son

ought to use about his mother—still the spirit of the
letter was neither 'treacherous', 'dishonorable,' or untrue—& was written moreover in anger & haste—&
never intended for your eye—The Duke's letter to
Randolph is such as no man should write to another—
not even a father to a son—All I can do is to repeat
how dreadfully sorry I am—& that whatever happens
I hope you will believe that I am most grateful—both
to you & the Duke—for all yr past kindness to me—&
that I shall ever remain Yrs. most affecty

J Spencer Churchill

This could be considered quite a tactful letter, under
the circumstances. Jennie admitted Randolph's fault,
pointed out the Duke's intemperance, and said how
sorry she was. A loyal wife could hardly do more. That
was not, however, how the Duchess saw it. Her outburst in reply is extremely revealing about the tensions
and suppressed emotions within the Marlborough
family:

Dearest Jennie   Nov. 5
I thank you for writing to me & am very sorry for the
annoyance which this must cause you—You talk of
it as a quarrel but it is much too serious for that. It
is a bitter sorrow to find both our sons turn against
us & reward our affection & kindness by insult & abuse.
I fear Randolph's words are but an instance of the
way he has got into with Blandford of abusing &
ridiculing us. I cannot trust myself to write all I could
abt. if for I do not wish to be harsh but I cannot think
that his Father's Language though strong was not
deserved—Randolph did misrepresent what I said abt
the ring & the way I said it & it was not true to say
Rosamond expressed annoyance when she never mentioned it at all—Randolph also spoke of 'our pretended views, looks & insinuations' which was perfectly untrue & he did this knowing it would rouse
Blandford's angry temper. It was treacherous & dis-

honourable towards us but indeed he has got himself
so into the habit of abusing People that I think he
hardly knows how far he goes, & he will surely get
himself into trouble. I never was so upset as when
these dreadful Letters were put into my hands as we
were leaving Home & it was such a blow to me that I
cld not control my emotions and the Duke was
naturally indignant. I will not argue abt it for I feel
too cut up. I believed Randolph to be loyal & true &
to find him otherwise cuts me to the heart. Nothing
can change it. Randolph has trampled on my affections & God forgive him for it. As for you dearest
Jennie Time will prove to you that I have treated you
as a daughter in word & deed. I love you & your dear
little child & I shall never cease to take a loving interest in you. Nor can I accuse myself of anything but
kind intentions respecting you since I have known you.
It is not in me to be false & though I may at times
have thought you unwise I have not intended to offend
or pass judgement on you. I wished to be more a
mother than a mother in law to you & perhaps I was
wrong—When you are away you will think kindly of
me. I quite feel that it is not in our Power to make
our sons love & respect us & to change their hearts
towards us & yet I have been brought up to think
strongly of Duty to Parents.
Sadly I admit therefore that it is perhaps well that
Randolph should see less of us for a time & perhaps
he may get to value more our affection & confidence.
                                        Yrs most affly. F Marlborough

The bitterness of this letter seems out of all proportion to Randolph's offence—which was, after all, unintentional, unless we accept the Duchess's highly improb-
able notion that Randolph was deliberately stirring up
Blandford's temper. Randolph, in fact, had found himself in an extremely awkward position, caught between
an upset wife and an insinuating mother—a situation
whose millions of historical precedents only showed
how unlikely it was that the husband and son would

emerge unscathed. The fact that he chose to defend Jennie against the Duchess was, surely, what caused the real offence. The Duchess thought he was 'loyal and true' to her; but he was more loyal and truer to his wife. Otherwise why should the Duchess have felt it necessary to defend her role as 'more a Mother than a Mother in law'? What else could have made her feel that her affections had been trampled on so badly that only God could forgive it? The Duchess had abandoned hope of Blandford: her maternal ambitions were for Randolph. Now she was desperately hurt, and showed it.

She also showed that she knew her son. Randolph had got himself into the habit of abusing people, and didn't realize quite how far he went: when he and Blandford ganged up together, they could get into serious trouble. Now, though, all that happened was that Randolph passed the Duke's letter on to his brother. There is irony in Blandford's suggestion that his father must have been writing after dinner: it was precisely the Prince of Wales's explanation for Blandford's own outburst against Randolph's marriage.

> Oak Dene
> Holmwood, Dorking
> Friday

My dear R.

His graces admirable composition is a disgrace to his intelligence as well as being 'eminently ungentle-manlike'. He contradicts himself flatly in his first and second points: 'misrepresentation of facts' & 'abuse of confidence' are two ideas in direct contradistinction to one another. I fear he must have written his letter after dinner judging from the haziness of the phraseology & the utter incongruity of all the nonsense he has endeavoured to string together. I think your reply quite sufficient, & if he does not see what a fool he makes of himself by entering into my mothers mischief I am only sorry for his intelligence & I leave him to his worst enemy 'himself'. If he expects respect from his sons he should learn how to treat them as gentle-men & not suppose that the overbearing manner &

assumption of superiority which for years he displayed
to us in our youth is going to be quietly submitted to
when we have attained maturer years, & I for one am
determined to make a start against it. / / I sent you a
wire today I shall not come to town tomorrow but
shall expect you by the 4.55 from Victoria

Yours affly
Bd.

P.S. I return you his graces composition herewith

This letter brings the sad state of family feelings out
into the open. Blandford thought his father overbearing,
and bitterly resented it; the Duchess, whom he seems
to have hated, believed *strongly* in Duty to Parents;
the inevitable result was a disturbed, rebellious son, for
whom maturer years had not tempered an early sense
of injustice and maltreatment. Unfortunately, he seems
to have had a strong influence over Randolph at this
time, and to have encouraged him to rebel, too. The
quarrel continued. It was still not over the following
January. Randolph wrote to Jennie, who was skating in
Paris:

Marlborough Club,
My darling   Pall Mall. S.W.
    I am staying at Almond's Hotel, Fanny[3] & I had a
row & I considered that she was vy impertinent so I
left. She informed me that she wld rather I did leave
her house than listen to a word against the Duke &
Duchess, so I took her at her word. I am quite decided
to stand no impudence of that sort from any of the
family, & the sooner they find it out the better we shall
get on.
    I have the same rooms we had the last time we
were here together. I thought of you so much last
night; I wish I was back with you, it seems an age
since I saw you. I am sure I cannot get away till
Saturday Pawle tells me he cannot conclude the

business sooner. It is vy tiresome as I have nothing to
do in London. The only thing is that Clayton[4] says
he wants to see me 2 or 3 times more, to put me quite
right.

I had a letter from Henri Standish this morning who
tells me that he arrives Tuesday morning. I shall try
& get him to wait for me that we may go back together.
I think we will be off to Nice vy soon. Clayton says it
will be vy good for me to go there. If you like we will
arrange to go Saturday week, & I will write to Sarace-
veski to get us rooms. Say in yr next if you approve. I
am vy anxious to settle about Cook's lodgings for next
season. I feel sure that it will suit us better than an
hotel & will be *much* cheaper than a house. I think I
can get the rooms, virtually the whole house for *20gs* a
week. & I am sure we shld be vy comfortable. If I
take them I shall engage them from the 21st of April.
Write me what you think. The frost has set in harder
than ever. Do be moderate my darling in skating &
dont overdo it. I am dying to get back to you. &
Skinny[5]

Ever yrs
Randolph

Sunday 16th

Randolph consulted Dr Clayton, then the family
doctor, for everything, including rheumatism. Presumably it was something more serious to require so much
attention. With Mr Pawle, Randolph was arranging a
loan, as we can see from his letter of the next day:

St James' Club,
Piccadilly, W.

My darling
I have to thank you for two letters received this
morning. I enclose you one from Fanny to me, from
which you will see that our little difference is made up.
I expect Henri Standish tomorrow morning & have
ordered him a room at Almonds. I think I may decide

upon Saturday for my return to you. I shall know for certain tomorrow. I hope to sign the necessary papers for the loan & *'toucher le magot'*[6] Thursday morning. I saw Clayton this morning who said I was much better. & I am to see him again Wednesday & Friday. . . . I forgot to tell you that Bill Cumming[7] paid me a visit the other day. He asked most affectionately after you, & expressed his intention of coming to Nice later. . . .

My mother wrote to Blandford the other day a sort of grandly forgiving letter which drove him wild. He had previously written to her a vy questionable sort of apology.

Cook has yr cloak ready & I am to bring it back. I have no news darling with ever so much love to you & the baby.

> Ever yrs
> Randolph

Monday, Jan 17th

Jennie thought the row had gone on quite long enough, and said so.

Dearest R. On awaking this morning Marie brought me yr letter of the 16th also one from Fanny—I was so distressed at hearing of yr new quarrel—that I was on the point of writing you a very cross letter—When luckily for me (as you no doubt wld have been furious) I received yr other telling me that it was all over —Really darling forgive me for saying it—but if you want to *éviter* discussions & quarrels on *that* disagreeable subject why dont you drop it—Why talk about or occupy yourself with it? I should like very much to go to Nice—but I am afraid it will be very expensive— & in this cold weather a long journey for Baby might be imprudent. . . .

It certainly needed saying, though alas, Jennie was not to succeed in persuading Randolph to avoid quarrels. However, he seems to have become rather apprehensive over the possible effects of this one. If his father had made his own brother resign the Woodstock seat over Church Rates, Randolph might well wonder about the consequences of being rude to his mother. The Duke's power over the majority of the constituents of Woodstock was great, but they still would not vote for his nominee without encouragement of a kind which was to be made illegal by the 1883 Corrupt Practices Act. A constituency was nursed with money, not love. Randolph feared that his father might withdraw his financial support. Since they were still not on speaking terms, he got the electoral agent to speak for him. The agent's report on his conversation with the Duke throws fascinating light on what was and what was not considered fair play in 1875:

> Woodstock,
> Oxon

Dear Lord Randolph Churchill   22 December 1875
   I have seen the Duke upon the subject of your letter, and stated what you wished me to represent.
   It is clear from the Duke's reply, that there is no intention whatever on his part, to recede from the offer which he made to you with reference to donations to Local Charities, and the necessary expences of maintaining the Registration.
   But, with regard to the former, the Duke appears to feel, that the subscriptions which have been given by your Predecessors in the borough, and which have been generally received as adequate, and liberal, are not likely to be regarded, less favorably when offered by you, my Lord; and therefore that a scale of appropriate subscriptions should be submitted for approval, as a guide for future years: and with this view, I am directed to ascertain what has been the usual amount of subscriptions throughout the Borough for some time past.
   Upon the subject of Game I had better state to you specifically what the Duke's views are.
   The Duke holds, in the first place, that presents of

Game in a Parliamentary Constituency are generally injudicious, and more likely to create enemies, than Friends, to a Representative.

The Duke's own practice, he assures me, has always been consistent with the opinion which He thus expresses: and the presents of Game which have been given from Blenheim, have been given entirely for non-political objects—objects in connection either with the Landed Estates, or with the Duke's own personal position, but never with a view to political favor.

The Tenants, the Duke says, and many of the Neighbours, usually receive presents, and the list may probably be elastic enough to include the Friends whom you have mentioned at Tackley and Wootton, as well as a few more at Bladon and Handborough: but the Duke maintains that it is absolutely necessary, on the ground of supply, as well as for other reasons, to draw the line somewhere: and if the line is not drawn in a most distinguishable manner, quite irrespective of the Register of Voters, the result will probably be the reverse of what is intended, producing instead of favor, jealousy, and dis-content!

With respect to the arrangement which you allude to for the sale and purchase of Blenheim Game at cost price last year, it seems, though I don't know whether it was made clear to you, that no special prohibition was intended to be made upon a similar arrangement this year: but the circumstances were altered, and a local Dealer was not the Purchaser this year.

Now, my Lord, may I make you a report as to your own kind gifts to the Poor. When the cold set in, with a deep snow, at the beginning of this Month, I sent £10 to Tackley, £10 to Kidlington, £5 to Wootton, £5 for Thrupp, and Shipton; and £3 for Begbroke—The gifts were very opportune, and could not fail to be acceptable—The Recipients best speak for themselves, and I enclose their own replies—You know what I have in hand, to be applied according to your suggestion to urgent cases, (if any appear)

as they may arise. But I shall be happy to fulfill any
further direction you may like to give with respect
to the amount, or any part of it—

I beg to offer my best wishes to yourself & Lady
Randolph Churchill—

> I have the honour to be
> yours very faithfully
> R. B. B. Hawkins

Lord Randolph Churchill M.P.

The Rector of Wootton acknowledged the Gifts in
person.

The Duke, then, continued to give his necessary support to Randolph as a Member of Parliament, and this
trivial family quarrel blew over. But almost at once
Blandford and Randolph were involved in a far more
serious affair, a full-blown Victorian scandal which
was to have disastrous consequences. Once again, it
was Blandford who started it.

NOTES

1. Lady Camden, Randolph's aunt.
2. The Duchess wrote to Mrs Jerome on December 3rd that
'the Milk is subsiding satisfactorily'.
3. Randolph's sister, married to Edward Marjoribanks, later
2nd Baron Tweedmouth. He became a prominent liberal
politician.
4. Dr Oscar Clayton, F.R.C.S., had a consulting-room in
Harley Street. He was Ext. Surg. in Ord. to the Prince of
Wales. He was knighted in 1882.
5. Winny.
6. Get my hands on the money.
7. Sir William Gordon-Cumming. His affectionate wishes
may not have been very welcome: he was notorious for pounc-
ing on newly married women.

4

THE AYLESFORD
AFFAIR

Three weeks before the Churchill family raged at each
other over a ring, the Prince of Wales had set off for
a grand tour of India. It was an impressive expedition,
for which the House of Commons provided £112,000,
and the Indian government another £100,000, but
though the Prince had three chefs, a studgroom, a
chaplain and the Duke of Sutherland's piper among his
retinue, he was much disappointed not to be able to
take a detachment of Life Guards, too. Queen Victoria said that would be too much. She also disapproved of most of the Prince's personal guests on the
tour, but they went all the same. Shooting elephants
and tigers, presiding over state banquets, exchanging
presents with Maharajahs and sticking pigs, the Prince
led his party in triumph all over India. On February
20th 1876 they camped on the border of Nepal, where
they were greeted by Sir Jung Bahadur with a turn-out
of 1000 elephants and 10,000 soldiers to assist less
than twenty sportsmen. It should have been a particularly splendid day. But in his diary the Prince
wrote: 'Letters!!!'

The letters were about Blandford. Among the Prince's
personal guests was Lord Aylesford, popularly known
as 'Sporting Joe'. His wife Edith had not wanted him
to go to India, but in the end she had given in. Shortly
after he'd gone, Blandford had moved himself and his
horses to an inn near Packington Hall, the Aylesford's

house near Coventry. Ostensibly he was there to hunt. But after a day in the saddle, he would make his way under cover of darkness to a side-door of the Hall. He had his own key. The affair was extremely serious. In February, deeply in love, Blandford and Edith decided to elope together. They would seek divorces, defy society, and marry.

It is very difficult for us, a hundred years later, with divorce made easier year by year, to understand the horror its very mention sent through the upper classes in the 1870s. An anonymous French diplomat wrote that the dominating idea of English society was not the cultivation of virtue, but the prevention of scandal, and he explained it as due to 'the extreme sensitiveness of the ladies and gentlemen prominent in London society to the public opinion of their inferiors'. But why were they so sensitive? Surely because they were fully aware that they belonged to an incredibly privileged class, and ever since the French Revolution privileged classes had looked anxiously over their shoulders. The only justification for their privileges was that they did, and were seen to do, their social duty; and that was to lead the nation not only politically but morally. Unfortunately, official Victorian morality, established by the Queen herself, and followed, at least in theory, by the respectable middle class, bore no relation whatever to upper class practice. Hence hypocrisy and cant now seem to be the chief characteristics of the period. Fashionable people were not in the least prudish or puritanical; they hardly could be with the Prince of Wales as their leader. Affairs were common and gossip was rife: known lovers were assigned neighbouring bedrooms on weekend parties: but it was felt, and passionately, that nonetheless a pretence of disciplined, loyal, married life must be kept up. A far worse sin than adultery was its advertisement. 'Society,' wrote the same Frenchman, 'regards as, in some sort, an enemy and a traitor to itself, the man or woman who puts it openly to the blush.' A public scandal—or Public Scandal, as the Aylesford affair was to be capitalized by one of the courtiers who kept it quiet—was thought literally to betray the whole social class. Hence the extreme punishments inflicted on those who let down the side by allowing their indiscretions to reach the courts and newspapers. Any divorced woman, innocent or guilty, was ostracized for life. The careers of such men as Charles Stewart Parnell, Sir Charles Dilke, and Oscar Wilde were ruined not so much by what they did—but by their failure to keep it out of the public eye. It is only by trying to understand the horror and fear attached to publicity rather than to sexual misdemeanour itself that one can see why Blandford's intended divorce caused such a hubbub. A divorce meant the Divorce Court, and the Divorce Court meant publicity. The Prince of Wales felt particularly strongly on the subject because he had been dragged into court himself in the Mordaunt divorce case of 1870. Though quite innocent, he had been strongly censured. Scandal must be avoided at all costs.

Thus the news of Blandford and Edith Aylesford's intentions caused consternation everywhere. In Nepal the Prince denounced Blandford as the greatest blackguard alive, and Aylesford set off home on the back of an elephant. In London counsels were held by both families, and eminent men were called in for advice. Edith's brother, Hwfa Williams, wanted to challenge Blandford to a duel. (Some years later he was shot, much to his own amazement, by a demented Post Office clerk as he was strolling through St James's Park.) Randolph, rushing to prevent his brother doing anything stupid, put detectives on Williams till it was agreed that the only person who had a real right to challenge Blandford was Aylesford himself. Aided by his brother-in-law, Edward Marjoribanks, Randolph succeeded in persuading Blandford not to proceed with his plans at least for the time being. It was not easy. Blandford was even more excitable than usual. But Randolph, Marjoribanks informed the Duke, 'is doing and has done all he can to influence' him. It was mainly due to Randolph's influence that Blandford had not taken any irrevocable step. But now Randolph took one himself.

Whether or not the Prince had himself had an affair with Edith Aylesford is not established. But he had certainly written her some indiscreet letters, which Edith had shown to Blandford who had passed them on to Randolph. They made Randolph very angry, for it is clear that he already believed that the Prince had deliberately encouraged Blandford's affair, and had insisted on taking Aylesford to India so that it could be carried on with greater freedom. He even thought that Aylesford connived at it, that there was collusion between him and the Prince; since the Prince was therefore in a large measure responsible for the impending disaster, he must do everything in his power to prevent it. Randolph had already telegraphed to the Prince in India to persuade Aylesford not to seek a divorce. Now, with the hotheadedness his mother had deplored in the affair of the ring, and the unscrupulousness with which he had intended to treat his father if his plans to marry Jennie were thwarted, Randolph went to Princess Alexandra and told her that, if Aylesford did sue Edith for divorce, the Prince's letters would be produced as evidence in court. He told her that it was the Solicitor General's opinion that if that happened, the Prince would never sit on the throne of England. It was blackmail.

It was a bad enough business already. Now it took on even more serious proportions. The Prime Minister, Disraeli, was called in. Queen Victoria was outraged —especially on Princess Alexandra's behalf. (The Princess herself seems to have behaved with exemplary calm throughout.) The Prince, still shooting tigers in India, sent the Master of the Buckhounds to convey to Randolph his 'just indignation'. The Master of the Buckhounds was Lord Hardwicke, and his chief claim to fame is that he invented the shiny top hat which was to become an essential prop for envoys all over the world. As an inner member of the Prince's set, and a friend of Randolph's and Jennie's, he would seem to have been a very suitable choice for ambassador in such an awkward affair. But it turned out he wasn't. A new element of unpleasantness now entered the dispute. Randolph and Hardwicke seemed to have some personal feeling quite apart from the official business at hand.

They met early in April. The Prince wanted an apology, or a duel. Randolph was prepared to apologize to Princess Alexandra, but not to the Prince, whom he virtually accused of cowardice for issuing a challenge he knew Randolph could not take up. (A subject may not fight his prince.) This was highly insulting, and no doubt angry words were exchanged. Later Randolph accused Hardwicke of 'having exaggerated much and invented more, and altogether done his best to embitter the quarrel'.

Meanwhile Aylesford had returned from India, and Blandford went over to Holland to avoid him, though he wrote to Randolph that 'if it is a question of having it out with him someday, I would 1000 times sooner it was now when H.R.H. can be nicely compromised than later when he has managed to slip out of it'. Though the Prince denied that there was anything scandalous in his letters to Edith Aylesford, it certainly looks as though Randolph and Blandford thought otherwise, and the gossip was that H.R.H. was staying away as long as possible. When Randolph went to see Blandford, Jennie stayed behind in London, apparently to supervise spring cleaning. Randolph found his brother a great bore. 'Blandford's eternal lectures & harangues always about himself are awfully wearying', he wrote to Jennie. '*Dieu! comme il m'ennuie.* I shall be so glad to get back to you darling & I am always thinking of you & the baby & wondering what you are doing.' He had a heavy cold, and felt quite sorry for himself.

On April 19th Jennie wrote with the latest news:

London
April 19th

Dearest—I dined with Fanny last night & Edward
did not arrive till quite late—so I cld not gather much
from him—particularly as Fanny's presence seems
to silence him—However I found out that yr father
& mother will not return before the end of next
week.[1] Edward took rooms for them at the Westminster for this Saturday—so I suppose they intend
remaining in Paris—The Duke it seems is in a fright
for fear you shld show his letter to Blandford he
received B's lengthy epistle & was much disgusted so
E. said nothing but ravings & appealing to him as a
friend to help him to get a divorce from Bertha—
At first the Duke thought of not answering it but he
has changed his mind—E. advised me to write to
the Duchess—& when I told him I had—he said
that she thought I ought to have written all along—
fancy!—However I think she will like my letter &
I hope it will put all things straight between us—
Edward enjoyed himself very much in Paris went to
the play with T. Trafford [2] and Rosebery [3] the former
has gone to Bordeaux to taste wines—& from thence
proceeds to Corsica This letter came for you this
morning I send it as perhaps you wld like to answer
it—there came also one from Henri Standish nothing
particular so I keep it—I think I shall write to Mr S.
—I feel so ill *'souffrante'* today that I haven't the
strength of a cat & feel all doubled up with cramps
so you will not be angry at this stupid erratic letter.
I shan't stir out today besides it is cold & nasty—
I believe Bertha is coming to stay with Fanny for
a few days. Fanny is the most 'bottled up' creature
I have *ever* met—Standish says he [is] coming here
next month in order to look for a house or lodgings
as they intend coming in June for the Season. E. says
he has heard that the Prince has been going on in
an extraordinary manner in India so he has heard
—& that it is very evident he wants to stay away as
long as he can—going to Spain etc—Of course he

will stay with Mme Murrieta [4] at Seville I suppose
—She has a house there I know & is there now—I
have no doubt Hardwicke will abuse us to H. Hatzfeldt [5] as most likely she will talk about us—Goodbye
darling I hope you dont mean to stay away long—
I am so lonely

Yrs ever
J.

Next day Jennie had even more important news:

April 20th
10 p.m.

My dearest darling R.
    I have just received yr letter of yesterday—You
ask me what I think of yr fathers 2d epistle. I think
it very bad—He is quite willing that you shld do all
in your power to prevent Blandford from disgracing
himself & his family—but is not at all willing to take
upon himself any of the responsibility—or share any
of the *désagrément* which must arise from being at
open war with H.R.H. But my dearest there are few
as generous as you & not many brothers wld risk
what you are risking for one so worthless as B. tho
he be yr only brother. A letter came for you tonight
from Hardwicke. I do not send it to you—as you
might miss it—besides you told me not to forward
any letters—I can hardly bring myself to write calmly
about it—so insolent & *disgusting* it is—It is just a
repetition of what he said to you in yr last conversation together—the only important part being that he
has heard from the Prince who wishes him to ac-
quaint you that he H.R.H. has sent yr letter to the
Queen—Hardwicke adds that he seems very much
annoyed at the tone of yr letter & that he (H) is
not astonished. The letter will keep till yr return I
think but it made me boil with rage—If you want
it immediately telegraph I have it locked up safely—
Au premier moment I thought of writing to him telling him that you had asked me not to forward any
letters—but that if *he* thought his letter important

enough or worth sending on to you to let me know
—However I thought better of it *'le silence est d'or'*.
Nasty hateful creature! Oh! I'm *so* angry—that a
man of that kind shld *dare* to write to you in the
way he has! *C'est trop fort*—My own darling dear
Randolph I wld give anything to have you here tonight I feel so wretchedly—if we are to have all these
ennuis—do for Heaven sake lets go through them
together—As long as I have you I dont care what
happens—Now dont say 'oh yes that is all very well
but you are weeping over yr Marlboro's House balls
—& yr O.M.'s F.K.'s & Hardwickes gone for ever'
No darling I assure you it is not so—how can I help
feeling sick at heart when you are away from me—
in difficulties *et pardessus le marché, avec un 'rhume
accablant'* [6] of which I'm sure you take no care—
Shall you return Sunday? I hope so *cher mari de mon
coeur—de ce pauvre coeur qui est si gros ce soir—* [7]
I shall write again tomorrow—

Yrs ever
J.

Jennie's loyalty to Randolph in this crisis was un-
swerving. Randolph was running, she knew, appalling
social risks. But she was prepared to go without the
Marlborough House set, without Oliver Montagu, Princess Alexandra's devoted admirer, and Francis Knollys,
who had been Randolph's best man; and above all,
without Hardwicke. If any evidence were needed that
Jennie was not simply a social butterfly, this letter
provides it. Randolph had not received it when he
answered her earlier letter from The Hague:

The Hague
April 20th

My darling I have just rcd yr two long interesting &
dear letters You seem to have been most industrious,
& to have found occupations for yrself in a wonderful
manner. I shall be awfully glad to get back to you;
first because I love you & dont like to be away from

you & 2nd because Blandford is a horrid bore. He came raving to me just now because Lady Aylesford had been told by Bircham [8] that she had much better make it up with her husband. I told him to go the devil, so he is rather angry. Really the heartless selfish way in which he talks is too much for me. He really is very bad. I am glad you wrote to my mother. I hope she dont intend to make herself disagreeable or give herself airs when she comes back

We have been to Amsterdam today, & seen a vy curious town, & some vy nice quaint pictures of the Dutch school. I bought there at a curio shop for 40 frcs, 4 oriental plates which hold hot water; vy nice for a mutton chop or Kidney. You will get them Saturday Please pay for them. I went into two or 3 curio shops but saw nothing which tempted me.

Tomorrow morning we go to Brussels & Sunday morning I hope to be en route for England. Please go to Carreras Princes St Leicester Sqr. & order me several boxes of cigarettes large & small sizes. Goodbye my own darling Kiss to the baby

Yrs ever
Randolph S.C.

Unfortunately Randolph does not seem to have answered Jennie's second letter, and by the time he got her next he must have been on his way home. She was having second thoughts, but was still furious about Hardwicke:

April 21st
London

Dearest,

I half regret my letter of last night I wrote it on the spur of the moment & I was dreadfully angry—I hope it wont influence you in any way—*if* you answer H's letter I am sure it ought to be in the most calm & dignified manner—Dont be angry with me for offering my advice it is really very presumptuous of me particularly as you are such a capital writer but notwithstanding I am glad you will have a day or 2 to think over it—for if you answered it immediately you might write something rash—Do you think the Queen will have an interview with Disraeli? if so perhaps you will have one with him in which case he wld be sure to see the clever way you have managed the whole thing—& you may get him on yr side (in a way) before H.R.H. returns—Am I talking nonsense? Yr letter to H. which the Prince has sent to the Queen—if I remember rightly was a very dignified firm one—& she certainly cant find fault with it if she is enlightened as to the whole matter—& if she shld—*Après!* what harm can she do? That does not prevent my feeling horribly anxious—& I feel so restless & worried I cant sit 2 *mts de suite* [9] in a chair & I have done nothing but read that nasty hateful letter all day—I am glad I am not going to spend the evening by myself I'm to dine with Fanny & Edward & go to the opera afterwards I have had such a *'démangeaison'* [10] all day to send word to Hardwicke to come & see me & then to *délivré* myself of a *pièce 'à la Blandford'* but discretion is the better part of valour I am only afraid I shall never have the opportunity—The idea of his talking about yr animosity to the Prince when his to you is a 1000 times stronger—I shall be so happy when you return darling—I daresay after all, things will turn out for the best *mais c'est une mauvaise cause* [11]—& not worth all the energy & brain you have spent on it. . . .

What was it that made Jennie so particularly angry with Hardwicke? Why did she call him 'a man of that kind' and a 'nasty hateful creature'? That does not emerge from her letters till later on. Meanwhile the Prince returned to England, had a private meeting with Princess Alexandra, in which he no doubt explained as best he could his own part in the business, then went to the opera with her, and was loudly cheered. There was nothing in the papers as yet, but there was a great deal of gossip, most of it in the Prince's favour. He had refused to intervene personally, as requested by Randolph at the beginning—that is, to ask Aylesford not to give Edith a divorce. But Randolph's blackmail had, indirectly, worked. Aylesford could not seek a divorce now, knowing that the Prince's name would be involved. The day after the Prince's return to London Aylesford asked Hardwicke to call on him. Hardwicke reported, to everyone's relief, that no Public Scandal would now take place. The Queen congratulated Hardwicke on his conduct, and asked him to urge the Prince to keep clear of all doubtful people in future; not a request that was to be granted. But the Aylesford affair was over in the sense that publicity had been avoided.

In another sense it had only just begun. Punishment for not sticking to the rules was ferocious. None of the principals was ever forgiven. Aylesford—an innocent party, at least in this business—was obliged to go to America, where he took up ranching. Outdrinking the Texan cowboys, he seems to have drunk himself to death at the early age of 36. The guilty Edith and Blandford lived together on the continent for some years, and had a child. But even after Aylesford was dead, and Bertha had (in 1883, when the scandal was stale) divorced Blandford, he did not marry her. Instead, not long before his own early death in 1892, he married a rich American widow. Leonard Jerome was a witness at their wedding in New York.

It was nearly ten years before Randolph was readmitted to the Prince's favour. For the time being, his social ostracism was almost complete. Albert Edward might not have any political power, but socially he was an absolute monarch, and he made it clear that he would not go where Randolph and Jennie were received. His honour had been impugned.

Randolph had never been to America, and Jennie had not been back since she was a girl. They decided that now might be a good time to pay a visit. The Duke of Marlborough was doing his best to arrange a reconciliation, and requested an interview with the Prince. On the day he was going to see him, Jennie went over to Paris for a few days to say goodbye to her mother and sisters. By mistake she took a bottle of Randolph's medicine with her:

Friday morning

Dearest—I have just received yr letter & cheque—I hope darling you didn't get my telegram too late last night—it was rather late before I cld send it—I got on all right till we came to Calais—& then we had to get into a tug before landing—& it was really very dangerous because the 2 boats made a tremendous swell & it was most difficult to get on board & it was *so* crowded that one cld hardly stand—I saw Schouvaloff [12] who made himself most useful—old Robert got me a coupé & I found the whole family drawn up at the *gare*—delighted to see me—I am so sorry about yr medicine it was Thompson's [13] fault *et par comble de malheur* [14] my own bottle was broken in her bag—luckily I have the prescription & am going to have it made up—You must write me all about the interview between yr Father & H.R.H.—of course I shall feel the greatest interest to know *ce qui s'est passé* mind you let me know—if you see Clemmy [15] please tell how sorry I was not to go with her yesterday—& that I hadn't time to write perhaps I had better do so now—I shall write to you again tonight & tell you what I've been doing Goodbye darling I feel homesick after you. Kiss the Baby they all send their love to you—
I send back the prescription yours. God bless you

Yours J.

Randolph seems to have taken this with him to some perhaps tactical conference, for on the back he drew what seem to be stumps and bails, and wrote the addresses of Disraeli and Delane, the editor of *The Times,* and the names of some of those involved. The interview between his father and the Prince had been a success, according to the Duchess: the Prince was peaceable and 'I believe that everybody in the Set are

sick of the whole Fight and the unpleasantness it makes
in society generally.' Randolph was to send an apology.
The Duke advised him to remember that a soft answer
turneth away wrath. Randolph was gloomy, and gave
a very different account of the interview to Jennie:

June 30th
8, Clifford Street,
Bond Street,
London, W.

My dearest

I was very glad to get yr letter this morning, I had
no time to write to you yesterday. Yr telegram was
delivered here at 2 A.M. Friday morning;

The interview between my father & HRH came off
yesterday evening. It led to no satisfactory result. The
Prince seems to have expressed the greatest animosity
agst me, but I believe my father stuck up to him well,
& told him that if he intended to remain so highly
displeased with me, he had better extend his displeasure to himself & my mother.

Hardwicke's account of his interview with me written to the Prince was read to my father. Hardwicke
appears to have exaggerated much & invented more,
& altogether done his best to embitter the quarrel.
I have written my father an account of what really
passed between Hardwicke & myself a copy of which
I will show you when you return. It is a vy good
letter, & my father will send it to H.R.H.

I have no particular news. HRH has declined
Ivor's [16] ball Fancy Ivor going a 2nd time to see
Francis Knollys to ask if he was coming. F.K.
shewed him all the correspondence, relating to late
events & also the letters & Ivor seems to have quite
chimed in with F.K. He had the impudence last night
to tell me that he thought I had been completely
wrong all thro. & when I said that whatever he
thought I hoped he wld keep his opinions to himself,
he replied that he shld do nothing of the kind He
must be mad.

Blandford has been going on in an extraordinary

manner. But it is much too long to write. He has been expelled from the Blues mess by the committee dont tell this to yr people.

The baby is vy flourishing. If you wld like to remain in Paris till next Saturday or Monday I dont mind vy much, as I think I shall go down to Broxmouth [17] on Wednesday or Thursday. I dine & lunch & breakfast at St James's Sqre.[18] I hope you are happy & enjoying yrself. What news do you hear of yr father, & when is he (PAGE TORN) I saw a most charming little house in Hertford strt. yesterday. A freehold. ½ the size of Charles Str [19] but wld hold us well. 16000£ they want for it. Which I think I see my way to managing. We must go & have a look at it when you come back. I took my father to see it & he liked it vy much. Give my best love to yr mother & Clara

Yours
R.

Jennie had not expected anything from the interview, as she wrote on July 2nd:

Sunday
Paris

Dearest R. Yr letter this morning did not surprise me as to the result of the interview with HRH. The fact is I am sure it is too soon to attempt any kind of reconciliation. I own I am rather astonished at Ivor's conduct—I suppose he is furious with you for being —(probably to him) the cause of the Prince's refusal to his ball—Hardwicke I've no doubt was only too delighted to give an exaggerated account in order to give himself more importance in the whole affair—

Has Disraeli done anything? I hope darling you dont worry over all this tiresome business. If you go to Broxmouth I will stay here a few days longer but if you don't I wld rather return Thursday as our stay in London will be very short & I want to see as much of Winston as possible besides having several things to do—It is very pleasant here & I am delighted to be with them all—yet I cannot help worrying a little at what is going on in London—& then you know I can never be quite happy away from you—& so Blandford has been going on in an extraordinary way—he must be mad. . . .

Randolph was feeling lonely in London. 'I don't like this house without you it is awfully dull,' he wrote. 'The baby is vy well. He came in to see me this afternoon & carried off the paper basket in triumph. Blandford came up to town last night, I did not see him. My mother tells me he is vy unhappy & desperate agst everybody.' On July 4th he wrote again, enclosing a copy of his letter to his father about Hardwicke which had been forwarded to the Prince of Wales. The Prince 'returned it, merely saying that he wld again see my father about it on my father's return to town'. The Duchess thought the house in Hertford Street was *much* too big. 'Dont you go and spend too much money,' Randolph said, more in hope than expectation, perhaps. Winston was flourishing. Next day he wrote again:

8, Clifford Street,
Bond Street,
London. W.

My dearest

I am off to Broxmouth tomorrow morning at 10.35. There is a dinner at St James's Square tonight for the Prince Imperial [20] also a Mr Blake Minister of Justice in Canada dines & I mean to pump him as to the attractions of Canada in the fishing line, as I hear he is a grt. fisherman.

Your letters are awfully short & tell me nothing what you are about. I am really vy disappointed about yr father after all his promises as to what he wld do for us if we went to America, he now will hardly see us there at all. I dont believe yr mother wants him to be there with us. Do you think the gentle Clara wld like to accompany us? ask her.

I think we have *remporté* [21] a victory over Hardwicke. I met him the other day. I was in a cab in a block in Bond Strt, & 'fixed' him from a long way off. I gave him such a prolonged look one of my worst scowls right at him. I fully expected a row, & indeed hoped for one, but he turned down his eyes after a second or two. He told Rosamond [22] last night that he had been vy badly treated that the family distrusted him, & that he had seen my letter to my father, which was most unfair & unkind to him. What a snake!! Knollys has written to my father that HRH wishes to see him tomorrow. I think it looks like peace. Cornelia's ball is tonight but I am not going. Do write me longer letters darling. You had better start Tuesday morning, & *nous arriverons ici tous les deux à la même heure.* [23] Love to Clara

Yrs ever
Randolph S. Churchill

July 5th

Jennie replied promptly, and at length; and at last giving us the clue to the personal feeling between Hardwicke and Randolph:

Thursday
Paris

Dearest R—You must not think that I write short letters—the fact is there is so little to tell you—& I am so little left alone that it is most difficult to write anything *'en suite'*—I have written for my cabin for Monday so I think I had better stick to that day— Can't you manage to meet me Monday night?—How delicious it will be—to be together again. I hope you have missed me & feel that you can't do without little J——?

It is no use talking to you in a letter—about Papa —but I believe he intends to be in America the end of August so we shall see something of him. I am glad you glared at Hardwicke—but do be careful— for I wldn't have him for *worlds*—think that you know what I told you—& if you are not discreet, it will somehow get about. Don't be angry darling but I am *so* afraid of my name being mixed up in it—& you must remember that last year people saw us a great deal together & thought he made up to me & so of course you must be extra careful not to let him or anyone else think that yr *brouille* [24] is about anything else but Blandford's affair. You've not written to me anything about Disraeli, *c'est-il passé quelque chose?* [25]—I wrote to yr Mother yesterday The Duc de Guiche called here today—& I made his acquaintance. He is very good looking only 23 & a widower with one little girl his wife was a Mlle de Beauman whom he married 2 years ago He is supposed to be a great *parti* here & all the Mama's run after him— I can't understand what his attraction can be here unless it is Clara—He has been here several times this week & today immediately proposed that we shld go to the Circus Saturday & I believe he is dreadfully afraid of compromising himself—& he treats Clara just like a *Jeune fille française* & she naturally '*posée's*' tremendously—He is the eldest son of the Duc de Grammont & his grandfather was the celebrated Count d'Orsay—he has now 80,000 frcs a year which is *beaucoup ici*—& will have more Mama & I both agree that *he* wld do admirably but of course it is ridiculous to think of it—

R de Fitzjames [26] came also this afternoon & amused me very much he *raffolléed* about '*cette petite horreur*' [27] & naturally I did not abuse her—*car cela serait de très mauvais gout* [28]—

Has Tommy Trafford answered yr letter?—I went over to the Bon Marché this morning with Mama & got some gloves—& I frittered to the extent of 6 francs in some rich silk nets which are *la grande mode* & which I think look very pretty *sur mes cheveux noirs—ne te moques pas?* [29] . . .

I hope darling *petit* R. that you will come back Monday. It will be so jolly—I have no news to tell you we potter about all day playing the piano reading

& driving—& pass the evenings quite alone so I can't
have much to say except that I love you & am longing
to see you. Have you quarrelled with Cornelia?—
Good night dearest I shld like to kiss you *grand
comme Ça*——

Ever yrs
J.

It is impossible to say for sure what Jennie wouldn't
for worlds have Hardwicke know she'd told Randolph,
but it is not hard to guess. If people thought Hardwicke had been making up to her, they may also have
thought he'd done more. Jennie's letter certainly suggests he probably tried. Given Randolph's quickness
to anger, he may well have taken the choice of Hardwicke as envoy, and Hardwicke's overbearing manner,
as especially insulting under the circumstances. He
may even have suspected the Prince of knowing of
Hardwicke's attempt (if that's what it was) on Jennie,
of sending him deliberately: Randolph's mind had its
dark suspicious corners, and he already thought the
worst of the Prince's behaviour over Edith Aylesford.
If the Prince *had* deliberately taken Aylesford to India
against Edith's wishes, so that Blandford should be
able the more easily to carry on his affair—then he'd
be perfectly capable of choosing as envoy to Randolph
a man who'd tried to seduce his wife. Furthermore,
knowing what Randolph did of Hardwicke, but unable
to reveal it to him—because Jennie had at all costs
to be kept out of the *brouille*—must have made him
seethe with even greater anger as he listened to Hardwicke's lectures on his own behaviour. So much is
speculation, of course. But Jennie's letter makes it clear
that something of the sort had happened.

Whatever the truth about Hardwicke and Jennie,
the whole unhappy business left Randolph very bitter
about high society: the bitterness was an important
element in his later political radicalism. He continued
to lead the privileged life, of course; but there is more

than a suspicion that he would have gladly sold the whole social world down the river.

The Prince was bitter, too. He would not accept the apology Randolph made, in spite of the Duke's second intervention. Negotiations went on for several weeks, through the Lord Chancellor. Meanwhile Jennie and Randolph were in America, and it was not till August 26th that the agreed text of the apology reached them. Randolph signed, but added a post-script which still further annoyed the Prince. The Lord Chancellor considered the Duke and Randolph had made their submission in the most ungracious and undignified way possible. The fact that Randolph signed at Saratoga, where General Burgoyne had surrendered to the Americans in 1777, was doubtless not lost on anyone. Randolph obviously considered his apology a defeat for British honour in 1876.

Meanwhile, the Duke, deeply mortified by his sons' dreadful behaviour, agreed to accept the post of Viceroy of Ireland as a way of withdrawing from English social life with some dignity. Even this disappointment was not without embarrassment, however, as the retiring Viceroy was Bertha Blandford's father. But it had one great advantage: Randolph could be given useful work as his father's private secretary. And as for Jennie—well, Jennie could look after Winston, and she could—well, in Ireland the one thing everyone could do was hunt. So she hunted.

Before the Marlboroughs left England, the Queen invited them to spend a night at Windsor Castle, on the strict understanding that there were to be no references to the 'domestic circumstances' which had caused Victoria 'anxiety and deep regret'. 'Its all most unpleasant & humiliating', wrote the Duchess. 'Oh dear —when will all this annoyance be at an end?' The visit went off very well, though the Queen was 'much grieved to see the alteration in both of them since she saw them at Osborne a year & 4 months ago. They looked so *distressed, wretched* & the poor Dss especially, who cd scarcely restrain her tears.'

On 10 January 1877 the new Viceroy, accompanied by his Duchess, Randolph and Jennie, the guests, and his three unmarried daughters, made his public entry into Dublin. Winston was one of the party, too. His earliest memories were to be of his time in Ireland. He wrote of his mother in a famous passage:

My picture of her in Ireland is in a riding habit, fitting like a skin and often beautifully spotted with mud. She and my father hunted continually on their large horses; and sometimes there were great scares because one or the other did not come back for many hours after they were expected.

My mother always seemed to me a fairy princess: a radiant being possessed of limitless riches and power. . . .

But Jennie had neither riches nor power. She was the wife of a disgraced second son. While Randolph was in London, attending Parliament, she often felt 'blue'. 'I don't find it dull', she wrote to him, 'except when I think of London and its amusements.' She must have thought of them a good deal. The Vice-Regal court was hardly lively, and though Clara often came over, there wasn't much to do. She painted and played the piano and rode. She saw more of the Duchess than perhaps she liked. When she took singing lessons, the Duchess seemed surprised: 'Have you any voice?' she asked. Jennie had married for better or worse, and this was definitely the worse. But for all that, she still shone for Winston 'like the Evening Star'.

NOTES

1. The Duke and Duchess had been cruising in the Aegean. They did not feel tempted to hurry home.

2. Tommy Trafford was a close friend of Randolph's, and frequently travelled with him. He had a Parisian mistress whom he later married.

3. Lord Rosebery, a friend of Randolph's from Eton, later Prime Minister.

4. The Murrietas, Spanish nobles, took a lavish part in English social life, in London and at Wadhurst, in Sussex.

5. Helen Hatzfeldt, wife of the German Ambassador in Madrid and, in 1885, London. The Hatzfeldts were friends of the Jeromes in Paris.

6. And in the bargain! with a 'dreadful cold'.

7. Dear husband of my heart—of this poor heart which is so heavy this evening.

8. Lady Aylesford's solicitor.

9. Two minutes on end.

10. Longing.

11. But it is a bad cause.

12. Russian Ambassador to Great Britain.

13. Jennie's maid.

14. As a crowning misfortune.

15. Lady Camden.

16. Sir Ivor Bertie Guest, later Lord Wimborne. He was married to Randolph's eldest sister, Cornelia.

17. Broxmouth Park, Dunbar, was the home of the Marquess of Bowmont, eldest son of the Duke of Roxburghe. Bowmont was married to Randolph's sister Annie.

18. Where the Duke and Duchess lived in London.

19. Randolph and Jennie's house in Mayfair.

20. The son of the Emperor Napoleon III, killed by the Zulus while fighting for the British in 1879.

21. Won.

22. Randolph's sister.

23. We will both arrive here at the same time.

24. Estrangement.

25. Has anything happened?

26. Charles Robert, Comte de Fitzjames, was a descendant of James II's illegitimate son by Arabella Churchill, sister to John, first Duke of Marlborough, and thus a very, very distant relation of Randolph's.

27. Was infatuated with that little horror.

28. For that would have been very bad taste.

29. On my black locks—don't mock me?

5

THE FOURTH PARTY

The Churchills were over three years in Ireland, and easily the most important thing that happened, as far as Jennie was concerned, was the birth of her second son, Jack, in February 1880. But if these were dull years for her, for Randolph they were a time of important personal development. Before he went to Dublin, he had been an MP for three years but made little mark: he had not begun to take either himself or politics seriously. But now, with Society closed to him, he began to think about society in a larger sense. Ireland could not have been a better place to be exiled to, for then, as now, the Irish question was the most intractable in British politics. Randolph took the opportunity to examine it in the greatest detail. He explored the country from end to end. He met the politicians of all parties and religions. Famine, as so often, loomed over the land, and the Duchess dutifully organized a charitable fund. It was Randolph, though, who administered it, who learned at first hand what poverty and starvation were. As a result, he became one of the few English MPs who had any real understanding of Irish conditions. (It is scarcely credible, but Disraeli never visited Ireland at all, and Gladstone only did so once.) Almost inevitably, Randolph began to think for himself about Irish matters, to develop his own ideas, very different from the conventional wisdom of his father the Viceroy. On one occasion he actually expressed them in public, much to his father's distress.

But for the most part he seems to have learned his lesson: he was a dutiful son and secretary.

Early in 1880 Disraeli was defeated at a General Election and Gladstone became Prime Minister for the second time. As a result, the Duke had to give up his Viceroyalty, and Jennie' and Randolph returned to London. Randolph was delighted to be in opposition: it gave far more scope to his natural combativeness. Furthermore, it gave him a chance to attack his own party leadership as well as the government, and he loved to fight on several fronts at once. The Conservative leader in the Commons was a dull but distinguished statesman called Sir Stafford Northcote, the vigour of whose attacks on the government was severely moderated by his very great personal admiration for Gladstone, whose secretary he had once been. Randolph despised this softness, and nicknamed Northcote "The Goat'. Then, with the help of three friends, he launched a brilliant independent attack on Gladstone's administration. The friends were Arthur Balfour, later to be Prime Minister, Sir Henry Wolff, and John Gorst. Borrowing their tactics from the Irish party, who had outraged the previous Conservative government by obstructing its legislation with endless delaying tactics in Parliament, Randolph and his friends provided a far more entertaining and successful opposition than anything Northcote could bring himself to organize. Quite soon, they were established as 'The Fourth Party'— the other three being the Conservatives, the Liberals and the Irish.

"Our house', wrote Jennie, 'became the rendezvous of all shades of politicians. Many were the plots and plans which were hatched in my presence by the Fourth Party, who, notwithstanding the seriousness of their endeavours, found time to laugh heartily and often at their own frustrated machinations.' Ironically, Northcote lived next door to the Churchills in St James's Place; if he heard the laughter that summer, he must have known that much of it was at his expense. By the end of the session the whole House of

Commons was laughing with Randolph—except those, of course, who were gnashing their teeth. Within a few months, from being no one of any political importance, Randolph was a public figure.

For all that, Jennie and Randolph were still excluded from the smartest parties. The Prince of Wales had not yielded an inch. Nor, it would seem from a letter he wrote to Jennie while they were still in Ireland, had Randolph:

My dearest,

I enclose you two letters from my mother from which you will perceive that there is a vy pretty quarrel between myself & the Guests. I reserve all comments on the matter till I am with you again. There is no doubt however that Cornelia behaved vy piggily, as she has done before on more than one occasion. As long as she chooses to go out of her way on every possible occasion to toady those who are not ordinary enemies but most bitter foes, so long I shall have a right to think that not merely does she totally disagree with me on most essential points, but also that she cannot have the least feeling or affection for me. & while I do not dispute her perfect liberty of action, I at the same time uphold my right under these circumstances to forget that she is my sister. . . .

Jennie must have been glad that his pugnacity was at last being usefully channelled into politics. She was now twenty-seven, had been married six years and produced two sons. In the thinking of upper-class society she was now 'fair game' for amorous adventurers— always provided, of course, that no Public Scandal should ensue. But though men doubtless tried, there seems no evidence that Jennie did anything more than flirt in the accepted manner of a beautiful woman, and her marriage was certainly *not* foundering, as has recently been suggested. She seems to have been quite open with Randolph about her admirers, and he with her. For instance, while in Ireland, she was much bothered by the attentions of the young and handsome Lord Rossmore. One day she felt obliged to write to Randolph:

I hope you wont be angry to hear that Rossmore called here today—& that I saw him quite by mistake—I was annoyed because it was luncheon time & I had ordered next to nothing—besides being in the midst of my accounts—He did not stay long as I had ordered the carriage at 3—I told him he must not call here any more as living alone I cld not receive any gentlemen & cld not make an exception for him.

Back in England, Randolph felt obliged to write to her in August 1881 about one of the 'continental cusses' Leonard Jerome so much disliked:

As I was writing to Castellane [1] this morning I opened the enclosed in order to find out his plans. I now send it to you with my reply to it. He is a little blackguard & we must have nothing more to do with him, and indeed I think all those French people are great brutes; But I really do think my darling you ought to be more careful in yr manner to men, who are always too ready to take a liberty. I have such confidence in you that I never bother you, but these kind of things are very annoying & vexatious.

Neither of these trivial but flattering incidents suggests a marriage in trouble—except, perhaps, to a fevered imagination. But in 1881 Jennie did meet the man who was to be the great tragic love of her life. Count Charles Kinsky was an attaché at the Austro-Hungarian embassy, a brilliant rider who was the first foreigner ever to win the Grand National—and that on his own horse, Zoedone, in 1883. He was not strikingly handsome, but he had one of the big moustaches which women found so endearing in those days, and even in photographs there is a great intensity about his dark eyes. He was very musical, which must have been something else which Jennie found attractive. That he was soon paying regular calls on Jennie is clear from the brief diary she kept at the beginning of 1882. The entries for January 3rd and 4th are particularly interesting for they mention not only Kinsky but Lady Blanche Hozier, who was shortly to give birth to a daughter called Clementine. Twenty-five years later Clementine and Winston were to marry.

Tuesday, January 3
Beautiful day. Went out & tried on my habit—took a little walk—lunched alone wrote a lot of letters—Charlie Fitzwilliam [2] & Kinsky called later Col. B.[3] who had had a good day's hunting with the Baron [4] at Leighton—They wanted me to dine & go to the play—but I couldn't make up the party—went to spend the evening with Blanche Hozier but she had gone to bed—Am longing to get down to Oakham & hunt—

Wednesday, January 4   Oakham
Fine—Randolph arrived from Ireland—had a long talk & then went out & breakfasted with Blanche Hozier—only Emily Yznaga [5]—took a little walk then went home. The Star [6] & Cornelia turned up—Sir H. Wolff & Gorst came to luncheon—took the 5.30 train to Oakham went to bed very early—had a long talk with Custance [7] before going.

Randolph had been spending Christmas, as he always did, with Lord Justice Gerald FitzGibbon, one of the friends he made in Ireland. Now he and Jennie went hunting for ten days, then returned to London to lunch and dine the Fourth Party. After that they went to Blenheim, where the children were staying.

Tuesday, January 17
Cold and raw—Gave Winston his lessons, then painted till luncheon—went to the stables—then

walked with R & the Duchess till 5—read to the children . . . played billiards with the Duke & Ld. Alfred Churchill— [8]

Wednesday, January 18
Very cold & foggy—Randolph & George [9] went out hunting—Drove with the Duchess to Stonesfield to give away blankets etc—practised a bit in the afternoon—wrote letters & read to the children—Ld. Lytton [10] & Sir Henry Wolff arrived—

Thursday, January 19
Dull. Went out driving with the Duchess—painted all the afternoon—went to a meeting at Woodstock to hear Lord Lytton—very good speech & delivery—but voice weak. Randolph & Sir H. Wolff, also made speeches—

The diary gives a revealing glimpse of Jennie's life. She has a small circle of London friends, otherwise it is politics, hunting, and charity with the Duchess. That she did *not* neglect her children seems obvious. Winston was now eight: one wonders what lessons Jennie felt herself fit to give him. She did not care for Blenheim: 'Dull,' she wrote on 30 January. 'Most uneventful week.' The truth was, as she had written to her mother a year earlier:

I quite forget what it is like to be with people who love me. I do so long sometimes to have someone to whom I could go and talk to. Of course Randolph is awfully good to me and always takes my part in everything, but how can I always be abusing his mother to him, when she is devoted to him, and wd do anything for him—The fact is I *loathe* living here. It is not on account of its dullness, *that* I don't mind, but it is gall and wormwood to me to accept anything or to be living on anyone I hate. It is no use disguising it, the Duchess hates me simply for what I am —perhaps a little prettier and more attractive than her daughters. Everything I do or say or wear is found fault with. We are always studiously polite to each other, but it is rather like a volcano, ready to burst out at any moment. . . .

She must have been glad to get back to London. But on 26 February Randolph fell ill. Lots of people came to see him, which cannot have helped. After dinner he was worse, and Jennie went to fetch Dr Clayton. On Tuesday 28 February she wrote: 'Up half the night with R.' He was seriously ill, though that did not stop her going to a small dinner party with friends at the Café Royal the following evening. Nor did it stop streams of people calling, including the ever faithful 'Star', and Kinsky. But on 2 March Jennie noted: 'wrote letters & sat with R. who nearly fainted tonight after hot bath'. She did not write in her diary again till the 14th, and on the 16th she took Randolph to recuperate near the Crystal Palace. Doubtless the idea was to remove him from the excitements of London, but 'The Star' still called every day. They paid £80, Jennie complained, to eat old roosters surrounded by black sausages. In April Jennie took Randolph to America for a month, but on their return he was still not right. Though they stopped briefly in London, and saw Sarah Bernhardt in *La Dame aux Camélias,* Jennie took another house in the suburbs, this time at Wimbledon. It was not until 3 July, more than four months after he first fell ill, that Randolph returned to the House of Commons.

In the next four years Randolph was to become a dominating figure in the Conservative party, and to hold great offices of state. He made speeches all over the country, as well as in the Commons, and he intrigued night and day. It was a very exhausting life, even for a fit man; but Randolph was never quite well. He smoked far too much—Jennie's first note to him at Cowes begged him not to, it will be remembered—and people often commented on how ill he looked. He was not one of those people who pretend to be all right when they're not, and he consulted doctors frequently, though to little avail. All they ever seem to have recommended was holidays. Randolph was glad enough to take them, often with Tommy Trafford or some other masculine companion. Once he went abroad with Blandford. Jennie took her own holidays, too—usually going to see her mother and sisters in Paris. In their class, husbands and wives led very independent existences, and it should not be thought, though it has been, that separate holidays meant any more serious form of separation. That Jennie and Randolph still loved each other is clear from their letters when they were apart, most dramatically in a series written in December 1882 and January 1883. Randolph, still not recovered from his illness of the spring, was in Algeria. Jennie was in London, furnishing their new house, 2 Connaught Place, at Marble Arch. Usually she had wonderful health, but now she fell ill herself. On 17 December she scribbled a little note:

Dearest R—

I am sorry to say I am in bed with a slight feverish attack. Laking[11] says I will be all right in a day or 2, if I remain perfectly quiet, so here I am an angel—taking my medicines and not stirring. I like Laking—He says in yr absence, he must be very strict & wont allow any imprudence—By the time this reaches you I shall probably be as well as ever—Mind you enjoy yrself—Mama & Leonie are here & are nursing me. I wrote to yr Mother today—everything is going on well—drawing room a success parquet nearly done. I will write you a letter every day—but until I am up dont expect [a] long epistle—It is no use my trying to write with ink, I always make such a mess—

Yours
J.

Dont you worry I am taking great care of myself—

The note is in pathetic and feeble writing, for Jennie's 'slight feverish attack', though no one told her, was typhoid. She managed another note two days later:

2 Connaught Place, W.
Tuesday 19th

Dearest R I hope it wont distress you to hear that I am still in bed & I am afraid am likely to be for a little while longer—Mama thought she wld like Gull[12] to come & see me just to be sure that Laking was treating me right—& so I saw Sir W. who was very kind—he says I've got a low fever what he called a febrile attack—which wld keep me here a fortnight, & then I shld get up perfectly well—I've got a nurse & am taken the greatest care of—& not allowed to do anything—When you see me you wont know that I've been ill—Now *dont* worry about me please—Write & tell me that you are happy & enjoying yr holiday— otherwise I shall be miserable—If you were here you couldn't do anything for me, so like a darling, dont worry—yr Mother has been to see me today & will tell you all about me—I shall write a line now & then—in fact I think a short line every day wont hurt me—I was so glad of yr letter. Take care of yrself & mind you enjoy yr little trip.

Yours
J.

Randolph did not get these letters for several days, in fact not until the 28th. He telegraphed in great alarm for news; but there was a muddle about the address and he did not at once receive the reassuring message Jennie sent him. She wrote again on the 29th:

2 Connaught Place, W.
Dec. 29th

Dearest R Yr telegram distressed me so—particularly when I found from the one to Mama that you had not received the one I had sent you—The fact is I cld not make out the address, it looked like Batna, & of course I thought that you were going on to Biskra and wanted

to find a telegram on arrival[13]—I had misgivings but
Dr Laking brought me the telegram you had sent him,
& that was even more illegible—so after much consideration & looking at map & geography books—we
came to the conclusion that it must be meant for
Biskra You poor darling I did feel so for you last night
& until the hour when I thought you wld get my telegram I was quite miserable. I know how you worry—
How naughty of you!—No news is always good news
—& if I had been seriously ill, dont you suppose they
wld have telegraphed it to you at once? I hope now
your mind is *quite* at rest. Today my temperature is
quiet normal & if it will keep so for 2 days, I shall get
up—It has been a mild attack of fever—& I have
never once been bad. . . .

Randolph's letters, once he knew Jennie was all right,
show not only how much he loved her, but how dependent he was on her. They are, for the most part, on
Connaught Place writing paper, but from the South of
France. The first was on New Year's Day, 1883.

My darling
I have been in such a state of mind about you ever
since last Thursday. I did not receive your letters telling me you were ill till just as I was starting for Batna,
& when I first read them it did not appear to me that
you were vy bad. I therefore telegraphed to you &
Laking to telegraph to me at Batna how you were;
this was at two oclock in the afternoon & on arriving
at Batna at eight I fully expected to find an answer.
There was none however & I waited all the next day
till nine oclock in the evening without getting any
reply. I got perfectly wild with anxiety & alarm. I made
sure the most dreadful things had happened, & that
I shld never see you again. I never passed such a day
& on reading yr letter over again I saw that you must
be vy seriously ill to have had Gull & a nurse and I
made sure it was typhoid fever. Well the whole day
from morning till night I worried & fretted at getting
no answer. I don't know what wld have happened to

me if dear Wolff had not telegraphed to Constantine
that he had seen you & that you were much better.
The telegram arrived at Batna just as the office closed
at nine oclock. I cant tell you my relief & joy, for I
had quite given you up. I daresay you will think this
vy foolish but you must remember that being so far
away added to my anxiety & getting no answer to my
telegrams was inexplicable. I had had such a fright
however that I determined to return to England, & I
cld not bear the idea of yr being ill without my being
with you to look after you; particularly when I remembered how you used to look after me when I was
ill. So I left Batna on Friday & got on board a steamer
at Phillippeville[14] which landed me here last night
when again I had the delight of receiving good news
of you and I have just received a telegram from Sir
W Gull saying that you are going on well. I am so
thankful darling I cant tell you; and as you & all my
people do not wish me to return I will go on to Nice.
But you must come out there as soon as you are able
to travel. If you will do so, I will throw over the
Birmingham meeting & stay with you here till you are
quite set up again. What a bad illness you must have
had. I am afraid you are not out of bed yet & you
must be awfully weak. I am sure for my sake you will
take the greatest care of yrself & not do anything
imprudent. Why dearest if anything happened to you
my life wld be broken. I cant think of that day I
passed at Batna without a shudder. I worked myself
up into such a state. I was all alone you see & cld not
get back till the next day. The trains telegraphs &
posts in Africa are abominable. I cld not have
travelled there with any more pleasure & enjoyment &
felt I must place myself within reach of you. Up to
that Thursday last I had enjoyed myself vy much. The
drive from Algiers to Constantine five days was delightful, beautiful scenery fine air & splendid weather.
Rather cold than warm however. It did me a lot of
good and I shld be vy well now if I had not caught a
cold at Batna which I have not got rid of yet. I shall

go on to Nice tomorrow & hope to find Trafford there.
Gorst too is at Mentone. I have been quite unable to
write to you or to anyone else since I heard of your
illness. Please thank Wolff for his letters & particularly
his telegrams. I dont [know] what I shld have done
without his telegrams of last Friday. I wld give anything to see you again. Mind I order you to come to
Nice the moment you are well enough to travel. Write
to me Poste Restante Nice, to say when Laking thinks
you will be strong to move. I hope in ten days or so.
We had a lovely passage across from Phillippeville
here; sea quite smooth & warm weather. Today is vy
fine & bright. Please thank dear Leonie for her letters
to me. It has been such a comfort to me to know that
yr Mother & Leonie were with you. I am sorry poor
little Winston has not been well, but I dont make out
what is the matter with him. It seems we are a sickly
family & cannot get rid of the doctors. I think Laking
seems to have been vy clever and attentive. I dont
make out yet what has been the exact nature of yr
illness but am writing to Laking to know all about it.
I am sure you have been getting seedy for some time,
& that accursed house in St James Place poisoned you.
I hope poor Clara will be none the worse for living
there. I hope some time or other we may go together
to Biskra. I believe it is a most lovely place, an immense plantation of palms in the middle of the desert
& such a climate. A much better place to spend the
winter than the Riviera. I am vy glad I went to Algeria
it is a charming country. Constantine is one of the
finest situated cities I ever saw. Such rocks & preci-
pices & hills all round. I saw an English paper for the
first time this morning for a fortnight. There does not
seem to be any great news, except about poor Gambetta[15] who seems to be in a bad way. Goodbye my
darling, Do get well quickly & be vy careful write or
make Leonie write every day to say how you are.

Yrs ever
Randolph

P.S. I wish you all a vy happy new year.

Jennie was on the mend, but slowly; she had been much more ill than she realized. Her convalescence was not helped by money worries:

2 Connaught Place, W.
Jan 3rd

Dearest R—I have just this moment received yr letters & telegram, & am delighted to think you have gone to Nice—but you poor darling I am *wretched* to know that you have been so worried—how cld you get so alarmed—you wld have been telegraphed to instantly had there been the slightest cause for anxiety—dearest *petit* R—I cant bear to think of yr being unhappy—& on my account—However now it's all over thank heaven—& we have I hope but our meeting to look forward to—

As I telegraphed you I am still in bed, & this makes the 20th day—but my temperature has been very erratic the last few days, & this morning it is 2 degrees below normal so Laking thinks it is the 28th day, as he reckons that I had the fever a week before I sent for him—if so this is the turning point & I shall be up in a couple of days Of course there is always the danger of a relapse but he has no fear of it—as I lie here perfectly quiet & there are no complications of any kind—Gull said I had a splendid constitution & even Laking is surprised at my strength—I dont feel at all weak, tho' of course I cld not walk—I get rather depressed—but feel quite cheery to-day—I dont know if you wld like me to stay at Cannes with Clemmy[16] Of course I wld much rather stay with you at Monte Carlo—but I cant help thinking of the expense—indeed I am more worried than I can say when I think of our money difficulties—R. Payne[17] has sent a bill for £246 for wine & I shall have to pay over £500 before I leave England—& that does not include *one* bill for the house—I mean furniture—I have not had any from Cooper[18] as yet—I dont allow myself to worry much—for fear of putting myself back I am so anxious to get well—but sometimes these thoughts *will* press on me. . . .

I'm a bag of bones—but both Gull & Laking tell me I shall have to guard against getting too fat, once I get well—You may imagine I am tired of being in bed & being fed every 2 hours on the same slops—soup—milk & brandy—& medicine—the sight of jelly makes me sick—*Mais on se fait à tout dans ce monde*[19]—I dont find it so irksome now—tho' every day my bones get more tender—I have had heaps of letters from all my friends. . . .

That Jennie really *was* feeling better comes out in a little bit of gossip she passed on. Randolph's sister Georgiana had just got engaged to Richard George Penn Curzon, later fourth Earl Howe, who was only twenty-one:

I was told they call yr mother now—'the Baby snatcher' on account of young Curzon—How ill natured people are—She has been awfully kind to me, & writes & telegraphs continually to know how I am.

Jennie's letter ends: 'Now goodbye *cher petit* R—your letter made me cry—you must never worry about me again—*à bientôt* I hope. Yours J.' Randolph was overjoyed by it:

My dearest   Jan. 5th
I have just got yr darling letter of the 3rd. Such a joy to me. I had had a horrid thought that yr little pencil scrap which I received at Constantine written when you first got ill was perhaps the last I shld ever get from you. I cant tell you how I felt about it. I cld not bear to read it. However I am rather angry with you for writing to me so long a letter for it must have tired you vy much. I know who it used to tire me to write when I was ill. Pray dont write any more. Get Leonie to write to me. I was overjoyed at Laking's telegram received yesterday saying that your 'progress

was most satisfactory'. I had been vy anxious again till
I got it. You must certainly in any case come here for
a few days as this place will cheer you up; we might
stay with Clemmy afterwards if she likes to have us. I
am afraid you have been vy ill indeed poor little darling & I think I ought to have been sent for. It wld have
done me good to look after you. As it is the worry &
anxiety about you has made me rather seedy & the
cold I caught pulled me down, but the fine weather
here will set me up again. The weather is vy bright &
sunny but the air in the shade is cold. Mind you bring
yr *fourrure* with you. I hardly dare however expect
you in a fortnight after such a long illness. I shall go
to Marseilles to meet you. My darling child do take
great care of yrself & get well quickly. I am so anxious
about you still. I dont know what I shld have done
without yr photograph which you know I brought
away with me. It has been such a comfort to me. Yesterday I went over to Mentone to see Gorst, & I drove
back in a carriage. It is such a beautiful drive. I
stopped ½ an hour at Monte Carlo on my way back
but did not see anyone I knew. Tommy Trafford has
not turned up here yet. Perhaps he has altered his
plans. Gorst comes over here today to stop the night
on his way to England. I shall tell him to go and see
you on his arrival to tell you all about me—so you
may look out for him on Monday. I am going to write
to Milward[20] to tell him I cannot go to that Birmingham meeting I dont feel at all inclined to begin politics
again. I am afraid our money affairs are rather in a
mess, but it is not worth while worrying about money.
Milward must arrange. You need not pay all Payne's
bill. Pay half. My tour has been rather expensive. I
have spent about 150£ up to now. What an escape
Leonie had from that little beast Gebhart.[21] You know
I never liked the appearance of the youth. I feel vy
lonely sometimes particularly at breakfast and dinner.
It is so horrid eating alone. & the time passes slowly
when one is alone. Do make haste & come out to me.
But still dont travel till you are really fit. Mind you see

Gull before you start & get his leave I keep wishing so I had gone home from Marseilles. We cld have gone to Torquay or Bournemouth together. I am afraid of the long journey here for you. Perhaps Wolff cld make the Rothschilds get the P&M to give you one of their new 'salons'.[22] They are vy comfortable. Tell Clara to write to me. I wonder when you can have caught yr fever. Is it possible that the drains are not right in the new house. You shld inquire abt this from Laking. I am so glad to hear Winnie is right again. Give him a kiss from me. Goodbye my darling I think always of you

Ever yrs
Randolph S.C.

Randolph sent a note to Jennie next day via Gorst. He also sent her a present—though he had forgotten it was her birthday on the 9th. Jennie was delighted with her oyster-knife: 'I think it is lovely, so quaint & so effective—I hope you did not give too much for it—I think it was so sweet of you to think of getting it for me —it [is] just what I wanted I was so tired of my arrow.' She was 29, but 'I shall not acknowledge it to the world 26 is quite enough.' She had walked her first rather shaky steps and was determined to come out and join him. Randolph sent her careful instructions about the journey:

Villa Carmen,
Monte Carlo,
January 11th

My dearest
    I was so glad of your letter yesterday & to learn that you liked the little 'oyster knife' which I sent you. I am ashamed to confess I forgot all about yr birthday. What a brute I am, but my memory is so bad. I hope next year you will have a more cheery one than this last. Well now when you start, you had better go by tidal train to Paris; telegraph to the station master at Folkestone the day before for a cabin. The steward on board the boat will get you a coupé at Boulogne.

Stop that night & next day in Paris, & leave in the evening by the 7. oclock train if you are coming straight thro to here, or by the 7:15 if you mean to break the journey at Marseilles. You must send to the station in Paris in the morning for a 'SALON' this is one of the new coupés—which will cost you 500 frcs. but will take yr maid. It is the only carriage to travel in, & if you cant get one you must wait in Paris till the next day. The sleeping car places are always taken some days in advance. 50£ will pay yr journey here with yr maid well. I almost wonder whether you cld manage to come when my father comes. I think he starts abt the 16th or so. I dont think the journey will tire you vy much. But perhaps you had better break it at Marseilles. I am sure you are not so much pulled down as people usually are, but still you must not be imprudent. There is a capital little doctor here who will look after you if necessary. I think we won't be in a hurry to go to Clemmy's at Cannes it is much pleasanter here, & vy dull there. . . . I had such a nice letter from Leonie. Please thank her vy much for it, she wont mind my not writing to her as I tell you what little news I have to tell. Fancy Annie being Mistress of the Robes.[23] She will be more uplifted than ever. The weather is a little better today & may take up now. The last 3 days have been unparalleled for 4 yrs. I had a long letter from Gorst telling me all about you & two from Wolff who *'entre nous'* does write such dull letters & never tells me any news. However don't you tell him this. Well now darling I have nothing more to say. Telegraph to me when you start, & also when you leave Paris. I will meet you at Marseilles. Such a joy to see you again darling. Take great care of yrself. Bring all yr warm clothes. I dont think you will be too hot. If you are you can get something at Nice where there are vy good shops. Goodbye my darling love to the children.

> Ever yrs
> Randolph SC

I suppose Winston will go back to school in a few days. Give him a little money from me before he goes.

Jennie had overestimated her capacity to recover from such a serious illness, and worry probably held her back. First there was Randolph's own health: 'I cant bear to hear of another new doctor—I do hope you dont mean to try any fresh treatment—the fresh air & sun & above all a quiet mind will do more to put you right than any amount of medicines.' Then there was money: 'I have had my *quart d'heure de Rabelais*[24] over my house books', she wrote on the 11th, and on the 12th: 'I do hope Milward will be able to settle with them for the £15,000. I suppose there is no chance of our laying our hands on the surplus—how handy it would come in!' Randolph wrote admiring some of the ladies he saw. 'Wait till you see how nice *I* look!' she replied. But she could not join him as soon as she had hoped.

Jan. 16
2 Connaught Place, W.
Dearest R I'm afraid I have been rather remiss about writing the last few days—& you are so good—I get a letter nearly every day—But since I go downstairs somehow it seems quite difficult to write. The last 2 days it has been fine for a couple of hours so I have gone out with Leonie for an hour in a hansom—& it was delightful but my whole morning seems to be taken up in dressing—such a business & such a lot of things I have to put on—& I cant wear any stays or any of my dresses on account of my 'stomachino' being tender & my waist is about 2 yards around—but I daresay it will all get right—I am already fatter—& shall look quite respectable by the time I get to you —but when will that be?—I had hoped to have started today, & had made Perry begin to pack—but Laking wld not hear of it, & was quite cross with me—& said he certainly wld not allow it before Sat. I feel quite in despair—However if I leave Sat I can be with you

Monday—but I will telegraph to you—Yr Mother
came to see me Monday, & was very kind—she pro-
poses that I shld travel with the Roxburghe's who
leave for Paris on Sat—Annie wrote to me this morning & said they wld look after me—but I don't think
they can be of much use to me, & I can get on better
alone with Perry—However if I go in the same train
of course we go together but I mean to be quite independent If I go Sat—I shall have to go by Dover as
the tidal train from Folkstone leaves at the unearthly
hour of 6.30 a.m. I see in the *Morning Post* this
morning that Sir H Wolff's 2nd son is laid up at
Rome with enteric fever & that Lady W. has gone out
to him—I shall write to poor Wolfino at once—both
he & Gorst came to see me the other day—tho not
together—Wolff told me he had had a talk about you
with Chenery,[25] who said you were the only man who
cld lead the Conservative party—also Cairns[26] praised
you up. . . . Laking never told me that it was typhoid
till a day or 2 ago—I had no idea one cld have it so
lightly—but I am glad he did not tell me it wld only
have worried. I think now I have had an escape—
Well *cher petit* R. I must get up it is nearly one—This
is a dull letter but I feel stupid & no energy to think—
Winston is pretty well—Laking advises Herne Bay
for a week—before he goes back to school—I'll write
tomorrow I do so wish I was with you.

                                          Yours J.

The weather on the Riviera remained bad, but Randolph's doctor told him it was doing him good. If he
had been well, it seems likely that he would have gone
straight back to England. As it was, he would not

feel really happy till I have got you safe out here.
Dont draw any cheques except what you want for the
journey. We may want to make a little tour later to
Venice or somewhere & shall want money. I have
written to Milward to tell him that the money put by
for furnishing the house is practically gone & that he

must find some more. So please dont reduce the balance you know we dont get any more till the 15 March. . . .

Next day he wrote again, delighted to hear Jennie would at last be coming soon:

Villa Carmen,
Monte Carlo,
My dearest   January 17th
I have just received your telegram & am delighted to hear that you may be able to start on Saturday. I just got a letter from Gorst saying how much better he had found you & that you were going to start Wednesday but I thought that was too good news to be true. I think I shall go to Toulon on Saturday to meet my father & probably remain there Sunday. But I will telegraph to you before I start. This morning being very fine I went out at 8, and ascended M. Agen on a donkey; it is over 5000 ft. high. & the last thousand feet being vy steep I had to walk. The view was lovely & I enjoyed it immensely. I did not get home till two oclock, & then I dressed myself & went to sleep for an hour & dont feel a bit tired. so I am sure I am getting much stronger. I have not seen anything of anybody today. Shall you be able to do all my commissions for me? I do wish you wld just see Gull before you finally leave London just to be certain you are all right & fit for the journey. I must say I think Gladstone is in a bad way & Gorst tells me he is told that all the news about Northcote's complete restoration to health is all humbug. I have told Gorst I shall do as he & Wolff wish about returning for the meeting of Parliament. You had better have a parting interview with Wolff before leaving to hear what he says. Goodbye my little darling I do hope & trust you are vy careful of yrself & shall continue to feel anxious about you until I get you under my own care.

Ever Yours
Randolph S.C.

This touching correspondence reveals how much Randolph and Jennie still loved each other. One can see him, sitting in his Batna hotel room, miles from anywhere staring at Jennie's photograph, thinking she might be dead, that his whole world had collapsed; while she, feverish with typhoid, the most dreaded illness of the Victorian age, lay on her sickbed and worried that *he* would be worried. They, and Winston, might be sickly, but the marriage was strong indeed. Further evidence comes from the final letter: what Wolff and Gorst couldn't commit to paper, they could tell Jennie. She was trusted with Randolph's political secrets. She was trusted altogether.

NOTES

1. The Castellane family was ancient and noble, with several branches. This blackguard may have been Marie-Eugène-Phillipe-Antoine-Boniface de Castellane, grandson of a Marshal of France, monarchist politician, novelist and playwright. He was the father of the Marquis Boni de Castellane, who married an American heiress, and was a friend of Jennie twenty years later.
2. Son of Earl Fitzwilliam, and passionate admirer of Jennie's sister Leonie. When rejected, he went to India.
3. Probably Colonel Burnaby, a dashing soldier whose interest in politics was such that he stood for Birmingham in 1880, and would have done so again in 1885 with Randolph, only he was killed, sword in hand, at the battle of Abu Klea.
4. Baron Ferdinand de Rothschild.
5. One of three American sisters who, like the Jerome girls, did very well in English society. Emily did not marry, but Consuelo became Duchess of Manchester, and Natica married Sir John Lister-Kaye.
6. Evelyn Edward Thomas Boscawen, later 7th Viscount Falmouth, had been on the Duke of Marlborough's staff in Dublin. He was an admirer of Jennie for many years.
7. Harry Custance, a jockey.
8. The Duke's brother, with whom he had quarrelled over Church Rates.

9. Randolph's fifth sister, Georgiana, as yet unmarried.

10. Lord Lytton had been Viceroy of India from 1876-80. He was the son of the novelist Bulwer-Lytton.

11. Francis Henry Laking practised at 62 Pall Mall and 13 Addison Road, Kensington. Dr Clayton seems to have been given up as useless.

12. Sir William Withey Gull, Bart, was one of the most eminent physicians of his day. He practised in Brook Street, Grosvenor Square.

13. Randolph was on his way from Constantine to Biskra, on the edge of the desert. Batna was about halfway. It was there he got Jennie's two letters.

14. Now called Skikda.

15. Gambetta, the French statesman, died on New Year's Eve.

16. Randolph's aunt Clemmy had married again and was now Lady Clementine Green.

17. Randolph Payne & Sons, Importers of Wines, Spirits and Liqueurs, 61 St James's Street. S.W.

18. Probably Henry & John Cooper, upholsterers, cabinet-makers, art decorators and designers, 8, 9 & 10 Great Pulteney Street, W.

19. But one puts up with everything in this world.

20. Robert Harding Milward, unfortunately, was a solicitor employed by the Churchill family. Though a JP, he went bankrupt for £97,000, was struck off the rolls, and sentenced to six years penal servitude for fraudulently converting to his own use monies entrusted to him. He died almost immediately after entering prison in 1902.

21. Freddie Gebhart was a wealthy American whose party trick was to crow like a cock. Leonard Jerome liked his company, but was glad when Leonie rejected him. Gebhart consoled himself with Lily Langtry.

22. The Paris-Marseilles railway. See next letter.

23. Annie's husband had succeeded to the Dukedom of Roxburghe in 1879. She herself was Mistress of the Robes from 1883-5.

24. Quarter of an hour of bad language.

25. Thomas Chenery (1826-84), editor of *The Times*.

26. The Lord Chancellor under Disraeli, who had found Randolph's apology to H.R.H. so ungracious. This passing remark shows how Randolph had won the attention and admiration of the senior members of the Conservative party.

6

TRIUMPH

By December 1884 Randolph's position in the Conservative party was such that Lord Salisbury, the Tory leader, had to come to terms with him. Part of the deal, not committed to paper, was that Randolph should become Secretary of State for India in any future Conservative administration. Randolph had, again, not been well, and a visit to India, it was hoped, would serve both to prepare him for government office and to give him a chance to get fit again on the long voyages there and back. There was no place for Jennie on such a trip, which involved so much meeting of politicians and Indian administrators and dignitaries, so he took with him his secretary, Frank Thomas. The family went to see him off:

Dec. 5th, 1884
Brighton

My dear Papa

I hope you had a good passage and were not sick at all on board?

Was it rough at all?

I should like to be you on that beautiful ship. We went and had some Hotel soup after you went, so we did not do amiss. We saw your big ship steaming out of harbour as we were in the train. I cannot think of anything more to say. With love and kisses I remain yours affect

Winston

P.S. I had not any foreign Paper, so you must excuse me.

By 'foriegn Paper' Winston meant the special thin paper which was used for writing to distant parts, like modern airmail paper. Jennie had some, and she used it the same day:

Dearest R. I have just received yr little letter, & feel so sorry for you—but the gale seems to have abated, & I hope by this time you are all right—You poor thing I am afraid the first few days will be anything but pleasant—it certainly is rather a wrench to go at the last moment—We got back all right but the children were half starved—however they made up for it when we got home—The house looked so melancholy I cld not bear to stay in it—so went off to Clara's for dinner. . . .

While Randolph was away, Jennie was to see a lot of Clara, who had married the dashing but unfortunate sportsman Moreton Frewen in 1881. (His speculations in such ventures as gold-crushing machines were to earn him the nickname 'Mortal Ruin'.) She was to see even more of Leonie, who had married John Leslie in October 1884 much to the distress of his parents. Leslie was in the Guards, and while his family remained huffy, he and Leonie lived with Jennie at 3 Connaught Place. After retailing family gossip, Jennie went on:

The children have both gone—I shall have Jack back before Xmas as I cld not undertake to manage Winston without Everest—I am afraid even she can't do it. . . .

Mrs Everest was Winston's devoted nurse, of whom, in *My Early Life,* he wrote with the deepest affection. She was, he said, his confidante, and it seems to have been she who drew Jennie's attention to the marks of the continual beatings he had received at his first appalling preparatory school. That autumn he had been removed to the gentler atmosphere of Brighton and the more tender care of the Misses Thomson, where his health and spirits soon improved. Not so, however, his behaviour, which remained lamentable. He was just ten.

Years later, when he wrote his biography of his father, Winston printed many of Randolph's highly entertaining letters from Malta, Suez, the Red Sea and India. But he omitted all reference to an incident concerning himself. On 18 December 1884, Jennie received the following letter from Winston's headmistress:

29 Brunswick Road
Dear Lady Randolph Churchill   Dec. 17th

Soon after writing to you this morning, I was called to see Winston who was in a trouble that might have proved very serious. He was at work in a drawing examination, and some dispute seems to have arisen between him, and the boy sitting next to him about a knife the tutor had lent them for their work. The whole affair passed in a moment, but Winston received a blow inflicting a slight wound in his chest.

Dr Roose assures me that he is not much hurt, but that he might have been. As this was not the first time we have to complain of a very passionate temper in this boy, I decided to send him home at once. He is a candidate for the *Britannia*,[1] and if it is known that he is expelled, he will be disqualified. I have told his parents that if you wish him to be publicly expelled, I shall do it: but I leave that decision to you. If you approve the milder course he will quietly disappear from the school, and we shall think the punishment sufficient. I am quite sure that it is very necessary to impress upon these young boys the necessity of their learning to govern their passionate impulses, and so serious a punishment falling on one of their school fellows, will I hope, help to do so.

Dr Roose tells me that Winston is going to town with him on Friday: so he will be able to give you his medical report.

Believe me
very faithfully yours
Charlotte Thomson

Dr Edward Charles Robson Roose, who practised in both Brighton and London, was to be the Churchills' doctor for the next ten years. His son was at the Misses Thomsons' school, too, and a friend of Winston's. Writing to Randolph the following day, Jennie took a thoroughly realistic view of the incident:

> Jack came back from Bournemouth yesterday look-ing most fit—Winston arrives with Dr Roose today—I was much startled yesterday by receiving the enclosed from Miss Thomson—I had a telegram from Dr. Roose at the same time saying that Winston was all right— but fancy what a serious affair it might have been!—I have no doubt Winston teased the boy dread-fully—& it ought to be a lesson to him—I will not close my letter until I have seen him & can tell you how he is—His holidays are not over until the 20th of Jan. I hope I shall be able to manage him—I mean to make him do a little writing etc every morning. . . .

She went on to talk of Leonie and John Leslie, who had offered to pay £20 a month towards the house-keeping. Leonie had hired a second piano, and she and Jennie played all day 'until our fingers ached'. Then she added:

> Dr Roose & Winston have just arrived—the latter is all right—the penknife however went in about a quarter of an inch but of course as I thought he began by pulling the other boy's ear—I hope it will be a lesson to him. . . .

Randolph was in Bombay when he got this news. He wrote to Jennie on 9 January 1885:

> My dearest
> I have just telegraphed to you wishing you very many happy returns of the day, & now reiterate the same with every wish that you were out here with me. I got your long letter of the 19th on Tuesday on

arrival here from Beejapore; What adventures Winston does have; it is a great mercy he was no worse injured. . . .

It was his only comment, except to add on 24 January, from Luck now:

Also tell little Winny how glad I was to get his letter which I thought was vy well written. I suppose he is back at Brighton now. I hope there will be no more stabbing. . . .

He seems to have been resigned to Winston's bad behaviour, but not too much bothered about it. It was only later, when he was near the end of his life, that he became so angry with his son. Meanwhile, he was thoroughly enjoying himself, though he had again been unwell. Mr. Thomas wrote to the Duchess from Indore, on 15 January:

Dear Duchess,
  I fear you will think I have forgotten my promise to write to you. I did however, commence a letter some time ago, but finding that Lord Randolph was writing by the same mail I thought it useless to proceed with it. I ought to tell you first that Lord Randolph is quite well, though he does not *look* as well as I could wish. This is no doubt owing to the long railway journeys we have undertaken. He has also lost that feeling of giddiness which attacked him at home, & which returned for a few days after landing at Bombay. . . .

Jennie's letters are full of domestic details, mainly about the house which she was thinking of selling. It was 'abominably built', and the nasty smell which she had succeeded in removing from her room had reappeared ten times stronger in the library. In fact 2 Connaught Place remained the Churchills' home till 1892. On 13 February she wrote:

I went to Brighton to see Winston yesterday—&
took Jack with me—They were so happy together &
Winny was wildly excited but I thought he looked very
pale & delicate, & Miss Thomson said that she thought
he was far from strong—What a care the boy is!—He
told me that he was very happy, & I think he likes the
school but I fancy that he does not get out enough—
We witnessed the performance of a play in which
Winston appears as a woman 'Lady Bertha' & he acted
quite wonderfully & looked so pretty—I shall see
Roose in a day or 2 & will have a talk about him. . . .

Jennie had been to a party and met Lord Hartington,
the Liberal Secretary of State for War who 'chaffed me,
& said he hoped you were not coming back too soon—
"Quite soon enough to worry you" I said'. Everyone
was asking after him. She sent him all the political and
social gossip.

She had been to see Lily Langtry in *The School for
Scandal*, '& I see today in *St Stephens Review*—a sketch
of me in a box—with Harry Chaplin[2] & a lady—&
underneath is written "Mr Chaplin interviews Ly Randolph" '. But there was not much to report. 'How
quickly the time passes when one leads a quiet life. The
winter is slipping away without my realising it. Jack
Leslie is again at the Tower on guard & Leonie & I
left to our own devices.'

Jennie looked forward to Randolph's return. She was
lonely without him, even with Leonie and Jack Leslie.
On 20 March she wrote her last letter of this series:

London
March 20th
Dearest R—I sent you a telegram yesterday which
I hope you got before starting today—& this epistle
I trust you will find at Suez—I can hardly realize
that in 3 weeks you will be nearly home—Living
like a mouse here without stirring—the time has
passed very quickly for me—but I daresay to you it

seems ages—when you think of all you have seen
& done—Remember you promised me never to go
on another such a journey without taking me—Life
is too short for such long separations don't you think
so?

The letter ends 'Shall you be glad to see me?' There
seems no reason to suppose that Randolph wasn't.

II

Randolph returned in April 1885. In June Gladstone
resigned and Lord Salisbury agreed to form a minority
Conservative government. He was most anxious to include Randolph, whose standing was now very high
in the country as well as the party. But Randolph had
his terms, and was not at all sure they would be met.
His talk, according to Rosebery, was both striking
and despondent. 'I am very nearly at the end of my
tether', he said. 'In the last five years I have lived
twenty. I have fought Society. I have fought Mr Gladstone at the head of a great majority. I have fought
the Opposition Front bench. Now I am fighting Lord
Salisbury. I have said I will not join the Government
unless Northcote leaves the House of Commons. Salisbury will never give way. I'm done.' It was a strange
mood to be in, for as Rosebery told him, Salisbury
could not form a government without him, but it indi-
cates how exhausting Randolph felt his career had been
already. Now it was to become far more so, for Salisbury did yield, Northcote did go to the House of Lords,
and Randolph became Secretary of State for India.

In those days it was necessary to seek re-election on
appointment to government office, so there had to be
a bye-election at Woodstock. Randolph had recently
quarrelled with Blandford over the sale of treasures
from Blenheim, a process begun by their father who
had died in 1883. Randolph decided it might be wisest
to keep away. His new office gave him an enormous

amount of work, and the result of the election was
not in doubt, so he sent Jennie to conduct his campaign
for him. Though she stayed at Blenheim, she made her
headquarters the Bear Hotel at Woodstock. Helping
her was Randolph's sister Georgiana. They felt most
important, as though the eyes of the world were upon
them. Jennie, revelling in the hustle and bustle of the
committee rooms, felt like a general conducting a battle. But her greatest effectiveness lay, literally, in the
field rather than the committee room. Georgiana had
brought down her tandem with her, and she and Jennie drove about the countryside canvassing the electors,
their horses gaily decorated with ribbons of pink and
brown, which were Randolph's racing colours.

Sometimes we would drive into the fields, and, getting down, climb the hayricks, falling upon our un-
wary prey at his work. There was no escaping us.
Many of the voters of those days went no farther
than their colours. 'I votes red' or 'blue', as the case
might be, and no talking, however forcible or subtle,
could move them. Party feeling ran high, and in out-
lying districts we would frequently be pursued by our
opponents, jeering and shouting at us; but this we
rather enjoyed. We were treated to jingling rhymes,
the following being a specimen:

'But just as I was talking
With Neighbour Brown and walking
To take a mug of beer at the Unicorn and Lion
(For there's somehow a connection
Between free beer and election),
Who should come but Lady Churchill, with a turnout
that was fine.

'And before me stopped her horses,
As she marshalled all her forces,
And before I knew what happened I had promised her
my vote;

And before I quite recovered
From the vision that had hovered,
'Twas much too late to rally, and I had changed my
   coat.

'And over Woodstock darted
On their mission brave, whole-hearted,
The tandem and their driver and the ribbons pink and
   brown.
And a smile that twinkled over,
And that made a man most love her,
Took the hearts and votes of all Liberals in the town.

'Bless my soul! that Yankee lady,
   Whether day was bright or shady,
Dashed about the district like an oriflamme of war,
   When the voters saw her bonnet,
   With the bright pink roses on it,
They followed as the soldiers did the Helmet of
   Navarre.'

It was an exhausting business, but years later Jennie
remembered this election, of all the many she fought
for Randolph and Winston, as the one she enjoyed
most. Thanks to her efforts, Randolph was returned
with an increased majority, and when the result was
announced she appeared at a window of the Bear
Hotel and made a speech to the crowd, thanking them
from the bottom of her heart. She was so delighted at
her success that she felt as though she had been elected
herself, and when she got back to London she was
quite disappointed that she wasn't acclaimed in the
streets like a national hero. Doubtless she was much
teased for this, but she received many gratifying con-
gratulations, too. Among them was a letter from Randolph's close friend, though political opponent, Sir
Henry James. He had been Attorney-General in the
Liberal government, and introduced the Corrupt Practices Act of 1883.

My dear Lady Randolph,

You must let me very sincerely and heartily congratulate you on the result of the election, especially as that result proceeded so very much from your personal exertions. Everybody is praising you very much.

But my gratification is slightly impaired by feeling I must introduce a new Corrupt Practices Act. Tandems must be put down, and certainly some alteration —a correspondent informs me—must be made in the means of ascent and descent therefrom; then arch looks have to be scheduled, and nothing must be said 'from my heart'. The graceful wave of a pocket handkerchief will have to be dealt with in committee.

> Still, I am very glad.
> Yours most truly,
> Henry James.

Jennie was particularly pleased with this letter, which came from a man who had proved a very good friend indeed. The previous year he had given a dinner party at which Randolph and the Prince of Wales were formally reconciled. Randolph's manner, according to Francis Knollys, 'was *just* what it ought to have been'. Thus in five years, from almost nothing, Randolph and Jennie were not merely restored to favour, they were one of the leading political and social couples in England.

The Duchess, naturally, was delighted with the way events had turned out. Since the Duke's death, Randolph's career had become the overwhelming interest of her life. Another who followed it closely was Dr Robson Roose:

Private   9 Regency Square,
                             Brighton
                             20 June 1885

Dear Lord Randolph Churchill

Permit me to congratulate you on your Victory, and to wish you health and happiness for your great

office! I feel *now* you will have an additional strain
upon your strength and I shall feel so deeply grateful
if you will permit me to come and see you if you are
ailing or over-worked not only in London but any
part of England in fact *anywhere,* and let me render
my services as a complimentary labor of *deep respect,*
as well as of *grateful* appreciation of your many acts
of kindness—Please do not be offended at this request; or think me pushing, I am only *so* desirous of
helping you and yours, and, apart from my respectful
regard, I am desirous for your country's sake of
helping with my small abilities to maintain in health
your invaluable life—Forgive me if I have annoyed
you, I mean so kindly by this letter. With compls.

> Yrs Faithfy
> Robson Roose

P.S. I venture to send a copy of my book which you
were good enough to say you would accept.[3] It is
dedicated to Gull as I belonged to his Hospl. and
etiquette demanded it.

I have been quite seriously ill and have been ordered to go to America and back in a White Star
Liner and I propose leaving July 16th. for 1 month
only. but if the pressure of the end of the session
is trying you I will gladly put off my voyage.

Randolph's health remained very doubtful. In September the Queen wrote to Jennie through a lady in
waiting to enquire how he was. Everyone was anxious.
But he set to at the India Office, and was soon making
a generally good impression.

III

The political events of 1885 and 1886 are extremely
complicated, and in spite of an immensely detailed
recent work on the subject, still not entirely clear.[4]
There was not only a struggle between the two main
parties, but within each of them a ceaseless manoeuvr-

ing for position among the leaders. Furthermore, politicians of both sides intrigued with each other quite as much as with their colleagues, in an effort to establish a new centre party which would command wide general support and give a new generation of men the chance to seize power from the old leadership of Gladstone and Salisbury. Ireland was the main issue on which manoeuvre and compromise could take place, as both parties were uneasily split.

Randolph took a leading part in these intrigues, trying one policy, then another, in an effort to gain a dominant position for himself, but it would be unrealistically glib to see his behaviour as simply opportunist. He believed that the old order of government by a small and wealthy class must give way to a new and more democratic one: hence his invention of 'Tory Democracy'. Nonetheless, like any politician, he had to start from the situation as it was, and throughout this period he was scheming and plotting night and day with an energy and single-mindedness which left him very little time for ordinary life. For a significant part of the period he held high office, with all the burdens that entailed. Furthermore, he was making many speeches, both in and out of Parliament, and speeches as calculated as his take a long time to write. It cannot be emphasized too strongly that he was driving himself exceedingly hard. Not only his health, but the enormous amount of work he got through must constantly be borne in mind throughout the events which follow.

His first spell of office was not lengthy, for Salisbury's government fell in January 1886, though not before Randolph had presided over the British annexation of Burma. In opposition again, he turned his attention to the burning issue of Ireland. Although he had earlier made overtures to Parnell and the Irish Nationalists, he now completely switched positions, and in February made his famous, or infamous, speech in Belfast in which he declared that 'Ulster will fight, and Ulster will be right.' Political passions were running extremely high. But in the midst of all the excitement, Randolph and Jennie were suddenly summoned to Brighton, where Winston had fallen dangerously ill with pneumonia. It was touch and go. Dr Roose gave up his London work to stay by Winston's bedside. When the danger was over, Mrs Jerome wrote to Jennie: 'Yr whole life has been one of good fortune & this the crowning blessing that little Winston has been spared to you.' Randolph and Jennie must have been enormously relieved: Randolph sent Roose a substantial cheque. Roose gushed his thanks:

> 45, Hill Street,
> Berkeley Square, W.

Dear Lord Randolph Churchill 31/3/86

In acknowledging the receipt of your too kind and thoughtful letter with its munificent enclosure what am I to say? When I realize, as I do daily, that through *you* I have opportunities introductions, and a kindly sympathy which is making for me a leading London career, I feel I *cannot* do too much for you and yours, and with this feeling of deep gratitude, I accept your cheque almost with pain! I cannot refuse what you wish to send, but I do feel that *without fee* no attention I can shew to you or yours can fulfil in any way the debt I owe to you—Please do not be offended with me for saying again and again that I have no desire no anticipation of fees from you, and that no amount of work I can do for you will redeem the immense service you have and do render to me by your mention of my name to so many

> Ever yours gratefully
> Robson Roose

P.S. I could write *so* much more but I think you understand what I feel.

The private crisis was soon over; the public one continued. On 8 April Gladstone introduced his Home Rule Bill: the fight over it was to last almost two months. Just before Easter, Randolph and Jennie both took brief breaks. Jennie went to stay with friends in Ireland, while Randolph went over to Paris for a few days. Most interestingly, his companions there included Charles Kinsky:

> Hotel Vendôme,
> 1 Place Vendôme,
> Paris

My dearest   April 20 1886

I write a few lines to tell you I am all right and find the change vy pleasant. I hope this will find you tomorrow safe back from Dublin. There were no apparetments at the Bristol sufficiently spacious for me & Harry Chaplin and Kinski who arrive tomorrow, so we have moved here where we are all together. I have been to the races today with Henry Hoare.[5] Very few people there. Last night I dined with Trafford & his wife & daughter & we went to the new Cirque. Tomorrow Ferdinand Rothschild gives us dinner and we go to see the Fiacre 117.[6] I have been to see Lady de Grey [7] who is looking vy well indeed. She is stopping with the Jancourts.[8] I met Minnie Paget [9] at breakfast at the Rothschilds yesterday also looking most flourishing.

That horrid young Cairns [10] is here. He tried to speak to me but I snubbed him. I shall return Sunday so you might get some one to dine. If possible Henry James as I shall want to hear the news. I hope you had a good time in Ireland.

> Ever yours
> Randolph S.C.

Then it was back to the Home Rule debate, which went on throughout May. Randolph played a leading part in the defeat of the Bill, which came on 7 June. A General Election was called immediately. In those days, a General Election took place over several weeks. There was no single day on which everyone voted, or on which all the votes were counted. Results came in

in dribs and drabs, and it took some time before it was
clear who was going to win.

Randolph was exhausted. He decided to make only
two speeches in his new constituency, Paddington.
(Woodstock had been abolished.) In them he violently
denounced Gladstone, and said the Home Rule Bill
was simply 'to gratify the ambition of an old man in
a hurry'. He was much cheered. When he and Jennie
and the Duchess attended a meeting together, the crowd
rose and sang *Rule Britannia*. It was all very heady
stuff, and Randolph was sure the Conservatives were
going to win, and there would follow a long term of
Conservative government in which he would be a
dominating figure. He determined to take another holiday while he could. Early in July he left to go fishing
in Norway with his old friend Tommy Trafford. It was
a remote place, with only two posts a week, and they
reckoned it was 1500 miles from Connaught Place.
He wrote to Jennie on 10 July:

I have heard no election news since Tuesday, when
things seemed to be going well. I am expecting the
post with telegrams every moment. This is doing me
a lot of good. I felt vy seedy leaving London & it
took me some days to get right. We had one rough
night in the North Sea which decidedly upset me.
This is a most lovely spot & very solitary; no tourists
no natives. The House which is rough to look at is
comfortable enough inside. & Tommy is as amiable
& charming as ever. He sends you many messages. . . .
. . . Are you having some good fun with dinners
or balls? Post just come in; with telegrams from
Moore [11] and Rothschild. Certainly most satisfactory
news which confirms all my expectations. . . .

Three days later he was still delighted with the news,
but worried over his and Jennie's financial situation:

I expect the Tories will now come in & remain in
some time. It seems to me you want the 5000£ a

year badly. But really we must retrench. I cannot understand how we get thro so much money. . . .

The answer was simple enough: by never stinting themselves of anything. Clearly their debts at this time were beginning to worry both of them. The political situation, however, could not have been better. The Conservatives won the election handsomely, and on 21 July Gladstone resigned. Three days later Randolph was back and bombarding Salisbury with suggestions for the new administration. There had been a good deal of speculation in his absence about what post he himself would be offered. Gossip had even reached Dr Roose, who wrote Randolph a significant warning letter:

> 45 Hill Street,
> Berkeley Square, W.
>
> Dear Lord Randolph Churchill 23 July, '86
> I hear rumours that you may be induced to take the post of 'Irish Secy.' or 'Foreign affairs' and I venture to send you this note, as your responsible medical adviser, of warning not to do so! Apart from the great anxiety of Ireland you would have *frequent railway journeys* most trying to one of your constitution, of course there is not this objection to the post of Foreign Minister but *that* entails, I am told, an increasing work and unceasing anxiety which you ought to avoid!
> I would respectfully suggest that you should go back to your old post 'India' as *that,* altho's arduous, is liable to be less trying to your constitution than the others I have mentioned—I hope you have returned better for your change? I go for 3 weeks rest from August 14th—
>
> yrs gratefully
> Robson Roose
> Please forgive this letter written in the interest of your health.

The previous September Randolph had been advised to take a rest. Overwork had made him irritable and the doctor prescribed digitalis as a sedative, which he proceeded to take in large doses. The effect of this drug is to depress the heart's activity; but it can be dangerous, as the action can be accumulative, and giddiness, acute depression and other nervous symptoms follow. We do not know for how long Randolph continued with this treatment. However, instead of avoiding work and anxiety, he now accepted a double load of both. Within a week of Roose's clear warning, Randolph was Chancellor of the Exchequer and Leader of the House of Commons. Furthermore, it was generally recognized that he was next in line to be Conservative Prime Minister. It was an astonishing triumph for a man who six years earlier had been a back-bencher.

Lord Salisbury had wanted Sir Michael Hicks-Beach, the previous Conservative Leader of the House, to take the post again, but Beach refused, saying that since Randolph would in fact *be* the leader, he should have the official position, too. But, he wrote, 'I had very great difficulty in persuading Lord Randolph to agree. I spent more than half an hour with him in the Committee Room of the Carlton before I could persuade him, and I was much struck by the hesitation he showed on account of what he said was his youth and inexperience in taking the position.' Here was the crux of the matter: Randolph's inexperience meant that he had to make excessive demands on his energy. Lord Rosebery said it used to take Randolph up to forty-eight hours to compose a speech and during that time he was unapproachable. He drove his staff as hard as himself. His very able secretary, A. W. Moore, collapsed from the strain at the end of the year and was sent away for a rest, but he never recovered from his exhaustion and died two months later at the age of forty-six. Randolph was living on his nerves, and smoking cigarettes incessantly. He was capable of sustained exertion, concentrated on the problems in hand, but was left with no energy for anything else. He knew he was taking on far too much. 'How long will your leadership last?' Rosebery asked him. 'Six months', Randolph answered gaily. 'And after that?' 'Westminster Abbey!'

Jennie's family were delighted at Randolph's success, though Jennie herself had again not been well. Her mother wrote to her on 5 August from Buxton, in Derbyshire, where she had been visiting Chatsworth and Haddon Hall and taking the baths.

Dear Jennie,

I was so pleased this morning to get yr letter I do hope now the excitement of both society and politics, are in a measure finished, that rest, and quiet will make you feel all right again. Do try to take care of yourself my dear Jennie—I cant tell you how pleased I am that Randolph got the Office he wished. I have done nothing but read the newspapers the past three weeks. I think I have seen everything that has been written about Randolph, both in praise & against him. I am so delighted that he has triumphed over his enemies. I know he will do great credit to himself & party in spite of the predictions to the contrary. Let us pray for health & strength for him, his duties will be so trying—I do so hope to live to see Randolph Prime Minister. . . .

She ended: 'I do hope that you will get well & strong, and be able to enjoy all yr autumn pleasures.' But for Jennie that autumn was to offer no pleasures at all.

NOTES

1. H.M.S. *Britannia* was the training-ship for cadets in the Royal Navy: now the Britannia Royal Naval College, Dartmouth.

2. Conservative MP and political friend of Randolph's, later Viscount Chaplin.

3. *Gout and Its Relations to Diseases of the Liver and Kidneys.* One doubts whether Randolph read it very carefully, but others did. It went into seven editions.

4. *The Governing Passion,* by A. B. Cooke and John Vincent.

5. Sir Henry Hoare, 5th Bart, b. 1824, had been a Liberal MP, but was now better known as a social and racing figure.

6. A play.

7. Gladys, daughter of Lord Herbert of Lea. Lord de Grey was the heir to the Marquess of Ripon.

8. Friends of long-standing. Jack went to stay with them at their home in Presles in 1898.

9. Minnie Stevens, an American, married to Arthur Paget, the son of a general who became a general himself.

10. Lord Chancellor Cairns had died in 1885. This is his son, the second Earl.

11. Mr A. W. Moore was Randolph's secretary.

7

TRAGEDY

In August something went very wrong indeed with Jennie's marriage. She was convinced there was another woman. Her mother, Clara and Leonie were all away from London. The only people she could turn to were her in-laws. She went first to Randolph's sister, Lady Cornelia Guest, whose intervention only made things worse. Then, swallowing her pride, she went to the Duchess, the woman who had made her early married life so trying, and who still openly disapproved of Jennie's smart social life. Jennie's letters to the Duchess do not seem to have survived, but the Duchess's to Jennie have. The first is dated 8 September, from Huntercombe, the Duchess's house in Buckinghamshire, near Burnham.

Confidential

Dearest Jennie

Huntercombe
Sept. 8

I thought so much about you that I was very glad to get your Letter I will begin with the end of it. Rely on one thing which is—I may not be able to do any good but I will do no harm & not like poor Cornelia put the fat in the Fire in my desire to help you. Meantime I PRAY you do not breathe thoughts of Revenge agst *any one*. It will bring you no blessing. Accept your present worry & anxiety patiently & strive to dispel it by the exercise of DOMESTIC VIRTUES!! looking after the Children & the new cook etc.—avoiding excitement & the Society of those

144

Friends who while ready enough to pander to you would gladly see you vexed or humbled as they no doubt are jealous of your success in society. How dull & tiresome you will think me & how little comfort—I think Ly Mandeville [1] would be true—but oh she is indiscreet & things do come round so. I wish so much you had your sisters for they are to be trusted & I really would trust no one else. Try dear to keep your troubles to yourself—this is hard for you have a tell tale Face—though you do tell little Fibs at times—It is a horrid time of year for you to be in town. If you do not go to Scotland with him dear Jennie do come and vegetate quietly here. Bring Jack & we will try to make you as happy as possible. I am sure it will show R—you care for him & he has a good Heart & will give you credit for it—If I were you I would not if it killed me let the heartless lot you live with generally see there was 'a shadow of a shade of a shred' wrong only *He* should know it & feel that it makes you miserable—And meantime though it is a hundrum task try to make yourself so essential to him that he must recognize it. He hates trouble—& yet he likes things to be nice & well managed. Oh dear Jennie you are going through a great *crise* of your Life & on yourself will depend whether your hold & influence becomes greater than ever or not—But the question is—Is it not worth it & you who are clever & young & attractive can do it if you choose. You must now sacrifice yourself & your pleasures & give yourself steadily up to the task—perhaps for many a day. I have no doubt of your success for I *know* in his Heart he is truly fond of you—& I think I ought to know—But I have told you all this & will not preach any more. Sunny [2] came ysy & looks well and gives a good Acct of your Boys.[3] Perhaps it will be as well for you to go there for next Sunday. But pray be very careful with Blandford. He is so indiscreet to say the least of it and does set people by the ears. I dare say there is some ground for Ly M's story. I can believe any thing of

those sorts of women. They seem to like to spoil a
menage. But that *species* of proceeding will defeat
its own end. God bless you I pray for you & my dear
R. every Day that God may give you patience strength
& gentleness & that He may watch over dear R. &
keep him straight

> Believe me
> Yrs most aff
> F.M.

I had such a nice note from dear Col Boscawen [4]
—Perhaps you might look out for a very tiny token
for *me*—in some old shop—There are 2 in Davies
St—something he could use to *suit* my poverty
striken *Pouch*.

It seems that Jennie did take the Duchess's advice
to go to Blenheim, but not the rest. She wrote the
Duchess three letters in the next forty-eight hours. She
was desperate. Whom she suspected is not clear—but
she obviously thought there was someone. The Duchess was less convinced; she thought the indiscretion
might have been Jennie's.

> Huntercombe
> Sept. 10

Dearest Jennie
I have your 3 Letters & they make my Heart ache.
I know not what to advise except patience—I cannot
make it out. Have you told me everything? Can anything have got to his ears, or some Diabolical Mischief been made—I must see him—I shall go up on
Monday Morng but I think its better you should not
be there & He cannot think it a Cabal. His Letter
does not allude to you—He only says he shall be
glad to see me Monday—Perhaps it would be well
for you to stay for the Show—or until your Mother
comes to you—for I dread your being left alone in
London & she is sure to give you good advice. I could
tell you more after I have seen him—You will have
the Children at Blenheim & could you not write to
him from there. Even if he does not answer he must

read your Letter & you could tell him how miserable you are & appeal to him not to break your Heart. Do not be afraid of my saying a word to make matters worse. I may indeed do no good but He will listen to me so Pray try & be calm dearest Jennie, its a heavy trial for you—worse for an impetuous disposition like yours—take it dear as quietly as you can & pray for strength to bear it—I never preach but in heavy sorrow only God can comfort one & He will help you dearest Jennie I do feel so sorry for you. All words seem so cold. If you wish to see me in London Monday please let me have a telegram at 46 Grov. Sq. otherwise I shall return here to lunch. I can say no more. You will have your Children to cheer you—After seeing Randolph will write you a long letter. I cannot understand his being so hard if he realizes all you suffer. Perhaps he is full of other things. I *cannot* believe there is any other woman . . .

The state of relations between Jennie and Randolph at this moment is clear from a curt note Randolph sent from the Treasury to greet Jennie on her return from Blenheim. The Duchess had been to see him, and Lady Mandeville seems to have tried to put things right, with no success.

> Treasury Chambers,
> Whitehall. S.W.
>
> Dear Jennie
>
> I have ordered lunch for you. My mother has been up this morning & has gone back. She is coming up Wednesday for Primrose League meeting.[5] Read enclosed which is vy droll & return it to Consuelo who sent it to me. I shall not be in till late tonight
>
> Yours ever
> R.S.C.

Randolph was wrong: the Duchess had not gone back. She had stayed in London and had lunch with Jennie. No doubt they had thrashed the whole thing

out in detail. She scribbled a note from Paddington
station on her way home:

> Missed the train dear & saw it just go out of the
> station. Am waiting till the 5.10—thought it no use
> to go back & bore you. I cannot say more & can only
> hope you will take my advice. I know how hard it is.
> But do try dear—& once more be *very* close & dis-
> creet & have patience & God bless & guide you
>
> Yrs most aff
F. M.
>
> You can tell R. I found so much to do I went to you
> for lunch.

So the Duchess was not above telling little fibs herself at times. It is clear that she was genuinely sorry
for Jennie, but also that she was very anxious that
nothing should get out, particularly now, when Randolph was doing so well. And he was doing well,
though as Leader of the House of Commons he was
having a very awkward time with the Irish, who were
obstructing government business in almost as masterly
a manner as Randolph himself had employed in 1880.
But he won high praise, even from the Queen, who
never trusted him, for his geniality and patience. He
was also extremely busy at the Treasury. But if in
public he was all self-control, in private he sometimes
gave vent to temperamental outbursts which deeply
shocked his colleagues, and made them think him unfit
for his high office. After an incident in which he
berated Hicks-Beach in front of Lord George Hamilton, for which he apologized next day, inviting both
men to dinner, Hamilton wrote:

> It is said, 'All is well that ends well', but after this
> experience of Churchill's waywardness I looked with
> great anxiety upon his future leadership. On thinking
> the matter over, I could only come to the conclusion
> that his nervous system was overstrained and that

we might soon again have an outburst which would be irremediable.

What outbursts there were at 2 Connaught Place we can only guess, but that the atmosphere was tense and unhappy is certain. Even if, as seems probable, Lady Mandeville had now denied the rumour she originally spread, Jennie still suspected someone—though it is hard to see how Randolph could have found the time to carry on an affair. But what other explanation could there be? He was still keeping his distance. Jennie, meanwhile, was trying to keep up a front by continuing her social round. Randolph wrote her another cool note from the Carlton Club on September 25th:

Dear Jennie

I think the Allsopps' [6] will be vy pleasant but Wilton [7] dull & cold, so advise you to refuse the latter. I go to Huntercombe this afternoon & to Newmarket on Monday by 2.30 train. We finished Parliament finally this morning. A great relief. I think you are quite right not to come up to London but to go straight from Duncombe Park [8] to Newmarket. Everybody has bolted from town. I had a long interview with the D of Cambridge [9] yesterday, and also a vy satisfactory one with Hatzfeldt. I fear Russia means business which will be awkward. Accounts from Ireland are fairly good. Au revoir at Newmarket.

> Yours ever
> Randolph S.C.

I had a vy gracious letter from The Queen yesterday.

The Queen had written to congratulate him on the skill and judgement he had shown in leading the Commons through a difficult session, but his behaviour outside the chamber caused much irritation to his colleagues. His frequent conversations on foreign affairs with Count Hatzfeldt, the German Ambassador, may have been satisfactory to him, but they annoyed Lord Salisbury very much indeed. It seemed that Randolph wanted to meddle in everyone else's business as well as his own. There were mutterings about him in the Cabinet. Meanwhile domestic matters continued to go badly. As always when a marriage is under strain, money troubles came to the fore. While Randolph was visiting his mother at Huntercombe, she received another letter from Jennie. Her reply was sharp:

Huntercombe
Sept. 26

Dearest Jennie

Thanks for your letter. I am glad you have enjoyed yourself. Randolph came yesy & seems in good Health & spirits—He has been very affect. & cheerful though Sarah [10] & I were quite alone. I leave him very much to himself & I really think he likes it best. I am much concerned & grieved to find that there has been a new settlement of his Affairs required & more money borrowed of Mr Montagu.[11] It has come about accidentally my knowing abt. it as my signature was necessary & it made me rather sorry that you have never been able to confide entirely in me though I do not see how I can shew you more affection and sympathy than I do—I reproached R. for his extravagance gently enough for God knows I cannot bear to add to his anxieties & he said he had relied on *you* doing for him as I used to do for his Father keeping things straight. Now dearest Jennie I would not for the world pain or judge you harshly—But indeed if you wish to regain your influence over him & make him fonder of you, you *must* sacrifice yourself & lead a different life. You must feel now that life cannot be all pleasure & oh dearest Jennie before it is too late I do pray you to lay my advice to heart & give up that fast lot you live with racing flirting & gossiping. Indeed it is real affection that dictates my words. You will be happier I know if *once* you break off with the past & live for a better and more useful existence. I believe you are as I told you at a great crisis of your life. I should be so glad if I could be of use to you & persuade you—But I have told you all this before & I do not want to lecture & bore you. If I could be of any use to you in Household matters you know I would. He tells me he is now going to give you an allowance for Housekeeping etc—But I do not like to seem inquisitive & you have never confided to me your money difficulties—As to other matters I feel sure you have no cause for jealousy in that quarter. But I feel there is a great deal of talk & I fear dear you have not been able to conceal things as you should have done. Mrs Stirling [12] Ly Mandeville Ly Londonderry [13] & others have talked & it has come round to me from Mary & my Children I do pray you to be *very* discreet this week I hope & trust for both your sakes that nothing will be observed at Newmarket. But you must be very careful Dear—And now God bless you—I shall think constantly of you & only wish it was in my power to do you any good.

We expect the Curzons this Evg which will be nice—Randolph seems quite satisfied abt. things in general & he has cause to be—Ever

Yr most afft
F.M.

Did he, though, have good enough cause? He was behaving in the most extraordinary way for a Cabinet Minister, enraging his colleagues, interfering, causing ceaseless trouble. On 2 October he went to Dartford and delivered what was virtually his personal programme for the government of which he was a member. It seemed deliberately designed to upset everyone with whom he was supposed to be working. And then he did something even more astonishing: as though to challenge his colleagues to see how they could manage without him, Randolph set off for a European holiday,

under the instantly penetrated disguise of 'Mr Spencer'.
He was now a famous politician on the continent as
well as in England, and many people quite wrongly
believed the pseudonym was to enable him to conduct
secret negotiations with European statesmen. Cabinet
Ministers were not amused. When the Duchess came
up to London to say goodbye, Jennie was not there.
She had not answered the Duchess's letter about their
financial problems, it seems:

Huntercombe
Oct. 3
8 o/c

Dearest Jennie

I was sorry not to find you in town. . . . I saw
Randolph but only for a very short Time as he appeared full of business & thought—He said he should
go today or Monday for a fortnight. I said would you
take Jennie & he said No only T. Trafford was going
with him but that you were going to Bradford [14]—
I said no more dear Jennie feeling it was wiser to
trust to Time to put things straight. I still believe
you have no cause for jealousy of that Lady—& that
you have the future in your own Hands—only there
must be sacrifice & self denial & great patience & can
you *will* you exercise it? Meantime dear you say
nothing abt. the *Money* question which I wrote to
you & which worries me very much. However perhaps when we meet we can talk it over. I have little
to tell you. If you feel inclined to come here you
know we shall be glad to see you. But I fear its very
quiet. The Lawn Tennis is at an end & so we shall
not have many visitors. . . . I do so like being here
so quiet & so cheery. The Days fly by. Blandford is
coming today for a night. I am longing to read Randolph's speech & hope it will be a great success. The
Londonderrys seem doing very well in Dublin I get
an Irish Paper daily & it reminds me of the old Times
—I went to a very successful Primrose League Meeting the other Day with Georgie where they recd. me
like Royalty!!—Georgie & I were so amused. She is
very popular & we both *orated*—God bless you Dear

—I hope your Mother is better—I wish I could put a wise cold Head on your shoulders! Its easy to preach to others I know though as you say very hard to do right oneself.

Yrs aff.
F.M.

I have just finished reading Dear R's magnificent speech & never have I read one more statesmanlike tactful & forcible. It must go down in the Country as it has done on my mind—so straightforward & yet discreet—so eminently *common sense*. It has been a great treat to me to read it—the story abt. the Dutch Generals—the Return of political Economy from the Starry regions to which Mr Gladstone consigned them & above all his words abt. the Unionists *must* forcibly strike everybody. I have no words to express my admiration & approval. If he is not gone will you give him this little bit of my Letter as I will not bother him I trust & pray he is well & will now get rest.

Tell me his address abroad.

Rest does not seem to have been Randolph's object, for he travelled rapidly round the capitals of Europe. His first note to Jennie came from Berlin:

Der Kaiserhof,
Berlin

Dear Jennie   October 6, 1886

You will like a line to let you know we got here safely after a vy long journey. From 6.30 am leaving Flushing to 11 oclock PM here. It was a vy hot day travelling. This is not much of an hotel rather dirty & bad waiters, but we discovered a restaurant this morning where we got a vy civilized breakfast. It is certainly not a vy lively town but worth seeing. Tommy & I spent an afternoon in the Zoological Gardens which are even better than ours. Tonight we go to a theatre where the attraction is a big ballet & tomorrow we leave at noon arriving at Dresden at five in the evening. It is certainly vy pleasant getting away from England and if the weather only keeps as fine as it is now travelling will be vy pleasant. My cold has not troubled me and is practically gone.

                                    Yours ever
                                    Randolph S.C.

The next letter is slightly warmer in tone, and reveals that he and Kinsky were still friends:

                                    Hotel Bellevue
                                    Dresden
Dear Jennie   October 8, 1886
   We arrived here yesterday afternoon glad to get away from Berlin which is certainly most dull and unattractive. I was much amused to get this morning a message through Iddesleigh [15] from H. Bismark [16] hoping I would go and see him if I went to Berlin. I wired to Iddesleigh that I did not intend to go to Berlin but that from here I was going to travel in Bohemia. I found here a vy interesting letter from Kinski. Please thank him for it & tell him I will write & tell him how his house at Prague is looking. Yesterday we went to a kind of Music Hall vy stupid & bad, but crowded with Saxons who seemed immensely amused. Of course we have done the Raphael, which certainly exceeds all one's expectations. The gallery is immense and would require a month to go over it properly so we did it in 45 mts. We go on to-morrow to Prague & the following day to Vienna. Tonight we are going to the opera which is said to be well done here. How spiteful the Radical papers are. That *Pall Mall* most mischievous. I hope Lady Salisbury does not read it or she might take alarm for the position of 'Robert'.[17] Tommy is vy flourishing & most amiable. We have found a vy good hotel here. Unfortunately the day has been pouring wet so have been a good deal in our rooms.

                                    Yours ever
                                    Randolph S.C.

From Dresden the travellers went on to Vienna.

> Frohner's Hôtel Imperial,
> Wien
> October 12, 1886

Dear Jennie

We got here last night & I found yr letter of Saturday; I return Winnie's which you enclosed. I am hopelessly discovered; at the station yesterday I found a whole army of reporters at whom I scowled in my most effective manner. Really it is almost intolerable that one cannot travel about without this publicity. How absurd the English papers are. Anything to equal the lies of the *Daily News* & *Pall Mall* I never read. W. H. Smith [18] is here & we had a long talk last night. I have got him to go and see Paget [19] who wanted me to go and dine with him & tell him that as I saw no one at Berlin I did not wish to see anyone here. The reporters have been besieging the hotel this morning but I have sent them all away without a word. The weather is fine & bright tho there is an autumn chill in the air. We have got 'Gugel' Kinsky's cabdriver, and are going tonight to the theatre an der Wien & afterwards to the Orpheum. where I hear the programmes are vy good. Prague is a most interesting place. I got you some Bohemian glass things for flowers & also a toilette for myself. They will reach Connaught Place in about a fortnight. I expect we shall leave this for Paris on Friday or Saturday. This pottering about Europe *de ville en ville* suits me down to the ground if it were not for the beastly newspapers. Tell Mama all about me. Old Kodolitsch [20] called this morning but I said I was out. I thought he would be such a bore. I am going to try & find a Sandringham present for 'Tum' here.[21]

The tone of this, though not exactly warm, is certainly not hostile. Randolph is buying Jennie presents; later, in Paris, he saw to a commission of hers at a jeweller's. It is exasperating that he, who kept almost every letter Jennie ever wrote him, did not keep the ones he received on his European tour. In any case, he was playing the part of a correct husband, writing regular but non-committal accounts of his doings.

Among the reporters clamouring at the station was one from *The Times*. 'Mr Spencer', he said, looked fatigued. He refused in emphatic terms to receive anyone whatever, but walked about Vienna both morning and afternoon, and visited a leather goods shop, before going to see Millöcker's operetta *The Vice-Admiral* in the evening.

Meanwhile there had been a small fire at 2 Connaught Place. Randolph was unperturbed. He wrote from Paris telling Jennie to do what the carpenter recommended. He was rather bored, as Tommy Trafford had gone to see his wife and children, but there were several old friends about to keep him company. He had received a letter from Winston which pleased him: he replied enclosing stamps and some of the autographs for which Winston was always beseeching him. (Winston seems to have sold them to his schoolfriends to supplement his pocket-money.)

If Jennie was hoping for kinder treatment on Randolph's return, she was disappointed. Once again she appealed to the Duchess, who replied:

> Huntercombe
> Oct. 24
>
> Dearest Jennie
>
> Do not fear for anything you have said to *me*—for it will go no further. But I do intreat you to put such thoughts away from you & I quite agree that perhaps it is best not to talk abt. them for it intensifies them & I am sure it works you up to exaggerate things. I know well how impulsive & excitable you are & it will be very hard for you to keep a watch over your words & *thoughts* even—But do my dearest Jennie make a firm resolve to *seal* your lips & govern your thoughts & do not let any friend *male* or *female* beguile you henceforth into confidence & be calm & gentle with him—Keep your place as a Mat-

ter of course & do not rush about for destruction
I know so well how hard it is for you & pray believe
it's no want of sympathy makes me say this but simply that it is the only possible way of getting his
Love & respect & of preserving your own Dignity—
It will bring you a blessing if you accept patiently
this trial & look on it as a sort of retribution for indiscretions or errors—Also I fear there is already a
lot of talk abt. it & women who have long been jealous
of you & your success are ready to *carp* & rejoice at
what makes you unhappy. The Curzons are come
home. Rosamond leaves tomorrow. We have had a
quiet Sunday & Blandford who is here appears in a
peaceful Amiable frame of Mind. God bless you.
Please send me local Papers & a Telegram after his
speech.

Yrs most aff
F.M.

I am sure Leonie is a good guide & confidante. You
require NO other & must have *none* in future, I feel
sure of her Discretion & believe in her calm judgement.

Jennie accompanied Randolph to Bradford, but
they seem to have parted again soon afterwards:

Eridge Castle,[22]
Sussex

Dear Jennie   November 1, 1886
   HRH tells me he expects us to stay over the Sun-
day at Sandringham so you had better write to Mrs
Allsopp to tell her we cannot go down till the Mon-
day following. Please send brougham to Charing
Cross on Wednesday morningt at *10.20*

Yours ever
Randolph S.C.

The weekend at Sandringham was not happy. Jennie
was unable to conceal her distress:

Huntercombe Manor,
Maidenhead
Dearest Jennie   Nov. 19

My heart aches for you but I feel you intensify
Matters and worry yourself in vain. If you could only
be quiet and calm—I feel sure everybody at Sandringham saw your jealousy—& I know there is just as
much talk abt. it as abt. the Brooke [23] affair. And
people will not pity you the idea is that you who have
led so independent a life are foolish *now* to be so
jealous & you have been too successful & prosperous
not to have made Enemies.

I saw R. on Tuesday for a short Time & said a
few words for you which he took in a way that made
me hope for you. I only said I thought you were not
well—that you seemed to me very unhappy & that
I thought you fretted abt him—He muttered you had
no cause—you were so excitable—to this I agreed
but I said you were very warm hearted & affect. &
quite devoted to him & I hoped he would be good to
you—Something of that kind & he kissed me &
seemed to acquiesce & he said no more except occasionally referred to you, said you had a pretty Ball
Dress. I cannot exactly say why but I left him with
the impression he really could not get away from
London. Dear Jennie I can say no more—Rosamond
writes some friends of theirs went to the Ball & that
he was the great attraction & you were very much
admired. Will you come here dear any Day after Sunday—We stay till the 3rd or 4th. . . .

Goodbye—I can only pray for you & hope for the
best.

Ever yrs affct.
F.M.

Still Jennie's misery went on; and still she tried to
keep up appearances, though with little success. She
and Randolph went to dine at Windsor with the Queen,
who thought her very handsome and dark. Randolph,
Victoria thought, looked very ill. Then they went to

stay with the Salisburys at Hatfield House. On 29 November the Duchess wrote that she'd been told it was Jennie who looked ill there, with Randolph 'out of sorts'. The whole social world was buzzing with rumours.

So was the political world. Randolph's quarrels with his colleagues in the Cabinet were now an open secret. He enraged them, for instance, by passing pieces of information to *The Times*. Salisbury described him as having 'a wayward and headstrong disposition': nowadays he would be called manic. The crisis finally came over his budget. He insisted on cuts in defence spending, and threatened to resign if his demands were not met. People did not take these threats seriously.

Relations between Randolph and Jennie can be gauged from her account of what happened next. Randolph was again invited to dine at Windsor. Jennie did not accompany him this time. She was busy drawing up the guest-list for a reception they were to give at the Foreign Office. The cards had been printed, but she wasn't sure about one or two people, so she sought Randolph's advice on his return. They were just going to the theatre with Sir Henry Wolff. She was puzzled when Randolph answered by saying 'Oh, I shouldn't worry about it if I were you; probably it will never take place.' He wouldn't explain himself, and no doubt she did not dare to press him, things being as they were. So off they went to see *The School for Scandal*. Shortly after the first act, Randolph slipped away, saying he was going to his club. In fact he went to *The Times* and showed the editor the letter of resignation he had written to Salisbury from Windsor. The first Jennie knew of it was when she read it in the paper next morning. She went down to breakfast, the paper in her hand. Randolph was calm and smiling. 'Quite a surprise for you,' he said. Nothing more. Jennie felt too utterly crushed and miserable to ask for any explanation, or even to remonstrate. Moore came rushing in, pale and anxious. 'He has thrown himself from the top of the ladder,' he said in a faltering voice. 'He will never reach it again.' He was right.

Later, in Rome, Randolph confirmed Rosebery's opinion that the Windsor letter was not a resignation letter; he only meant it as the beginning of a correspondence. The real fact was, Rosebery stated, that nervous, impulsive, overstrained and impatient of opposition as Randolph was, he discharged this menace of resignation at Lord Salisbury as he had flung a similar threat in the previous year, without calculation, and as a warning rather than a positive act. Salisbury, however, this time took him at his word. The resignation was accepted, with relief, and the government found itself perfectly able to carry on without him.

The resignation caused an immense sensation, and at once all that had been whispered about Jennie's marriage became openly discussed. Gossip suggested a Public Scandal might lie behind Randolph's seemingly inexplicable behaviour. An American journalist heard the rumours and wrote to Jennie:

> Hotel Metropole
> Charing Cross
> Jany 14th, '87

My Lady,

An article furnished me this week for enclosure in my Saturday cable to the *New York Sun,* deals with the details of a separation which the writer alleges to be pending between yourself and Lord Randolph.

Unwilling to publish so grave a statement without having first made every effort to verify its exactness, I called twice, hoping to see either Lord Randolph or yourself in order to be guided in correcting, or entirely withholding the article in question, by what you might wish to say. If you will make an appointment for me before noon tomorrow, when my despatch is sent, I shall be pleased to wait upon yourself or Lord Randolph.

I endeavoured to see your Father, Mr. Jerome, whom I have met but could not learn whether he had gone from the Langham. I may add that a cable received today from New York informs me that rumours are current there of the story of which the article sent to me purports to be a confirmation.

Believe me My Lady

Very truly yours

Arthur Brisbane

Cable Correspondent, *The Sun, New York*

Lady Randolph Churchill

Jennie took the letter straight to Randolph. The draft of his reply survives:

2 Connaught Place, W.

Sir,   Jan 14, 1887

Lady Randolph Churchill has handed to me the vy singular letter which you have today addressed to her.

If as I assume you have regard to the credit of the newspaper in New York to which you act as correspondent I would advise you not to be a party to furnishing them with information and causing them to circulate statements which are utterly false libellous & unfounded.

It passes my comprehension how such rumours could have been started, how anyone of position or respectability could pay the smallest attention to such scandalous gossip, & how an American gentleman could write such enquiries as you have written to a lady & to one moreover who is a compatriot of his

I am

Yours obediently

Randolph S. Churchill

Arthur Brisbane Esq.

Brisbane did his best to defend himself:

The Hotel Metropole

London, S.W.

Jan 14, 1887

Sir—As London correspondent of *The Sun,* it is my duty to forward by cable such statements as are of public interest, and which reach me through the ordinary news channels. The assertion in regard to which I wrote to Lady Randolph Churchill was sent to me for publication in the usual way. Instead of publishing it forthwith, I called three times at your residence intending to place the communication before you, but was unable to see you.

I was informed this evening that you were not in London, and it was for that reason that my letter was addressed to Lady Randolph Churchill instead of to yourself—

I learn this evening that a duplicate of the communication addressed to me had been sent to a second American newspaper and would have been published in America as current rumor, had I not chanced to speak with the representative of that paper.

I thank you for your trouble in replying to my note, while regretting the interpretation which you put upon my efforts to save a lady and a compatriot from the uncontradicted publication of scandalous gossip—

> Very truly yours
> Arthur Brisbane

Lord Randolph Churchill

Randolph at first felt genuine surprise at the way events had turned out over his threat of resignation. The strain of the last few months had been too great and probably impaired his judgement. Having made the threat, and finding himself obliged to make it good, he did the honourable thing and resigned. Once the decision was made, and he was shorn of his responsibilities, he began to feel relieved. As he said later to Rosebery, 'I would not live the last four years again for a million a year'—and that was something coming from a man who was very short of money.

The immediate result for Jennie was a reconciliation with Randolph. For when, early in February, he once more went on an extended foreign holiday, it is clear from both their letters that all is well again. For Jennie the crisis was over, and when Randolph reached Biskra, from which he had turned back on hearing of Jennie's illness in 1882, he found long, effervescent, gossipy 'epistles', full of affection, and perhaps relief.

On 6 February, for instance, she wrote about a dinner party she had gone to at the Mandevilles, where she met Lord Dunraven, Under-Secretary of State for the Colonies, who was about to follow Randolph's example and resign from the government. Then she had had a visit from the Prince of Wales. 'He came at 5. & remained over an hour, & was most cordial—insisted on kissing my hand when he went away & declared himself our "best friend"!' (A cynic might suggest that perhaps he was hoping to take advantage of the troubled marital situation.) Randolph had written to the Queen apologizing for the fact that his resignation had been reported in the papers before she had been informed. The Queen's private secretary had replied briefly and coldly. The Prince thought the letter curt, but he explained that it would not be proper for the Queen to enter into a discussion on the subject, even if she approved. 'Of course Tum indulged in a few arrows—but they have not stuck into me,' Jennie wrote.

She had been to dinner the night before with Sir William Harcourt, who had been Home Secretary and then Chancellor of the Exchequer under Gladstone. The dinner was dull and nasty, the talk all political. George Goschen, a Liberal Unionist, had taken Randolph's place in the Conservative administration. (He is the man Randolph is supposed to have 'forgotten' when he resigned.) 'Harcourt was very pompous—he said he rejoiced when he heard that Goschen had joined for 2 reasons—that it kept *you* out—& wld break up the govt.' There was much chaff about the Chancellor's official robes. The tradition of passing them on from one Chancellor to another had been broken by Disraeli in 1853, when he refused to hand them over to Gladstone. Harcourt asked Jennie if Randolph was passing his on to Goschen. 'No,' she replied, 'they are put away in a tin box for a few months until they are wanted.'

After dinner Jennie went to a party being given by the Prince of Wales at the New Club in Covent Garden. Lord Hartington, leader of the Liberal Unionists and heir to the Duke of Devonshire, was there with 'a large party of lovely ladies'. He was most amiable, and talked to Jennie the whole time. 'Randolph is so right to go away,' he said. 'I envy him—he has had his day, and off he goes.' They talked of a speech that W. H. Smith had just given. Hartington thought Smith had spoken very well. 'No fireworks!' said the Prince, with a giggle at Jennie. 'I believe you,' she answered, 'but when you are in pitch darkness people are very glad of fireworks to show them the way.' Hartington told her she had scored, and indeed she defended Randolph splendidly.

At lunch that very day she had sat next to Joseph Chamberlain, who had broken with Gladstone over Home Rule, and was now a leading Liberal Unionist. He and Randolph had been intriguing together a good deal over the last two years. He was nice to Jennie 'for the first time', she wrote. 'I wish I cld remember all he said—However he is not in the least vexed with you—& thinks you are perfectly right to go away—that it is yr best game—you have but to wait—He quite agreed with me that you & he were the only 2 possible leaders in the future—but that you must agree in private, as to the amount of public abuse you were to shower on each other.' Chamberlain was very bitter about Goschen, and said he would *never* again be in a Liberal Cabinet or get in for a Liberal seat. Mrs. Jeune, the political hostess who was giving the lunch, told Jennie that Goschen was nervous and unhappy, and would be a failure. Dicey, the editor of *The Observer,* was there, and Jennie made a point of being civil to him. But the letter was not entirely political. In a PS Jennie wrote: 'The children are all right. It is Jack's birthday on Wed. 9th 7 years old! How time flies—'

When Jack was born, Randolph had been nobody: now the great moments of his career were over, though naturally neither he nor Jennie knew it. She wrote on the 15th about a dinner-party at the Dunravens. She had sat next to Hartington:

I asked him how he thought '*his*' Govt: were getting on—'Very badly the last week,' he said—'Randolph wld never have allowed the waste of time—5 days before a minister spoke'—He chaffed about yr robes & asked if he shld try & sell them for me to Goschen —I said I thought the bargain wld be too hard a one 'Do you mean Goschen wld go in for the "old clo" line?' everyone laughed—However, said Hartington, Randolph won't want them in the future, as he will be P.M. next time. . . .

The letter had a P.S., revealing the twelve-year-old Winston's passionate partisanship of his father:

Winston was taken to a pantomime at Brighton where they hissed a sketch of you—he burst into tears —& then turned furiously on a man—who was hissing behind him—& said 'Stop that row you snub nosed Radical'!!

Randolph was delighted with this news, and asked that Winston be sent a sovereign for his loyalty. A few days later Jennie was invited to dinner by the Salisburys. She was not sure whether she should go or not, and whether Randoph would approve, but she took her courage in her hands and went:

2 Connaught Place
Feb 21st

Dearest R. I was very glad of yr telegram today from Constantine or rather last night, as I had no idea where to write to. I hope you found Biskra warm. It is rather hard to go so far & find snow—I feel I have heaps to tell you, but don't know where to begin— First of all about my dinner at the Salisbury's—There were a lot of small tables & Lady S. made me sit at hers next to Abercorn[24]—She wanted to be very amiable & said she hoped you were well & enjoying yrself —After dinner Ld S. came and talked to me for nearly an hour about every imaginable thing except you—He was very nervous & jerky & after a time the conversation turned on you, a propos of the cold weather abroad. I told him that you wrote you did not give 2 thoughts to politics & were quite happy—'I am sure the rest will do him good,' he said—'Randolph's brain works so quickly that it must wear out his nervous system.' 'I don't think so,' I said, 'but it is true that his brain works with rapidity so rapid—that he generally arrives at a conclusion 6 mths before most people.' I can't repeat all he said but my impression was that he wanted to be friendly—but not in a political line—He evidently did not want to discuss you—so of course I did not force it. He abused Henry James & said that he was very jealous of Goschen— Meanwhile I hear on every side that the Liberal Unionists are very low, even Hartington, as they know they will never be re-elected & things are going *very* badly in Ireland—I do so hope dearest that you will not disapprove of my having gone to the Salisbury's if it does no good it can do no harm—& I am sure it will stop some of the carping—There were lots of the enemy about & they looked so astonished at seeing me in confab with Ld S. . . .

Jennie had been to dine with Mrs. Jeune. Henry James had been there, and Harcourt, Chamberlain, and Ritchie, President of the Local Government Board. Mrs. Jeune thought there had been a great change in Randolph's favour in the last few days. Even Ashmead-Bartlett, a long-standing enemy of Randolph's in the party, now believed that the Conservatives could not get on without him. Ritchie had only one refrain— Randolph must come back. Goschen was not a success: 'He looks like a man who has got on a kilt for the first time', Ritchie declared. But Randolph's supporter, Dunraven, had made a hash of his resignation: 'it was a fiasco'. Chamberlain sent his love.

Jennie gave a slightly different version of her dinner with the Salisbury's to Leonie, and incidentally revealed her mixed feelings about Randolph's resignation:

I had a long talk with Ld. S. after dinner but I did not get much out of him. He was very shy and nervous and I had the greatest difficulty to get him to speak of Randolph. It is too long to repeat but I rather had the impression that they could never come together again. Don't repeat this, of course it is impossible to say what may happen in the House. As Arthur Balfour said— their difficulties haven't commenced yet and when they do—they may have to go to Randolph. But Sniffy I feel very sick at heart sometimes. It was such a splendid position he threw away. In the bottom of my heart I sometimes think his head was quite turned at the moment and that he thought he cd do *anything*. However 'it is an ill wind that blows *no* good' and R. has been so much easier and nicer since that I ought not to regret the crisis. He writes most affectionately and very often and I hope all will be righted when he returns. . . .

Jennie felt she could speak her heart to Randolph again now. A letter of 5 March says all that need be said about the end of this unhappy episode:

I was very glad to get yr letter from Tunis & to hear such a good account of you. It is a blessing to think that you are well & happy. It reconciles me to much that is disagreeable here—where people are as venomous & ill natured about us as possible—But you are good to me & I trust you utterly, & don't care twopence what they say—Enjoy yrself as much as you can & come back well, ready to fight the whole lot— And if you are only glad to see me, & understand how much I think of you & all that you are to me—I shall be quite happy—

NOTES

1. Consuelo Yznaga. Lord Mandeville became Duke of Manchester in 1890.

2. Blandford's eldest son.

3. Who were staying at Blenheim.

4. Jennie's old flame 'The Star' was marrying the Hon. Kathleen Douglas-Pennant.

5. Jennie and the Duchess were both founder-members of the Primrose League, a Conservative Party organization founded in memory of Disraeli at Blenheim in 1883.

6. Samuel Charles and Georgiana Millicent Allsopp. He became the second Baron Hindlip the following year.

7. Wilton House, Salisbury, home of the Earl of Pembroke.

8. In Yorkshire, home of the Earl of Feversham.

9. Cousin of Queen Victoria, and Commander-in-Chief of the British Army 1856-95.

10. Lady Sarah Churchill, Randolph's youngest sister, who later married Lieutenant-Colonel G. C. Wilson.

11. Probably Samuel, head of Samuel Montagu & Co., foreign bankers. He was the Liberty MP for Tower Hamlets, Whitechapel Division: later Lord Swaythling.

12. The Hon. Mrs Norah Stirling, daughter of Lord Rossmore. Her husband was in the Royal Horse Guards.

13. Lady Theresa Susey Helen, daughter of the Earl of Shrewsbury. Her husband was Lord-Lieutenant of Ireland from 1886-9. She was a famous hostess.

14. Where the conference of Conservative Associations was being held at the end of October.

15. Sir Stafford Northcote had taken the title of Iddesleigh on his far from noble elevation to the House of Lords. He was now Foreign Secretary, and still a victim of Randolph's dislike and contempt.

16. Herbert Bismarck, son of the German statesman.

17. Lord Salisbury.

18. Secretary of State for War.

19. Sir Augustus Berkeley Paget, British Ambassador to Austria since 1884.

20. Colonel Kodolitsch once invited Jennie to inspect his Hungarian regiment on a charger. Like Kinsky, he spent much of his time in London.

21. Shortly after his return, Randolph and Jennie went to stay with 'Tum', the Prince of Wales, at Sandringham.

22. Now demolished, then home of the 5th Earl and 1st Marquess of Abergavenny.

23. Daisy Brooke, the beautiful Countess of Warwick, was having an affair with Lord Charles Beresford. Much scandal was to follow, before she became the mistress of the Prince of Wales.

24. Son of the Duke whom Randolph's father had succeeded as Viceroy of Ireland.

8

LOVING AND LOSING

'The moment a man is out of the Cabinet', wrote Randolph in 1894, 'he is lost, he is not a bit worth more than any other Member of Parliament.' It was something he had learned slowly and painfully. He remained in the Commons till his death, and for some years his reputation remained high. But as it declined, so did his health. He turned with some success from politics to racing, winning the Oaks with L'Abbesse de Jouare, popularly known as Abcess on the Jaw. But typically he was abroad at the time, and missed his biggest racing triumph. Jennie wasn't there, either—she was boating on the Thames and got the news from a lock-keeper. In April 1891 Randolph decided to go to South Africa and try to make some money. 'I was a very poor creature after your departure,' wrote Jennie, but she perked up when he bought some shares in the Rand Mine, and sent her some diamonds. She was delighted:

I suppose by now you are comfortably established at Fort Salisbury and are 'prospecting' to any amount —I was agreeably surprised & delighted by receiving another diamond from you—it is a beauty, & for the present I have had it made into a pin, with a screw at the bottom for safety—How *dear of you* to send it to me. . . . Last July in London Clara had the fortune teller Mrs Soundy at her house—& after telling me my character etc. she looked into a glass ball & asked me to wish something—Of course in my mind I

Jennie's parents, Clara Jerome and Leonard

Opposite, above, Randolph's father, the 7th Duke of Marlborough
Opposite, below, Randolph's mother, the Duchess of Marlborough

The three Jerome sisters, from left to right, Jennie, Clara and Leonie

Winston aged ten with his younger brother Jack

The Marquess of Blandford,
Randolph's elder brother, later
to become 8th Duke of Marlborough

Opposite, Jennie and Randolph in 1874

Jennie dressed for a ball

The drawing room at 2 Connaught Place

Jennie with Jack and Winston

Jennie with Lady Curzon at the Woodstock Election in 1885

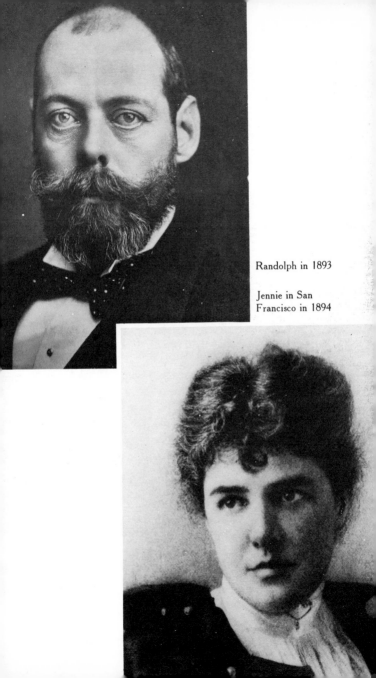

Randolph in 1893

Jennie in San
Francisco in 1894

Count Kinsky

Below, Jennie with
Winston and Jack

The Executive Committee of the Hospital Ship "Maine".
From left to right: Lady Essex, Mrs. Griffiths, Mrs. Van Duzer,
Mrs. Von Andre, Mrs. Ronalds, Mrs. Leslie, Jennie,
Mrs. Arthur Paget, Mrs. Blow, Mrs. Moreton Frewen,
Mrs. Halderman, Mrs. Field

The Hospital Ship "Maine" at Durban

Jennie with the staff of the "Maine"

Opposite, Jennie as the Empress Theodora at a ball at Devonshire
House. She later signed the photograph for her son Jack

Jennie with her injured son Jack, aboard the "Maine"

Jennie with Winston in 1912

Opposite, above, Jennie writing letters in the drawing room at Brook Street

Opposite, below, Jennie with her children and grandchildren

Jennie with her grandson Peregrine, co-author of this book

Thames Television

presents

Lee Remick

as

Lady Randolph Churchill
1854-1921

in a new series of seven one-hour plays
written by **Julian Mitchell**

with

Ronald Pickup as Lord Randolph Churchill
Warren Clarke as Winston Churchill
and **Rachel Kempson**
Barbara Parkins
Dan O'Herlihy

Jennie

Lady Randolph Churchill

ENNIE JEROME was born in Brooklyn in 1854. Her father was a rich speculator and racehorse owner. Her mother had social aspirations. In 1868 she took Jennie and her other two teenage daughters to Europe. And when the Franco-Prussian war started, she brought them to England. The Jerome girls were launched into British society.

The girls were beautiful and vivacious. But from the start it was the dark and sparkling Jennie who made the running. Within weeks of her arrival in England, she met Lord Randolph Churchill. Three days later she accepted his proposal of marriage, to the dismay of both their families. He was 23. She was only 19. They were married in April the following year, and in November Jennie gave birth to their first son, Winston Churchill.

Now, in a new series of seven one-hour plays made to coincide with Churchill Centenary Year, Thames Television tells the love story of Jennie and Randolph. But it was a love story which turned to tragedy. For, after years of illness which cut short his brilliant political career, Randolph died when he should have been at the height of his powers, leaving Jennie a beautiful widow at the age of 41.

After Randolph's death, Jennie's towering political ambitions centred on Winston. She never missed a chance to further his career, campaigned tirelessly for him, and dreamed of seeing him become Prime Minister. But she still needed to be loved as a woman. In her later years she made two further marriages, both to men no older than Winston.

The series shows dramatically what it was like for a lively young American girl to find herself suddenly thrust into the stuffy atmosphere of the great houses of England. It tells how Jennie both dazzled and daunted the whole of society from the Prince of Wales downwards. And how she matured into a beautiful woman who put her own indelible stamp on her times.

Like all society ladies Jennie was a prolific letter writer. Julian Mitchell was given full access to her letters and researched his subject thoroughly with the help of members of the Churchill family, to enable him to tell the story of Jennie as it has never been told before.

1
Jennie Jerome

ENNIE'S parents Leonard and Clara Jerome, although devoted, understood each other perfectly. Clara, who had social ambitions, was happiest in Europe. Leonard, ever anxious to make a deal, preferred the bustle of New York. So he happily settled his wife and three beautiful daughters in Paris,

THE JEROME FAMILY
Linda Liles, Dan O'Herlihy, Helen Horton,
Lee Remick, Barbara Parkins

LEONIE
Barbara Parkins

RANDOLPH & JENNIE AT THE ARIADNE BALL
Ronald Pickup, Lee Remick

PRINCE OF WALES & DUKE OF MARLBOROUGH
Thorley Walters, Cyril Luckham

where they stayed until the fall of the 2nd Empire forced them to flee to England.

The girls, all beautiful in their different ways, were much courted. But Jennie was the most striking of all. She played the piano well. She was brilliant and witty in conversation, with perhaps more outward sparkle than was thought proper then. Men of all ages and nationalities adored her. She in return flirted outrageously. But only when she met Lord Randolph Churchill, at a Royal Ball on HMS Ariadne, guardship of Cowes Regatta, did she really fall in love.

Cowes Week, 1873, and the invitation which brought Jennie and Randolph together, at a ball on board HMS Ariadne. Jennie later noted the fact between the lines.

Randolph, younger son of the Duke of Marlborough, had not shown much interest in women until then. At 23, he had neither deep convictions nor high ambitions. His only passions were for the horse and the hunt. But he fell in love with Jennie on the night they met. She was a passionate 19-year-old, eager to experience all that life had to offer. And she was unlike any of the girls Randolph had met before in the great houses of the English aristocracy. He proposed on the third evening of the acquaintance and Jennie accepted.

Ronald Pickup *as Lord Randolph Churchill*

Both families were shocked. Marriage was out of the question. The Marlboroughs were appalled at the thought of a 'vulgar' American daughter-in-law. Clara Jerome, who might otherwise have been thrilled to be getting a titled son-in-law, knew that Randolph, being a younger son, would inherit nothing of the Marlborough estate. But Leonard Jerome, even though strongly biased against the in-breeding and over-breeding within the British aristocracy, adored his fiery and beautiful daughter, and was delighted by her choice. He also knew that the accumulating obstacles would only fortify Jennie's determination. And he was right.

The wedding took place in Paris the following year. But the Duke and Duchess of Marlborough were not present.

2
Lady Randolph

THE NEWLY-WED Churchills, idyllically happy, took London society by storm. Not the society still revolving sedately round Queen Victoria, but the gayer, more flamboyant set of the Prince of Wales. The couple had all the graces: beauty,

LORD RANDOLPH CHURCHILL
Ronald Pickup

charm, intellect, energy — and the Prince himself saw that they were welcome wherever they went.

But Jennie viewed Randolph's mother in the same light as the staid court of Victoria. Her American upbringing had not prepared her for the stuffiness of the great English houses — especially Blenheim, to which her visits rapidly became a matter of joyless duty, and she often caused embarrassment with her naturally outspoken manner.

It was while she was staying at Blenheim that she gave premature birth to Winston on 30 November 1874. She was so unprepared that the baby's immediate necessities had to be borrowed from villagers in Woodstock. The family stayed at Blenheim for Christmas and the baby was baptised Winston Leonard Spencer Churchill in Blenheim Chapel by

Nº. 28,176.

BIRTHS.

On the 30th Nov., at Blenheim Palace, the Lady RANDOLPH CHURCHILL, prematurely, of a son.

Birth announcement in *The Times*

the Duke's chaplain. They moved back to their London home early in the New Year, and Jennie was able to take her dominating role in the society life she had so desperately missed.

But suddenly, without warning, scandal struck. Randolph's elder brother Lord Blandford became involved in the famous Aylesford divorce scandal, and incurred the intense displeasure of the Prince of Wales. To protect his brother, Randolph put his own social position and career in jeopardy by calling on the Princess of Wales and threatening to publish some love letters the Prince had written to the lady in question, Edith Aylesford. Society was outraged. The Churchills were immediately ostracised from the Prince of Wales' set.

Jennie stood by him. From now on she would focus all her attention on furthering Randolph's political career, tragic as it seemed to be excluded from the social scene.

3
Recovery

OSTRACISED from British society, Jennie and Randolph moved to Ireland. Randolph acted as private secretary to his father, who had become Viceroy of Ireland at Disraeli's request to save the face of the Marlborough family. While leading a life of comparative ease, Randolph became aware of the hopeless poverty of the Irish peasants. Jennie encouraged him to speak out on the Irish question in the House of Commons. His speeches upset not only the government but also his parents, who vented their annoyance on Jennie.

On Randolph's return to Ireland from Parliament, Jennie announced that she was pregnant again. She also wished her husband were not away so often. But when they returned to England Randolph became more and more occupied with the Parliamentary ambitions which led him to

RANDOLPH & JENNIE

DINNER AT BLENHEIM

JENNIE ARRIVES AT BLENHEIM

JENNIE CAMPAIGNING FOR RANDOLPH

attack both Government and opposition with brilliant success. They saw even less of each other.

One of Jennie's many admirers at this time was Count Charles Kinsky, a dashing Austrian diplomat who made the most of his chances to be with Jennie while Randolph was away. When apparent overwork finally made Randolph ill and he and Jennie took a house in Wimbledon, Kinsky became a constant visitor.

As soon as Randolph recovered, he resumed his political intrigues and continued his attack on the government. The Prince of Wales, impressed by Randolph's success during eight years of social exile, welcomed him back into his circle. Soon afterwards, Randolph was made Secretary of State for India, and went there for a long official visit. Without Jennie.

"HE COMPLETELY CARRIES THE HOUSE."

One of the political cartoons which charted Randolph's success

LEONIE & JENNIE

THE DUCHESS OF MARLBOROUGH
Rachel Kempson

RANDOLPH'S LAST SPEECH IN THE COMMONS
Ronald Pickup

JENNIE WITH THE BABY WINSTON
Lee Remick

COUNT CHARLES KINSKY
Jeremy Brett

But Jennie was not lonely. She now had two children, Winston and Jack. Her sister Leonie was staying with her. And Kinsky now became her constant companion as well as a much-needed father-figure for Winston.

Soon after Randolph returned, the Gladstone government collapsed and Randolph began to engineer his place in the new cabinet. Jennie resumed her campaigning on his behalf. After years of political and social obscurity, the couple were ready to take their places as leaders of society.

Patrick Troughton *as Disraeli,* with Jennie at a masked ball

4
Triumph and Tragedy

ENNIE, now fully aware that Randolph lived only for politics, began to see more and more of Kinsky, to the annoyance of the Duchess of Marlborough. The Duchess continued to campaign ruthlessly for her favourite son's future. He was made Chancellor of the Exchequer and Leader of the House. He drew attention as the most prominent statesman of the time. It was felt certain that he would become Prime Minister.

But to Jennie, the higher he climbed, the more cold and aloof he seemed. He separated himself from her physically and was prone to inexplicable attacks of fatigue and temper—mostly aimed at her. She suspected other women despite the assurances of her sister Leonie and the Duchess. Eventually Randolph told her that he had syphilis. She was mortified, but stood by him.

As Randolph's health deteriorated, Jennie gained increasing comfort from the friendship of Kinsky, and the two became lovers. But Jennie still found time to be a great source of strength and support to her husband who was obviously beyond help. She could not leave him now. Kinsky swore he would wait for her, even though he was under pressure from his parents to marry.

Suddenly, it was announced in *The Times* that Randolph had resigned. No one could understand

Jeremy Brett *as Charles Kinsky*, with Jennie

his action. Only Jennie, who had been equally taken by surprise, could see that he was making a last-ditch bid for immediate power although realising that his illness was steadily worsening. But Randolph had reckoned without the many enemies he had made during his rise. He had threatened resignation so often. This time Lord Salisbury accepted.

Jennie knew that this was the beginning of the end for her husband. The once brilliant man was now a pitiful sight, as madness and death approached. His judgment had gone and the debts were mounting. To prevent speculation and keep him away from the public eye she took him on a world tour, determined to comfort him to the end.

She needed Kinsky now more than ever. But

even he was to try her strength. At Rangoon Jennie received a telegram from Leonie saying that Kinsky had announced his plans to marry. He had been unable to fight off his family's insistence for quite long enough. Jennie failed to stop the marriage.

When Randolph inevitably died, pitifully and tragically, Jennie had never been poorer, and never so alone. But it was a merciful release for them both.

5
A Perfect Darling

NEVER a believer in letting misfortune get the upper hand, and still extremely beautiful in her forties, Jennie gradually began to enjoy life once again, notably with a young guards officer she had met during a weekend at Warwick Castle. At 24, George Cornwallis-West was just two weeks older than Winston. He found Jennie devastatingly attractive. She was flattered at first, then completely captivated. They saw more and more of each other, despite society gossip and strong opposition from George's family and even the Prince of Wales.

Meanwhile, Winston was carving himself a brilliant military career and was already planning his future as a politician. Jennie helped him all she could, as she had supported Randolph before him. But she still pursued her own interests. She launched a lavish quarterly magazine, *The Anglo-*

Saxon Review, which attracted contributions from many distinguished writers of the day. But Jennie, to whom quality always came before economy, made it too expensive to be a commercial success.

When the Boer War started and Winston, Jack and George all went to South Africa, Jennie embarked on an even more ambitious project: she would raise money (mostly from wealthy Americans) to equip a hospital ship and go with it to

The Hospital Ship *Maine*

Africa. It would not only be a worthwhile contribution to the war effort, but also a means of being closer to George. But this aspect of her vision was shattered when George was invalided home just as she was about to embark. It was impossible not to go ahead with her plan. She left George in London.

By the time she had made the journey to South Africa and back, Jennie had decided that it was foolish to let society gossip spoil what might be her last chance for happiness. She and George were married only weeks after her return. Again the groom's parents were conspicuously absent.

JENNIE & GEORGE CORNWALLIS-WEST
Lee Remick, Christopher Cazenove

MRS PATRICK CAMPBELL & GEORGE
Sian Phillips, Christopher Cazenove

WINSTON & CLEMENTINE
Warren Clarke, Anna Fox

JENNIE & WINSTON
Lee Remick, Warren Clarke

1915: TROOPS EMBARKING AT VICTORIA STATION

6
'His Borrowed Plumes'

GAINST all predictions, Jennie's marriage to George seemed successful and happy. George, more by necessity than by design, worked in the City and Jennie spent more and more time writing her memoirs. She had a keen critic in Winston, whose biography of his father and eloquent war writings had already earned him a high reputation. Eventually Jennie's 'Reminiscences' were published, and the warm reception the book received spurred her to try her hand at writing plays.

Meanwhile George, when not pursuing his hated career, often had to content himself with finding his own amusements. One of the people he met was Mrs Patrick Campbell, the most distinguished and radiant actress of the day. He told her about Jennie's play, *His Borrowed Plumes,* and 'Mrs Pat' enthusiastically volunteered to put it on. The play was a melodrama about two women fighting over a man – a prophetic theme as things turned out, for it became clear as rehearsals progressed that George was falling in love with Mrs. Pat. She was determined that he should.

After the play had opened, George asked Jennie for a divorce. To support his family and estates, he explained, he needed an heir and money. Jennie agreed not to stand in his way and wondered who his intended wife might be. She was shocked when later

Sian Phillips *as Mrs Patrick Campbell*
Christopher Cazenove *as George Cornwallis-West*

it was announced that George was to marry Mrs
Patrick Campbell, who was in even worse financial
straits than Jennie herself – and the same age.

Now it seemed that all Jennie had left was Winston and his political ambitions. He was now President of the Board of Trade and seemed set to make
even more impact than his father. For the second
time in her life, Jennie set her sights on Number

Mrs. GEORGE CORNWALLIS-WEST'S
MATINEES.

TUESDAY, WEDNESDAY, THURSDAY and FRIDAY AFTERNOONS,
JULY 6th, 7th, 8th and 9th,

Commencing at Three o'clock,

HIS BORROWED PLUMES

An Original Modern Comedy in Three Acts,

By Mrs. GEORGE CORNWALLIS-WEST.

Major Percival Sumner V C   Mr. DAWSON M

Ten Downing Street. But she realised he needed a woman who was more than a mother to him if he was to succeed. Her efforts at matchmaking were rewarded when Winston met and proposed to Clementine Hozier, the daughter of Jennie's great friend, Blanche Hozier.

But her own immediate problems were not so easily solved.

7
A Past and a Future

WITH no husband and no lover, much of the life went out of Jennie. She felt again the malice of the English upper class, against the 'upstart' Winston Churchill and his American mother. Like his father, Winston had made many enemies during his climb to office, and Jennie feared that her son's career might take the same drastic course. By 1915 he was First Lord of the Admiralty and the youngest member of the Cabinet by at least ten years.

Jennie busied herself raising funds for charitable causes, sitting on committees, contributing to the war effort and helping to run the American Women's War Hospital. But still she felt useless and empty. It took Leonie to sum up what was wrong: 'You're no good without a man.'

Determined not to be a burden to her friends, Jennie began to renew some acquaintances. One of them was Montague Porch, a young man she had met in Rome, where she had fled to escape the fuss after her divorce from George. Porch was even younger than George, but his pleasure at seeing Jennie again quickly turned to love and soon, at the age of sixty-four, Jennie surprised everyone by marrying him.

Charles Kay *as Montague Porch,* with Jennie

'I have a past and he has a future, so we should be all right,' Jennie told Leonie. And they were all right. Perhaps their devotion would have been tested in time, but Jennie was not to live long enough for such a trial.

One evening in 1921, hurrying down to dinner in the fashionable high-heeled shoes she insisted on wearing, she tripped on the stairs and broke her ankle. Gangrene set in and her leg was amputated. She went into a coma and died. Her face, in death, bore no wrinkles or any trace of pain.

'She looks so young,' said Jack Churchill as the family gathered round her bed.

'She was always young,' said Winston.

Cast

Jennie	**Lee Remick**
Randolph	**Ronald Pickup**
Duke of Marlborough	**Cyril Luckham**
Duchess of Marlborough	**Rachel Kempson**
Leonard Jerome	**Dan O'Herlihy**
Mrs Jerome	**Helen Horton**
Leonie	**Barbara Parkins**
Clara	**Linda Liles**
Blandford	**John Westbrook**
Bertha	**Barbara Laurenson**
Prince of Wales	**Thorley Walters**
Princess of Wales	**Joanna David**
Gladstone	**David Steuart**
Disraeli	**Patrick Troughton**
Charles Kinsky	**Jeremy Brett**
Winston Churchill (age 8-10)	**Paul Ambrose**
Winston Churchill (as a man)	**Warren Clarke**
Clementine	**Anna Fox**
Jack Churchill	**Malcolm Stoddard**
Gwendoline (Goonie)	**Ciaran Madden**
George Cornwallis-West	**Christopher Cazenove**
Mrs Patrick Campbell	**Sian Phillips**
Montague Porch	**Charles Kay**

and full supporting cast

Written by Julian Mitchell
Produced by Andrew Brown
Directed by James Cellan Jones
Executive Producer Stella Richman

Produced by Thames Television
at its riverside studios at Teddington in Middlesex and
on locations including Warwick Castle, Blenheim Palace,
York House, Salisbury Hall, and Cowes in the
Isle of Wight.

Thames Television,
306-316 Euston Road, London NW1 3BB, England. Telephone 01-387 9494.

wished that you might make a lot of money & succeed out there. After a pause she said 'Yes you will get yr wish but not easily—& it wont be realized for a year & a half' May she prove right!

After bringing him up to date with all the racing and social news, she ended: 'Well goodbye I have got on both yr diamonds they are much admired—I dont in the least mind being like an ape—& can accommodate any more you choose to send! Best love.'

In spite of diamonds and Rand shares, however, the financial situation went from bad to worse. In the autumn of 1892 Jennie and Randolph had to sell 2 Connaught Place, and move in with the Duchess at 50 Grosvenor Square. For Jennie it was very bitter, as she admitted in a letter to Randolph that December:

Quite between ourselves I don't think yr Mother cares about my staying here if she goes away & she has postponed her departure indefinitely. I am not going to bother you with it all & I shall try & do the best I can for myself & the boys—but I feel rather 'mis' over it all—I know 'beggars cannot be choosers' but I feel *very old* for this sort of thing. I have been to Hudson's[1] & settled what is to be sold—a certain amount will come here—but not all—as some things I do not want—and there is only room for very little— Yr mother does not want to part with any of her things & rather discourages us moving upstairs—But it really does not matter if you have what you want & I have my rooms all right—the boys can very soon manage with yr mother's furniture things will all settle themselves. . . .

During Randolph's South African trip, Jennie was living at Banstead Manor, near Newmarket, a house Randolph had first rented the previous year to be near his race-horses. A frequent visitor was Charles Kinsky. With Winston and Jack he played the part of a genial uncle, and they liked him very much. In 1890, Winston had given him chicken pox, but he doesn't seem to have minded, indeed he wrote Winston a friendly note. Sometimes he sent the boys stamps for their collections. That summer he took Winston to the Crystal Palace to see the German Emperor, some wild beasts and some splendid fireworks. Winston, aged sixteen, was tremendously impressed by the way Kinsky handled the head-waiter and crushed the fingers of an insolent Kaffir in his powerful grasp. They drank champagne, and on the way home, with Kinsky driving his phaeton with a fast pair of horses, they passed everyone on the road. Later, at Banstead, Kinsky set up a target for Winston and Jack to shoot at, and wrote from Vienna promising a gun. Jack, when he went to Harrow, had a picture of Kinsky in his room—probably the one of him on his Grand National winner Zoedone which Winston later offered a sovereign for. He wanted to put it in his rooms at Aldershot Barracks.

Jennie kept no letter from Kinsky of this period. Perhaps, when the affair was over, she sent them back; perhaps, in rage, or out of caution, she destroyed them. That she was discreet is plain. Writing to Randolph in October 1891, about a house party she'd been giving, and what a success it had been, she noted that 'Kinsky slept at the Farm opposite as there was no room for him & he did not mind—Everest has been ill with pleurisy—poor old thing, & of course I would not turn her out.' It's almost as though she wanted Randolph to know just how careful she was being.

Kinsky was not by any means in permanent attendance. He had his diplomatic duties (though they were hardly arduous), and was moved from embassy to embassy, though he always kept a flat in London and hunters in the Shires. He was discreet, too, and perhaps he kept his distance when Randolph was at home. But he and Jennie were often to be found at the same weekend house parties. Those in the know, in Edwardian England, kept it to themselves, but acted on their knowledge.

Though Randolph seems to have been unaware of the

progressively more obvious effects of his illness, the last years of his life were agonizing for all who knew and loved him. The time came when his speeches in the Commons made so little sense that friends went to Jennie and begged her to stop him coming. It was partly to keep him away, and partly in a last vain effort to help him recapture his health by travelling, that she set off with him in June 1894, against doctors' recommendations, on his final voyage. They were to go round the world. With them, as well as menservants and a doctor, they took a lead-lined coffin. It was necessary to be prepared. Jennie must have set out to do her duty in particularly low spirits, for her relationship with Kinsky had become unsettled. There was very little, anywhere, that she could any longer feel sure of.

They went first to New York, then to Maine, then across Canada to Banff Springs. From there Jennie wrote to Leonie about Randolph's urge to keep moving:

> As soon as he gets a little better from having a rest and being quiet he will be put back by this travelling—and *nothing* will deter him from doing what he likes. He is very kind and considerate when he feels well—but absolutely *impossible* when he gets excited—and as he gets like that 20 times a day—you may imagine my life is not an easy one. . . . I can't look ahead very far—Keith[2] thinks that R. will eventually get quite well, & I think so too—if only he would give himself a chance. Meanwhile I try to make the best of it.

From Banff Springs they went to Vancouver, and from Vancouver to San Francisco, and from San Francisco they took a boat to Japan. Randolph got no better, he got visibly worse. There were angry scenes, with the doctor 'énervé', and a manservant sent home. Randolph insisted on going to Burma, which in happier days he had annexed. It was there, on top of all the horrors of the voyage, that Jennie received a telegram from

Charles Kinsky announcing his engagement to Countess Elizabeth Wolff Metternich zur Gracht.

She was shattered. Even to Clara, to whom she never let herself go, she wrote: 'I HATE IT. I shall return without a friend in the world & too old to make any more now.' Leonie, who knew much more of what Jennie really felt, went with Winston to take Jack out for the day from Harrow. He wrote to his father, in a letter which Randolph probably never read:

Aunt Leonie and Winston came down to see me last saturday they [didn't] stop very long however. She told me Count Kinsky is going to be married and that he says he is the happiest man in the world. To think I have not been really happy for nearly 6 months since you left. O how I wish I could express my thoughts and soul towards you and Dear Mama, but I can't and if I try I only write bad English.

Kinsky can hardly have expected Leonie to believe him, but what she really thought she was too sensible to say to a fourteen-year-old. It was to her that Jennie could express all her 'thoughts and soul'. In a remarkable, but partly lost letter, written early in December, as she was steaming from India to Egypt, Jennie revealed everything:

... it is not likely—but of course in R's state anything is possible—Our mail comes in Tuesday & I hope to get letters from you—I suppose Charles has written to you about his engagement he wired it to me—& from his last letter I was not expecting it. Oh Leonie darling do you think it is *too late* to stop it? Nothing is impossible you know. Can't you help me—for Heaven sake write to him. Don't be astonished at my writing this—after my last letter—But I am frightened of the future all alone—& Charles is the only person on earth that I cd start life afresh with—& if I have lost him—I am indeed paid out for my treatment of him—The only thing I reproach F.W. for, is for telling me give Charles up—knowing that he himself did not intend to stick to me—Leonie darling use all yr cleverness & all yr strength & urge him to put off his marriage. Anyhow until I have seen him—He cared for me until quite recently—& if I am only given the chance—I will redeem all the past. The world wld forgive him knowing his devotion to me—& if he still cares for me—the girl I am sure wld be willing to give him up—particularly as there is someone else—she cld go back to—Leonie dearest rightly or wrongly work for this tell him that I am so suited to him that my troubles have sobered me & that I cld be all he desired—besides I cld help him in his career—The future looks too black & lonely—without him—Oh! why have things gone so wrong—Perhaps you can put it right—don't let him marry until he has seen me— It is only a month to wait—*P. & O 'Carthage' Red Sea—Dec 10th*—Dearest Snippy—As I found we were going as fast as the Mails, I have kept my letter back until Today—we part from this ship tonight at Ismailia—but it will take on my letter which will reach you the 18th if you are in London—We go to Cairo for 8 days, as we have to wait for our Messageries boat which we join at Alexandria for Marseilles where we arrive the 20th. We have had a very good passage & R. is very quiet. I think he will be easily managed henceforth. His will is very feeble—I had to give in about Monte Carlo as he set his heart on going there instead of Cannes—We shall go to the Metropole at first, & make plans later—Perhaps if we remain at M.C. we can take a small villa at Beaulieu. Write to me c/o Smith Bank on M.C. I don't know if the Duchess will come out or not it may be too long a journey for her —in which case we wld return to England after a bit —If she comes perhaps Winston will bring her out— He can go to Germany a little later—As for Jack if he does not stay at Deepdene[3] you might look after him if necessary—but I dare say the Duchess will have made arrangements for him—You will let me know all yr plans—Give my love to Mama & Clara—of

course I will write—*Don't breathe* what I have written
about Charles to anyone—

> Yr loving
> Jennie

So that was it. Pressure had certainly been brought
to bear on Kinsky by his family, who felt it was more
than time he married, and preferably a catholic with the
requisite number of quarterings. But he had resisted
that for years. Now that he believed that Jennie no
longer loved him, and knew she had betrayed him, he
resisted no longer. And Jennie was distraught. Who was
F.W.? We do not know. But it might have been
Frederic, Lord Wolverton: Jennie certainly knew him,
he has the right initials, he was one of the Prince of
Wales's circle: furthermore, he married in January
1895, which is suggestive. But there is no evidence, and
it may just as well have been someone else. Whoever
it was, his attraction had proved fatal.

Jennie and Randolph were back in London for what
must have been a grim Christmas. On 3 January Jennie
wrote to Leonie:

. . . Don't dream of coming over at present & until it
suits you. There is little to do here & I am really much
in a better frame of mind than you can possibly
imagine as regards this wedding. The bitterness if there
was any, has absolutely left me. He and I have parted
the best of friends and in a truly *fin de siècle* manner.
So darling don't worry about me on that score. I am
not *quite* the meek creature I may seem to you. Pity
or mere sympathy from even *you* is wasted on me.
No one can do me *any* good. He has not behaved particularly well & I cant find much to admire in him but
I care for him as some people like opium or drink
although they wd like not to. *N'en parlons plus.*[4]
Randolph's condition and my precarious future worries me much more. Physically he is better but mentally he is 1000 times worse. Even his mother wishes
now that he had died the other day. What is going to

happen I cant think or what we are to do if he gets better. Up to now the General Public and even Society does not know the real truth & after *all* my sacrifices and the misery of these 6 months, it would be hard if it got out. It would do incalculable harm to his political reputation & memory & is a dreadful thing for all of us. We cant make any plans for the next days. My life is dreadful here, so disorganised & uncomfortable, no place to sit, everything in confusion. I've got a cold which makes me feel 'like mud'. . . .

On 9 January, Kinsky was married. On the 14th Jennie wrote to Jack, who was staying at Deepdene with Duchess Lily:

My darling Jack

When am I going to see you again? Don't you think you might put pen to paper—I feel very lonely never hearing from you—You will have seen in the papers of poor Papa's sudden attack the other night. It was very serious but he has rallied altho' on the whole he is not so well—I am writing in bed which will account for this scrawl—Winston writes from Hindlip that it is pleasant there. I believe Sunny & his sisters go there today—I think he will probably come back Wed: give my best love to Aunt Lily—I wish I cld see her—but I do not feel I can leave the house for an hour at present—You might come up & see me one day if Aunt Lily approves

Yr. loving Mother
J.S.C.

Write to me about yr clothes—how are they?

Even at a moment like that Jennie could worry about her son's school clothes.

Ten days later Randolph died, of General Paralysis of the Insane, leaving substantial debt: his Rand shares, which would have made his children millionaires, were sold to pay them off. Within a few days Jennie had lost the two men she had loved most.

NOTES

1. William Hudson, household furniture remover and fire-proof furniture depositors, Hudson's buildings, Wilton Road, S.W.

2. The doctor who accompanied them.

3. Home of Blandford's second wife, know as Duchess Lily. Blandford had died in 1892.

4. Let's talk no more about it.

9

GEORGE

Jennie was resilient. She'd surprised her doctors by her powers of recovery in 1883, and she must have surprised her friends now. Instead of moping and mourning, she went to Paris with Leonie. She deserved a little fun after all she'd been through, and even the Duchess was only mildly disapproving. 'She carped a little at your *"apartement"* in "the gayest part of the Champs Elysées" but was otherwise very amiable—or rather not particularly malevolent,' wrote Winston in February 1895. A frequent visitor to the Avenue Kléber flat was Bourke Cockran, the celebrated American orator whose rhetorical style was to be such an influence on Winston's. But in April Jennie and Leonie had to return. Their mother, who had retired to a bleak life in Tunbridge Wells after Leonard Jerome's death in 1891, fell ill and also died. Jennie found herself even more alone. But she had her boys.

The story of how she took her parental duties more seriously after Randolph's death can be followed in the biography of Winston. But though he has naturally received far more attention from historians than his younger brother, Jack too benefited from Jennie's greater interest. In some ways he was closer to her than Winston, able, as he grew up, to tease her about her admirers and adventures in a way Winston never did. Also, at times, he and Jennie formed an alliance of amused exasperation against Winston's ceaseless demands and of mock despair against his perilous reputation-seeking as a young army officer. For all Jennie's endless social round and constant struggle against financial disaster, they were a remarkably united and loving threesome.

The social round hardly ever paused long enough for Jennie to catch her breath and collect her thoughts, but sometimes she felt dispirited. Her old friends George and Mary Curzon were going to India as Viceroy and Vicereine, and many parties were given to speed them on their way. One night, at Welbeck Abbey, home of the Duke of Portland, Jennie found herself next to Curzon:

In a despondent mood I bemoaned the empty life I was leading at that moment. Lord Curzon tried to console me by saying that a women alone was a godsend in society, and that I might look forward to a long vista of country-house parties, dinners, and balls. Thinking over our conversation later, I found myself wondering if this indeed was all that the remainder of my life held for me. . . .

This must have been in 1898. In June of that year Jennie was invited to stay at Warwick Castle by Daisy Warwick, who had had a long reign as the Prince of Wales's favourite mistress. The Prince enjoyed Jennie's company very much: he was getting difficult to amuse as he grew older, but she knew how to do it, and so was frequently invited where he was going to stay. Among the other guests was a handsome young officer in the Scots Guards, George Cornwallis-West. George was twenty-four, just sixteen days older than Winston. His father owned 10,000 acres in Wales, round Ruthin Castle in Denbighshire, and was Honorary Colonel of the 4th Battalion of the Royal Welch Fusiliers, but for all his rank, he was really something of an aesthete, and had spent his youth in Italy, copying old masters and begetting three illegitimate daughters. In 1872, having inherited and decided to become respectable, he married Patsy, the beautiful grand-daughter of the Marquess of Headfort. Patsy quickly produced two girls and

George, to whom she seems to have taken an early dislike. She was, however, ambitious for her children, and had married her elder daughter, Daisy, to the immensely rich Prince of Pless: Shelagh, younger than George, was to marry the Duke of Westminster, no pauper himself. It was, in shooting terms, a left and a right for a family who had nothing like the cash to match their acres. But Patsy wanted only the best: for George's godfather, she had acquired the Prince of Wales himself.

In his amiable memoirs *Edwardian Hey-Days,* subtitled *A Little about a Lot of Things,* George described that weekend at Warwick Castle. He was at Hythe doing a course of musketry when he received his invitation. Leave from a course was almost unheard of, but an invitation to meet the Prince was virtually an order, so George quickly got permission, and off he went. Warwick Castle is one of the most splendid places in England, standing on its bluff above the river Avon, and Daisy Warwick at this time was, as George put it, 'at the zenith of her beauty'. But it was Jennie, not Daisy, that took his eye. She was forty-four, but looked not a day over thirty, and her charm and zest for life were undiminished. She always, even when she was old, treated people of all ages as equals: George was enormously flattered by her attention. Before anyone knew what was happening, they were out on the river together. According to George, Jennie talked about Winston, about the great faith she had in him, and her ambitions for his career. He would rise to great things, she was sure. But they cannot have confined their conversation to Winston's prospects, for they had fallen instantly in love.

In his memoirs George leaves it there, and goes on to write of how he introduced the Mauser automatic pistol to the School of Musketry, the rise of French restaurants in London, and one or two polo-players he knew. He was discretion itself, in fact. But to Jennie he was quite uninhibited. He wrote from Newlands Manor, his family's other large country house, at Lymington, in Hampshire, on 3 July 1898:

Jennie Dearest, It is perfectly heavenly down here and I do so miss you, & long for you to be with me here. I wonder now what you are doing & who you are on the river with, I am sure Sweetie you are behaving yourself well. I have to go back to that dreary spot Pirbright[1] tomorrow, or rather have to be there, very early, so consequently leave this tonight. Dont forget tomorrow afternoon, if you possibly can, come & have tea with me at Burton's Court, & listen to the band. Good night you dear angel, *à bientôt,* yours always.

G.

Burton's Court is a large green place in front of the Royal Hospital, Chelsea, where the Guards have their cricket-field. To this day the Guards band plays on summer afternoons beneath the trees, and it must be one of the last Edwardian pleasures left in England to go and hear them while Guardsmen bat and bowl, their concentration apparently quite undisturbed by the musical accompaniment. For George, though, in 1898, the excitement of taking Jennie out to tea proved too much. He took to his bed almost at once: he often did in an emotional crisis. The rapidity of the affair was proving too much for his parents, too, who thoroughly disapproved:

In bed at
Dearest Jennie,   50 Park Street[2]

Excuse this scrawl but am still in bed, with every prospect of remaining there at present. Still darling I am better much. My temperature has gone down, it was 104 on Sat night. Much as I hate the idea of not seeing you, I dare not advise you to come here, as one never knows when my mother or father, who arrives today, may turn up. The former found out from my servant where the roses came from, though he had the sense to say they were sent with a note. We had a

scene, she required a lot of pacifying & then only by
assuring her that you were anxious for me to marry
M.G;[3] & had asked me to lunch to meet her. It appears
two *nice kind-hearted men* (D them) have informed
her I am devoted to you. God bless you dearest, I
longed to be with you at Eastwell,[4] but Fates are
against us. What time do you go to Newmarket tomorrow. Your ever.

G.

He was soon up again:

My dearest Jennie   July 13th, 1898
    I am much better today & am down for the first
time. The Doctor has ordered me home where I go tomorrow for a bit, how I do wish you were coming too.
How is Newmarket, I see your host won a race yesterday. My address after tomorrow will be Newlands
Manor.
 Lymington
  Hants.
Will you write me a line there like the angel that you
are. I have missed you so the last few days, I have a
picture of you before me now one in this weeks *Sketch*
sitting at a piano. I have got such blues today. I want
you to cheer me up badly. My battalion came up
from Pirbright today, so at any rate when I do come
up again I shant have to rush off to Pirbright every
other hour. I hope you are behaving nicely with your
old friend H.W. are you sweetie dear? It is such a
glorious day out my thoughts carry me back to Hamp-
ton Court & the punt & the river, how I enjoyed that
day, you make me forget I felt at all C.D.[5] Au revoir
Dearest.

                            yours always
                              G.

    H.W. was Hugh Warrender, one of Jennie's most
staunch admirers, who pursued her and pursued her,
and never married anyone else. His brother George,

later an admiral, was also an admirer. Their sister
Eleanor, another great friend of Jennie's, was a nurse.
George had no need to worry. It was high summer, and
Jennie thought of no one else. The lovers were only
thwarted by George's tiresome duties, such as having
to guard the Bank of England. On 19 July, Jennie
must have watched him marching off:

> Oh my Jennie darling I did so love seeing you to-
> day, how I do crave for you, and longed to rush
> out of the ranks & tell you so, when I saw you this
> evening, you are so much, so *very much* to me
> sweetie. . . .

The *very much* was underlined four times, but
George's passion still increased daily:

My Darling   July 25th, '98
   I have just this second got your second note, I am
so mis, I had not the *least* idea that you were waiting
in the carriage, when the 1st note arrived, or of
course I would have rushed down four steps at a time
to see my beloved Jennie, what a fool the waiter was
not to tell me, I cant tell you how fearfully disappointed I am, I would have given worlds to see you.
And the note I sent was such a cold formal note, as
there were some others writing at the same table, but
now they are all playing bridge, so that I can let my
heart overflow to my sweetie. Oh darling I do love
you, you are all the world to me, I cannot tell you
how I appreciate all your confidence in me. How are
you, '*Est ce que vos yeux sont un peu culottés*' [6] but
if they are its only because I love you, & my love
is reciprocated. Bless you my sweetie, from your own
                                        G.

Four days later it was:

> I thought about you all yesterday & built castles in
> the air about you & I living together, it was such a

nice castle, & somehow didn't fall to pieces as soon as most castles in the air do.

Then he was off to play cricket. He was besotted; there being no London mountains, he climbed balconies for her instead:

> 50 Park Street,
> Grosvenor Square, W.
> 8.15 a.m.

My Darling

Just off to parade feel so fit after a cold shower-bath.
An awful thing happened. I found directly I left I had left my latchkey, on a chain with a cigarette holder case, in your dressing room on the right hand side as you go in. Keep it a little then will you either send it or leave it here in a parcel. I had to climb up the balustrade to the balcony

> Bless you.
> G.

The lovers plotted to spend another week-end at Warwick Castle:

> 50 Park Street,
> Grosvenor Square, W.
> August 1st, '98

My Sweetie

Just a line before I start for Latimer, to tell you I am thinking of you & that I love you darling. I hated leaving you last night, I hope you are refreshed by your long sleep I am, & feel fit to make a hundred runs. What a happy peaceful day we spent yesterday, wasn't it delicious. I hope you will enjoy yourself at Cowes. I have just heard my people are going shares in a house there who with I dont know. Got a wire this morning from Lady W. Of course come Warwick any time you like Thursday. *A bientôt* my own sweetie, I long to be coming with you

> from your loving
> G.

Jennie, however, was not invited to Warwick, much to George's chagrin, and no doubt her own. Daisy Warwick was piqued, perhaps—not because she had designs on George herself, but because she thought they were being too obvious. Besides, no one in the Prince's circle would have looked with favour on a woman of Jennie's age carrying on so boldly with a man a mere fortnight older than her own son. When she arrived at Warwick, Daisy announced that she had put off the ladies of the party. 'It is too horrid', wrote George. Equally horrid was the interview he had with his father about money:

> Perham Down Camp
> (Really in the train on my way there!)
> August 23rd, '98

Darling little Missus,

As you see by above I am writing this in the train so that my writing will be even worse than it generally is. I left camp yesterday at 6.0 and after an extraordinary round about journey, including travelling by special and luggage trains I arrived home at 11.0 pm five hours to go 40 miles, wonderful speed! I had an unpleasant morning going through accounts with the the agent & my father, & found that a most unsatisfactory state of things existed. However I managed after some persuasion to get my father to agree to several things, which I hope will put matters straight for a time at any rate. There is nothing so unpleasant as my position of having to regulate my fathers expenditure, it is in most cases the other way round. How I long to be with you now, you who are so sensible, would I know give me such good advice, and all my petty worries would vanish at once if I were with you dearest. We march to Wilton on Sat next, and will be there about four days. I do wish you were going to stay with the Pembrokes, or somewhere near Salisbury, wouldn't it be nice. I hope you have had all my letters, the post at Perham is somewhat vague as regards delivery & collection. Goodbye my sweetie,

I love you so. I forgot to say I fear I couldn't manage to go to the Mintos [7] as well as the Guthries [8] so soon together. Excuse writing. Love from your loving
George

Jennie was about to set out on her autumn travels, starting at Blenheim. George wished he could have gone, as there was a Fire Brigade competition which would have interested him very much. Jennie wasn't too happy about leaving him alone for several days. George assured her she could trust him:

I love you, & if you think for one instant you cant trust me by myself in London, you are quite mistaken, but there I know you were only chaffing me. . . .

Perhaps she wasn't 'only chaffing', though. George was easily impressed by feminine beauty, and was already leading a full sexual life, it would seem, at eighteen. He and some fellow Old Etonians took three tarts out on the river at Maidenhead one day. When they reached Windsor, the 'Perfect Ladies' ('at the very top of their profession and all young and pretty') asked to be shown round Eton College, including the Chapel. There, one by one, the young men abandoned them out of shame: 'Somehow it seemed rather beastly—those three tarts in Upper Chapel.' Off religious premises, though, George seems to have had few qualms. His susceptibility to women and theirs to him made life very easy in some ways; but not for those who hoped for some steadiness of affection.

Jennie cannot have imagined the affair would last long at this time, for she tried to get George a post with Curzon in India. Curzon was not interested:

You recommended young Cornwallis-West. He seemed a nice boy at Warwick but I don't suppose there is a chance of my having room for him, as I fancy I can only take one English officer from here & I have 50 applications.

George seemed quite keen to go, too. He asked Jennie if she'd heard anything. Jennie and Patsy seem to have been on friendly terms, because he thought Jennie might have told Patsy first.

They met again at Duart Castle, the Guthries' house on the Isle of Mull. Jennie wrote to Jack with bad news on 20 September:

Fancy what a bore for me—I have sprained my ankle & can hardly put my foot to the ground—I was 4 miles from home when I did it—& managed to hobble back—but today it is so swelled I have to send for a doctor—

Her sisters said it served her right for pursuing George over the moors: a man should never be interfered with while he was at his sport.

There are many letters from George to Jennie over the next two years, mostly full of accounts of army manoeuvres, hunting and shooting. As letters, they do not begin to compare with Randolph's, any more than George compared with Randolph as a man. But they have a likeable boyish frankness, and moments of real tenderness, and George's absolute devotion to Jennie is beyond question:

You are such an angel, I know you understand, & even if you did feel hurt you would never show it. And I love you for it very dearly. There is no one like you, you never get what I call 'Heroics', and never want me to do anything you think I'd rather not, in fact you spoil me, you angel I should love to give you a big hug before [I] start. I will go direct from the station & dress & come to you, put on your dear Jappy dress if you are alone. My cold is much better, thanks to ammoniated quinine. . . .

I have just awoke from the 40 winks, you prophesied I would take; & feel all the better for them. You sweetie I hated leaving you last night; it seems un-

natural that I should have ever to go away. I am none
the worse, and got a cab almost immediately. Your
telephonic conversation was nice but very inadequate,
I wanted to be shot along the wires myself. . . .

I dreamt about you last night, only too vividly,
some-one tried to take you away from me, I can never
allow that, the mental pain was awful even in my
dream, Heaven knows what it would be if it actually
happened. . . .

The only bar to Jennie and George's happiness was
the strong disapproval of their affair being shown by
all their friends, and particularly by those who took
their social responsibilities gravely, such as the Prince
of Wales. He wrote to Jennie and told her she was
being foolish and compromising her social position.
George was miffed:

I really do think its exceedingly cool of H.R.H. to
write the kind of letter you mention in your letter.
I wonder why our friendship should annoy him. I
gain everything by your love for me, I fear you lose
by it. I wish it were otherwise. . . .

Jennie thought she was being unwise herself at times.
At any rate she would not even contemplate marriage,
and George accepted it:

> Ford Manor,
> Lingfield,
> Surrey

My darling little Missus,   November 9th, '98
   I was so glad to find your dear letter awaiting me,
when I arrived in from shooting this evening. You
must not be afraid Missus mine, I do really love you,
& appreciate your cleverness & good qualities; really
I would give up everything for you, I feel this more
when I am not with you, as when I am, you are always trying to make me realize the folly of it all.

I should say though only part of it, as there is no folly in being devoted to you my sweet, even if we cant get married. And I feel every day more & more like a creeper clinging to & growing on you. I may add that it is my prayer that this creeper may be 'evergreen'. We had a good day today about 600 pheasants, some high mostly otherwise. Tomorrow is to be the best day they expect to get 600 pheasants before lunch & 800 rabbits afterwards. If you want to bet, put a very little on Turkish-Bath & Chevy-Chase on Saturday at Liverpool, I heard from the trainer today, he thinks they will win. This is private as I never give away stable secrets, but there is no such thing as a secret between your loving George & my sweet little Missus.

No secrets, and no marriage. Marriage would be ridiculous and unbecoming. It was out of the question.

NOTES

1. Where his battalion was stationed.

2. The Cornwallis-Wests' London house.

3. Mary (May) Goelet, American heiress, who married Randolph's nephew, the Duke of Roxburghe, in 1903.

4. At Newmarket, where Jennie was staying with Lord William de la Poer Beresford, V.C., who had married Blandford's widow (Duchess Lily) in 1895.

5. Seedy.

6. Guards' Officer French for 'Have you got bags under your eyes.'

7. The 4th Earl of Minto, who was Governor-General of Canada 1898-1904, and later Viceroy of India, had a house at St Boswell's, Roxburghshire, where Jennie often stayed.

8. Walter Murray Guthrie was married to Olive Leslie, Leonie's sister-in-law.

10

LOVE AND LETTERS

I

1899 was the busiest year of Jennie's life. She was forty-five, looked thirty, and must have felt eighteen. She was bursting with energy, so that not even an affair with a man the same age as her eldest son, or that son's endless demands for her assistance in every aspect of his career, could use it all up. She continued to think about her conversation with Lord Curzon. What should she do *really* to fill her life?

Among her many accomplishments, Jennie was an excellent musician, and the picture George had admired in *The Sketch* showed her sitting at a piano with Mademoiselle Maria Janotha, a popular performer in royal circles, and Pearl Craigie, an American of thirty-one who wrote novels and played under the name of 'John Oliver Hobbes'. The three women had played Bach's Concerto in D Minor for three pianos at a concert at the Queen's Hall. It was the only time, Jennie said, she ever enjoyed playing in public, though she did so often for charity. Perhaps this was because of Pearl Craigie, whom she had met through the Curzons. Jennie made few friends with women outside the immediate family circle, but for Pearl she felt real affection: .

A woman of great sympathies, her unselfishness has been realized by all who ever came in contact with her, and her valuable time was always at the dis-

191

posal of anyone she could help. . . . A brilliant and
clever conversationalist, she could hold her own with
all manner of men, and yet in the more frivolous
company, which she often frequented and thoroughly
enjoyed, she never talked over people's heads. She
had the art of drawing everyone out and making them
appear at their best. So different to some clever
women writers I have met. . . .

That was in 1907. Some years later Jennie wrote of her
again:

It was impossible to know her and not love her.
She was so human, so sympathetic and her brilliant
and delicious mind so deep a well to draw from.

I remember a day we spent together in the country. We went for a walk. It was one of those days
the English climate never wearies of giving—grey,
raw, damp, odious. But we became so interested in
our talk that it was some time before we noticed that
we had wandered into a ploughed field. To me, it
seemed, listening to her, that the field was enamelled
with flowers, and that a warm sun beamed on us.
She had the rare quality of making you feel at peace
with yourself, and inspiring you with unfailing hope.

No other woman ever made Jennie feel like that; it
was men who led her into ploughed fields. But the
reasons why she found Pearl Craigie so attractive are
obvious. Jennie was no intellectual, but she was intelligent, and though George provided everything she required in a physical way, mentally he gave her nothing.
A talented, accomplished woman like Pearl Craigie
was precisely the sort of person Jennie felt could help
her with the problem of what to do with her life.

She had many literary friends. Among them had been
Oscar Wilde, now disgraced. Jennie was once accused
of misquoting from *The Importance of Being Earnest*.
She made a bet that she was right, and wrote offering

Wilde a beautiful pen-holder if he would vouch for her accuracy. He replied:

The Cottage,
Dear Lady Randolph,   Goring-on-Thames

'The only difference between the saint and the sinner is that every saint has a past and that every sinner has a future!' That, of course, is the quotation. How dull men are! They should listen to brilliant women, and look at beautiful ones—and when, as in the present case, a woman is both beautiful and brilliant, they might have the ordinary common sense to admit that she is verbally inspired.

I trust your bet will be promptly paid, as I want to begin writing my new comedy, and have no pen!
Believe me,

Yours sincerely,
Oscar Wilde

Now Jennie decided to start a new literary magazine, and Pearl Craigie helped in many ways.

She introduced Jennie to the people she needed: Sidney Low, who was to be Jennie's assistant editor, John Lane, the publisher, Cyril Davenport, who chose the covers—which were copies of fine bindings. Doubtless Pearl Craigie suggested contributors, too. 'On looking back at the early period of the *Review*,' Jennie wrote, 'I often wonder how I should have succeeded without Pearl Craigie's intelligent help and advice.'

The advice she got from other people was confused and contradictory, but Winston took a close interest and thought it an excellent idea. He wrote on 1 January 1899:

I have no doubt that the business will go on. If it does you will have an occupation and an interest in life which will make up for all the silly social amusements you will cease to shine in as time goes on and which will give you in the latter part of your life as fine a position in the world of taste & thought as

formerly & now in that of elegance and beauty. It is
wise & philosophic. It may also be profitable. If you
could make a £1,000 a year out of it, I think that
would be a little lift in the dark clouds.

The patronizing tone of that is breath-taking, from
son to mother, and as a New Year message it cannot
have gone down too well with Jennie. But Winston
was genuinely enthusiastic, and asked her to keep an
editorial chair available for him, should he choose to
take it. He shivered, though, at Jennie's choice of name,
The Anglo-Saxon Review. The idea of an Anglo-
American alliance was a wild impossibility, he said,
and would find no room among the literary ventures
of the day. Jennie and Pearl Craigie, both Americans,
obviously thought otherwise. Indeed, Anglo-American
co-operation was to dominate Jennie's thinking that
whole year.

It is sad to have to say that, though *The Anglo-
Saxon Review* was successful in giving Jennie something to do, as a magazine it was a failure. It was
extremely expensive, for one thing: a guinea was a lot
to ask, even with the fine binding, and there were never
enough people willing to pay it. Instead of making
money, it lost from the beginning. More important,
there was no real editorial principle behind the selection of material. Jennie knew everyone, and those she
didn't Pearl Craigie and Sidney Low knew, and they
bullied and cajoled and got people to write as editors
should. But the magazine existed to fill a gap in Jennie's life rather than one in the literary world. There
were plenty of reviews at the time, and most of them
not only cheaper, but frankly better. Not that *The
Anglo-Saxon* did not have some excellent material:
the first issue had a long story by Henry James, for
instance. (Henry James the author of *The Turn of the
Screw* and *The Golden Bowl,* that is; not Randolph's
friend.) Other contributors included Swinburne, with
a poem on the Battle of the Nile, and 'John Oliver
Hobbes' herself with a long poetic drama unpromis-

ingly called *Osbern and Ursyne*. There were pieces
about Lady Mary Wortley Montagu and Wireless Teleg-
raphy and the Treaty of Paris. There was an article
by Lord Rosebery on Sir Robert Peel. But somehow
it didn't add up to a magazine with any definite personality. Such as it was, the tone was vaguely aristocratic, and the review was mocked for having so
many contributors from high society. In later issues
such men of distinction in their different ways as Lord
Crewe, Edmund Gosse, George Bernard Shaw, John
Gorst, Stephen Crane, H. de Vere Stacpoole, George
Gissing, Maurice Baring and William Archer were
liable to find themselves between the same covers as
Angling Reminiscences in England and the Tropics by
Susan, Countess of Malmesbury. Daisy Warwick's contribution must have caused a few smiles. It was called
Some Minor Miseries of a Book Lover: no one had
imagined her problems lay in the field of bibliophilism.
But it is easy to mock, and *The Anglo-Saxon* did run
for twelve issues and fulfil its main purpose. It gave
Jennie a sense of a full and purposeful life. She wrote
to Jack on 24 February:

I am getting on very well with the review—but it is
anxious work—I have got the people I want for the
staff—which is important—& am getting money for
the syndicate—I am so tired of writing about it that
I don't think I will go all over it again—You will
have more than enough of it when you return.

Jack was in Egypt, acting as secretary to Sir Ernest
Cassel, the financier. He had been made to go into the
City. *Someone* in the family had to make some money,
and as Jennie only knew how to spend it, and Winston
was too busy, it had to be Jack. He hated, but accepted
it. He does not seem to have taken much interest in
the magazine. George took an interest, but thought he
knew his limitations:

I often wonder if you would object if I were to send

you endearing telegrams, I often want to when I pass a telegraph office. You angel I didn't like leaving you one bit yesterday. I wish I could be of more help to you in your enterprise, I fear my talents (if I have any) are certainly not literary.

As a matter of fact George was later to extend his range from the amorous telegram to several full length books.

II

At the end of April 1899 Jennie was invited to stay with the Cornwallis-Wests at Ruthin Castle for Chester races: the Prince of Wales was going to be there. 'H.R.H. appears to be very anxious to meet you. Odd isn't it?' wrote George. Perhaps he meant to lecture her between the races. Obligatory guests included Lord Marcus Beresford, who managed the Prince's horses, and Mr Reuben Sassoon, who placed his bets. Among those chosen for other reasons was Miss Muriel Wilson, daughter of Arthur Wilson, in whose house, Tranby Croft, the famous Baccarat Scandal had taken place in 1890. Muriel was an heiress on whom many mothers had their eye for their sons—including Jennie, who thought she might do very well for Winston. Patsy obviously wanted her for George, which must have caused some tensions in the party, though none between Jennie and George, whose devotion continued unabated throughout the summer. By this time Jennie was beginning to waver on the subject of marriage. On 16 February she had written to Jack, noting Lord Crewe's engagement to Lady Peggy Primrose: 'only 22 years between them!' But she had a conscience about the gap between herself and George. It gave her bad dreams. George would have none of it:

Dreams always go by contraries, and *yours* was no exception to the rule, and darling I feel it will always be the case as regards us two. No one shall come between us. . . .

Not even Winston, who was now back in England and had retired from the army to fight a by-election at Oldham. Jennie put on the dress she wore for her concerts and appeared with him at meetings. 'There are thousands of true hearts in this constituency which have a warm corner for Lady Randolph Churchill,' said the *Oldham Daily Standard* on 27 June, and on the 28th it recorded that 'Lady Randolph Churchill had a most enthusiastic reception as she accompanied Alderman Whittaker [1] to the platform. Her charming and graceful presence gave an added interest to the proceedings. She listened intently to the speeches, and seemed especially pleased and amused with Mr Bottomley's [2] vigorous and humorous address.' She did not, it seems, speak herself, but her very presence was thought to contribute to the Conservative cause. This time, however, it was to no avail, and Winston was not elected.

Soon after Jennie's visit to Oldham, she and George must have agreed that they would marry, in spite of everything:

> Pirbright Camp,
> Woking
> July 11th, '99

My darling little Missus,

I am sending my servant up for some things, so take the opportunity of writing you a line before you start for Newmarket. You are such a darling. I loved your bringing me to the station last night.

I was awfully chaffed this morning as someone saw me, and remarked I kept my head in the carriage some time. I passed it off by saying 'Well if a man cant be driven to the station by his own sister he cant be by anyone.' They believed me. Some day soon I hope to be able to say wife instead of sister. Dont forget you have a pony to play with for me. We had a parade this morning it *was* hot. Bless you my own Precious one, till Thursday. Your own

G.

Four days later he wrote saying:

I went to see Mrs Greaves [8] after I left you, I told her in the strictest confidence, that I was going to marry you, she was very pleased, and declared she had never known an instance of two people marrying when the man was the younger, that was not a success.

Their engagement was, of course, to remain an absolute secret, and, equally of course, it didn't. Things came to a head in August: George was invited on board the Prince's yacht *Britannia* at Cowes:

The Prince of Wales took the opportunity of taking me aside and pointing out to me the inadvisability of my marrying a woman so much my senior. He admitted that this was the only argument against our engagement, told me that no one could possibly say what might happen within the next three months, and begged me to do nothing in a hurry.

The Prince meant that the situation in South Africa was serious, and it looked like war. ' "If there *is* war", he added, "you're sure to go out. There'll be time enough to consider it when you come back." ' Unfortunately the Prince was too late; the engagement leaked into the papers, where much was made of George's closeness in age to Winston. The wedding was forecast for October. Though these reports were denied, some public comment was unavoidable, for Cowes had a strange effect on Jennie. It was there, of course, that she had met and become engaged to Randolph, and *their* romance had got into the papers, somehow, too. The Marquis Boni de Castellane explained how it happened this time. One evening Jennie told him about it, making him promise to keep it a secret. A few hours later he discovered she'd told his whole party.

After all this excitement, Jennie and George went to Paris for still more. They took a trip to Versailles, though that was not what excited George most:

> I did so enjoy my two days, & nights!! in Paris my love, they were the happiest I have ever spent in my life, & trust they were only a foretaste of what is to come. . . .

Jennie went from Paris to Aix, to take a cure and think. George went back to London, where he saw Jack. Jack did not always care for Jennie's admirers, but he seems to have got on all right with George:

> Jack came to dine, and we talked of you. You would have been amused at the menu, we had grouse for dinner, but as it was the 11th only, they were put down as '*Dindonneaux d'Ecosse*'.[4] I went to see my doctor today, as I was not quite well again after Paris, I suppose it never *had* got *quite* well, and overdoing it brought it on again, its so difficult to write what I mean without being crude. However he said it was nothing and would be well in a few days. Darling precious Missie I am counting the days before we meet again. . . .

In Aix, Jennie was regretting her indiscretion at Cowes and having serious doubts again:

> Arthur's
> St James' Street, S.W.
> August 14th, '99
>
> Little Missie mine, your letter today made me rather sad. You said in any case no matter what happens we will stick to each other, but precious you dont mean by that, we should not marry, do you? When I am away from you I feel all the more determined, but be as you wish, (whatever that may be) I'll al-

ways stick to you, and can no more bear the thought of our being separated than you can. The adjutant took me aside today & wanted to know if it was true I was engaged, and Col Paget [5] had written to him to find out. I told him it was true in this way, that I would marry you tomorrow if you would me, but that you were not willing, still at the same time it didn't follow that I did not intend to persevere in the idea. The opinion here is that *I* acted too prematurely & had it put in the papers, & that you evidently had it contradicted, it is unpleasant for me, and several sarcastic things have been said to me, but I dont mind one *little* bit dearest one, and am only telling you this, to make your mind at rest, & show you that you are in *no way* held up to ridicule. . . .

Jennie continued to have doubts, and to worry George with her letters. On his way from Scotland to stay with the Wilsons at Tranby Croft, he assured her that *his* mind was quite made up. When he got there he found trouble—though not from Muriel:

Tranby Croft,
Hull
August 20th, '99

My own precious little Missie, I cant tell you how delighted I was to find a letter from you, on my arrival here after having been travelling all day, and another one this morning, I do love getting your dear letters so. 'Missie mine', I have written to you every single day since you left, so that as you got no letter one day, you will probably get two on another. I had a letter from the adjutant today, saying that Col Paget wishes to see me on the 25th I know what this means he is going to have a go at me about you, but dont be afraid my darling love I shall be strong, as if possible I love you more than ever; still it is a bore if he uses threats I shall say I shall leave the regiment, you wont desert me Missie, will you? I couldnt bear it, it would break my heart. Perhaps he will try

& persuade me to go abroad, but I wont go, I cant leave you Missie, for I love you better than my life, and any prospects I might have would become empty & hollow without you to share them with. I've got such blues, & how I long to be with you, so that you could drive them all away. But enough of this strain. I am sorry to hear about your bother with American subscribers, it is such a bore being so far away, we must go over there in October together. Have you started your article yet? . . .

Coming back to London, he went out to dinner:

I compared all the women there with you or rather tried to, but it was impossible for me to do so; you are my idol my precious, and are set up far above anyone else in this world. When I went to bed, I cried out 'Missie! Missie! I love you, are you thinking of me?' were you? I wonder? . . .

Next day, though, he got another letter from Jennie that he didn't like. She reported that she'd heard from the Prince. 'You might have added that you didn't propose to carry out the Prince's suggestion,' George complained. But Jennie was wondering. The Prince, at another spa, was writing to her in a firm but kindly manner. A woman could do pretty much what she liked, he considered, so long as she wasn't mischievous, but a marriage to George would be not only mischievous but foolish, for it would never bring the happiness she fondly imagined. She was old enough to know better. Such advice was doubtless coming to Jennie from all quarters and by every post. When the story reached India, for instance, Mary Curzon wrote to ask whether to send a wedding-present or not: 'And shall you yield to prayer and persuasion then? Jennie solo is so delightful that I am still not reconciled to Jennie duet. . . .' It wasn't only prayer and persuasion, though, that Jennie had to consider. The Prince's advice contained a warning: if she went ahead and married George, she would cease to be his friend. History must have seemed to be repeating itself. The social life of the Prince's set meant even more to Jennie now than it had done in 1876: she certainly did not wish to give it up again.

Jack, meanwhile, was more concerned about Winston's romance with Pamela Plowden, a girl he had been pursuing for some time. He told George his doubts:

> Jack dined with me last night, and opened his heart to me about Miss Pamela, he doesn't often talk so I was pleased with his confidence. He doesn't think much of her, in fact he dislikes her, he says she is such an awful humbug, and is the same to three other men as she is to Winston. He tells me they went about at Blenheim as if they were engaged, in fact several people asked if it was so. I am sorry for Winston, as I dont think he would be happy with her, I cant make her out, she is certainly very clever, in a doubtful sense of the world. . . .

When Jennie returned from Aix, she and George went again to stay at Duart Castle on the Isle of Mull. There she seems to have told George quite definitely that marriage was off. He was desolate:

> Duart Castle, Craignure,
> Isle of Mull
> Sept 12th, '99
>
> My darling little Missie,
> I feel so low & miserable this morning, and I miss you terribly. I wonder what you feel. I hope you were not tossed last night, I heard the wind blowing as I lay awake. The little dog Jennie came to sleep in my room last night; can you guess why? They are all going to Oban for the games, but I am going stalking instead, more amusing I think. You are lucky in having a fine day to go through the canal, I have always heard it is quite lovely. The London papers have had a miscarriage today so I dont know

how matters are going in London. Bless you my darling Missie, I love you very dearly & will stick to you even if we dont get married. I cant write more now I'm too mis.

> Your loving
> Georgie

He went on being 'mis'. Two days later he wrote:

> . . . . Oh my little Missie I have been so depressed since we parted; to think that all our arrangements and little plans for the future, as man & wife, have burst like a soap bubble, and nothing will ever remain but a pleasant recollection in some ways, and very bitter in others, of what has proved to be nothing but a 'Castle in the air'. Little Missie I would have made you very happy despite all drawbacks, but if you think I would have injured you socially, and made you a subject of ridicule, had I married you, then you are right to let matters remain as they are. I love you dearly and shall never love another woman as much. Please God the day will never come when you will regret the decision you have come to.

She seems to have regretted it at once, for she sent him a telegram, to which he replied:

> WISH IT COULD BE SO TOO LATE BOATS ARE BURNT HAVE WRITTEN MY RELATIONS YOUR OWN FAULT GEORGE.

NOTES

1. Chairman of the local Conservative association.
2. Horatio William Bottomley, 1860-1933, journalist, company promoter, fraud, bankrupt, eventually imprisoned: MP for South Hackney 1906-12 as a Liberal, and 1918-22 as an Independent.

3. Mrs Rosamund Angharad Greaves, only child of Edward Lloyd of Flintshire. She married secondly Lord Henry Grosvenor. She lived in Scotland.

4. Young Scotch turkeys.

5. Colonel Arthur Paget, married to Jennie's old American friend, Minnie Stevens. He became a general in 1900.

11

WAR

While this private drama was being enacted, a public one, of rather greater moment, was just beginning in South Africa. The Prince of Wales had been right: war was coming with the Boers. In October, George's Battalion of the Scots Guards was sent out under the command of Lord Methuen. At his interview with Colonel Paget George had given a verbal undertaking not to marry or become officially engaged before setting out. For this he was well rewarded. He wrote to Jennie on 6 October:

I had a pleasant surprise when I went to the Orderly room this morning, but dont say anything about it, as it is not definitely settled. Col Paget has recommended me to a general as his aide-de-camp, he wouldn't tell me who he was, but only that he was certain to get a command, and he had asked him (Arthur P) to recommend someone. Of course I accepted at once. It would be far better to [see] the fun from a horse than from the flat of one's feet. Ah Missie I am glad to go out as a soldier, but I do hate leaving you my precious one. I saw Winston today in St James Str, dont tell him I said so, but he looked just a young dissenting parson, hat brushed the wrong way, and at the back of his head, awful old black coat and tie, he is a good fellow but very untidy. . . .

George was busy buying his kit, and looking spick and span. He didn't realize that pressure had been brought from a royal quarter to get him his job as A.D.C. He soon found out:

October 15th, '99

My dear George West,

I had the opportunity of speaking to Lord Methuen at the station yesterday when I took leave of Sir Redvers Buller, and strongly urged him to take you on his staff, so I hope it may be all satisfactorily settled.

I envy you going out on active service with so fine a battalion, and wish you good luck and a safe return home.

Yours very sincerely,
Albert Edward

Jennie had written rather crossly to the Prince, calling him a fair-weather friend, and pointing out the great sacrifice she was making in not marrying George. Perhaps the Prince wished to prove how deep his friendship really was. He was not only helping George in his military career, he was making sure he would mix with senior officers with the right ideas. When George came back, with any luck he'd have forgotten all about his romance with Jennie, and all risk of danger and ridicule would vanish.

George's regiment set off to South Africa from Chelsea Barracks at five o'clock on a dark autumn morning. There was a slight fog, and the streets were, in any case, poorly lit. Wives and sweethearts joined in the march, linking arms with the soldiers, and when they reached Westminster Bridge, on their way to Waterloo, there was a large crowd waiting to see them off. Bottles of whisky were pressed on the delighted troops, and in the semi-darkness it was difficult to prevent the march becoming a disorganized rabble. But at Waterloo itself the police prevented civilians going in with the soldiers, and there were many heart-rending farewells.

Though George went off, as a young soldier should,

with excitement and expectation, his own parting with Jennie had been pretty heart-rending, too:

S.S. *Nubia*
4.45 p.m.
21st Oct. '99

My own darling little Missie,

I did so love getting your two dear little notes before I started, I shall treasure them, and they will be always in the pocket next to my heart till we meet again. My precious one it was agony simply agony leaving you, but Thank God as you say, I know you love me dearly and it is returned as you, in your turn, must realize.

The ship was just starting when Mother came on board, she got out at Southampton and came to the docks on chance of seeing me, I wish in a way she had not as it upset me very much, she looked so ill & worn. Oh my precious little Missie how I do love you, you never have been more loved in all your life; your sweet face was such a comfort to me today, I am glad you came. I must not be low but its very hard having to be parted from THE one thing that is most joyful and beloved in ones life. I am sending this by the Pilot, who gets off when we pass the Needles. We touch at St Vincent, a port in the Cape Verde Islands. Au revoir my own darling precious little Missie, I *do* worship you so, and loathe parting from you, but it is fate, and I will return soon to your dear arms. Bless you again my true love, I love you I love you

your own loving
George

George took his own pony with him, called Toby, but the voyage was long and tedious. It took twenty-eight days to Cape Town, but the monotony was relieved, to some extent, by the fact that Alfred Rothschild had generously presented the Officers' Mess with twenty cases of 1887 Perrier Jouet.

Those were the days. Winston was also on his way

to South Africa, and also equipped with adequate supplies of liquor—including eighteen bottles of ten-year-old Scotch whisky, six of Very Old Eau de Vie, and twelve of Rose's Cordial Lime Juice, perhaps for hangovers. He had refused to intervene in Jennie's situation, though Colonel Cornwallis-West had obviously urged him to do so. 'After all I don't believe you will marry', he told Jennie. 'My idea is that the family pressure will crush George.' Meanwhile he had become War Correspondent for the *Morning Post*. Jack, too, though Jennie didn't know it, was planning to escape from the life he so disliked in the City and go to the war.

Deprived of her menfolk, Jennie found *The Anglo-Saxon Review* not nearly sufficient occupation, and getting restless again, she wondered how she could contribute something to the war. Mrs A. A. Blow, an American lady who had lived in South Africa, had the perfect answer: Americans in Britain could not do anything to participate in the war directly, as America was neutral. But why not send a hospital-ship? Furthermore, there was an American millionaire ready to provide one. Jennie responded enthusiastically, as the official report made clear:

It was on the 25th of October, 1899, that at her invitation the following ladies met at her house: Lady Essex,[1] Mrs Blow, Mrs Joseph Chamberlain,[2] Mrs Arthur Paget, and Mrs Ronalds, to formulate this generous idea, and to further cement with their active sympathy for the wounded that bond of brotherhood which exists between the Anglo-Saxon Nations, by establishing a fund destined to equip and maintain the Hospital Ship *Maine,* which vessel was generously lent to the British Government by The Atlantic Transport Company through Mr Bernard Baker, the Chairman, who has from the first contributed very largely towards the expenses, showing in this practical manner his public spirit and international sympathy in the cause of humanity. Thus, entirely at the cost of Americans not only in the United States, but those residing in England and other countries, has this vessel been sent on her errand of mercy in charge of American Doctors, Nurses and Orderlies selected for the Committee by Mrs Whitelaw Reid.[8]

Jennie was made Chairman of the General Committee, with Mrs Blow as Hon. Sec., and Mrs Ronalds as Hon. Treasurer. The last was a very old acquaintance of Jennie's indeed, from the days when Leonard Jerome had got her to sing for him in his private theatre in New York. Fanny Ronalds was a social figure of some eminence, as well as a singer, and in spite of her affair with Leonard, she had managed to remain a friend of Jennie's mother. She had lived in Paris when the Jeromes lived there, and then in London, where she fell in love with Sir Arthur Sullivan, the musical half of the team of Gilbert and Sullivan. Jennie had known her all her life.

With splendid American energy, the ladies set about raising £30,000 ($150,000). Subscriptions were implored, and firms badgered to provide free supplies. Lily Langtry gave a concert in New York, Mrs Ronalds raffled a diamond and moonstone pendant, 'entertainments' were put on at Claridges and the Hotels Cecil and Carlton, and Barnum and Bailey donated a performance at Olympia. The Queen took a great interest, and sent a Union Jack, presented to the ship by the Duke of Connaught, her third son, and the close friend of Leonie. The Committee had hoped for a Stars and Stripes from President McKinley, too, but there was strong anti-British feeling in America about the war, and the *Maine* had to go without. When the American nurses and doctors came, Jennie took them to Windsor, and the Queen talked to her for half an hour, asking about everything, and who had helped most on the Committee. Jennie wanted to say that Clara and Leonie had been a great help, but to Clara's great annoyance, she hesitated, and the chance was lost. Two days later she was bidden to dine and sleep at Windsor, and was again closely questioned by the Queen.

That there were great ructions on a committee of rich and self-willed women was only to be expected, but in spite of jealousies and back-biting the target was exceeded by more than a fifth. In the middle of all the work, Jennie suddenly heard that Winston had been captured. She received a deluge of sympathetic letters and telegrams; among them was one from Charles Kinsky, now in St Petersburg, and another from Patsy Cornwallis-West. Patsy remained friendly. Perhaps, like others, she believed the affair was over. Rosebery wrote, for instance: 'May I say without impertinence that I am sure you are wise after the crisis of which you spoke to me at Guisachan, to throw yourself into work and such good work as the *Maine*?' But Jennie had not forgotten George, nor he her. He wrote on 3 December with alarming news:

> Orange River,
> South Africa
> My own darling little Missie,   December 3rd, '99
>
> Stirring events have happened since I wrote to you a week ago, but, as is usually the case people in England have a better knowledge of facts than we have who are actually taking part in the campaign. I wrote to you last from Enseling siding, and two days afterwards we had the hardest fight that has taken place in any part of the colony since the war began. 13 hours hard fighting was the time the battle of Modder River lasted, and I can tell you it was a near shave, at one time I thought we should be driven back, but thanks to our Artillery we just managed to win the day. I went out with my General & his staff at 4-0 a.m. and we reconnoitred their position, at least as far as we could. It is impossible to see these Boers they hide themselves so successfully, and they are so cute that they will not open fire on our reconnoitring patrols, as by so doing they would give away their numbers and position. The other day, we could only see a few on our right flank partially concealed

in an old reservoir and in some trenches, as we could find no others, the General naturally concluded that the village of Modder River, on our left, was unoccupied, and therefore ordered the whole of his infantry to advance across an absolutely open plain, they got within 800 yards of their goal when suddenly a terrific fire was opened to them, this started at 6.0 a.m. and did not cease till 7 p.m. The men started without breakfast and went the whole day without food, and water, having finished their water long before noon. It was a terribly hard day, and the heat was terrific. I was knocked over by sunstroke at 3-p.m. and dont remember anything till the evening, when I found myself in hospital. I was sent down to De Aar where I remained for four days. I am all right now my darling Missie so dont be anxious, and am off to the front again first thing tomorrow. Oh my own little Sweet Missie I am so sick of this war, three big battles in six days is enough for any man, and I think most of us think the same. I want to be back to you my sweetheart, my love for you grows stronger every day. So far Thank God I am safe, but one can never tell what may happen to one. Well Missie mine if anything does, you will always know that you are the only woman I have ever given my whole heart & soul to, and that I love you better than anything in the whole world. How busy you must be Missie mine, what with your ship, which appears to be a great success, and your Maggie. I do hope this number will turn out well, I expect to hear from you as to the returns of the last number. I wonder if you will be able to come out here I wouldn't risk the *Review* not being a success if I was you, but my darling I would love to see you, and to have you to nurse me if I was wounded. This will reach you about Christmas time, I wonder if you will be at Blenheim again. How I do long to be with you, and hold you tight in my arms once more. I am yours precious one absolutely, and I know you are mine. I heard a cynic the other day say 'I like women and admire them they are so much more sensible than we are, They may like one man best, but they are quite happy with some one else when the other is away, and dont fret like men do over one woman.' I rose like a trout, and of course got awfully chaffed. Still in my case I was right wasn't I my precious one. Well my little Missie I must stop now as it is bed-time. God bless you my own darling. I kiss your sweet lips many many times,

　　　　　　　　　　　　　　　your own loving
　　　　　　　　　　　　　　　　　George
I have re-read this and it seems such a stupid letter, but I have so little time. Bless you darling.

George's sunstroke was entirely due to his own care-lessness. He had been galloping about with messages on Toby, and got roundly cursed by a senior officer for riding too close to the General, thereby attracting enemy fire and risking the General's life. George had therefore handed the pony to his orderly and lain down and kept quiet. When the General and his staff moved off, neither Toby nor the orderly could be found, and George started to wander about in search of them. He had forgotten to fill his water-bottle. In the intense heat this was fatal, and he rapidly became delirious. Luckily someone found him and brought him back to camp. But it was a serious case of sun-stroke.

George's letter makes it clear that Jennie had been planning to come out with the *Maine* for some time. In her *Reminiscences* she said that she felt the Com-mittee ought to be represented on board by 'a person of authority without a salary', but it seems clear that personal considerations played their part, too. She had nothing to keep her in England, and every reason to go, gossip or no gossip. The ship sailed on 23 Decem-ber. That day, though, Jennie received a telegram:

INVALIDED PROBABLY RETURNING ALMOST IMMEDI-ATELY REPEAT MOTHER GEORGE.

It was a staggering blow. What had happened was

that George had underestimated the seriousness of his illness and discharged himself from hospital too soon. He had gone back to the front. But after a few days he fell ill again, and was sent to Cape Town, and from there ordered home. The same day as his telegram he wrote:

Sanatorium,
Claremont

My darling little Missie,   December 23rd, 1899

I am too miserable for words. I have had no communication from you letter, or otherwise for three weeks, the last I got was a cable dated Nov 30th and nothing has come for me from you by the last three mails, although they have sent our letters here straight, & not up to the front; as is proved by my having received my other letters. Oh Missie darling what does it mean? I have been so C.D. and wanted your letters to cheer me up so much. I have sent you three cables in the last ten days, and have had no answer, the last one was selfish I confess. I wanted you to postpone your departure until I arrived, it was horrid of me to want it, when you are coming out to nurse the sick & wounded. Now I dont know when you leave, or whether there is a chance of my seeing you before you start. Oh please my little Missie dont stay too long here, come back to me do!! You dont realize how much I love you, and what it means to me to be going home feeling I shall not be greeted by your dear lips. I hope to be fit by April perhaps, & then I may come out here again if the war is still raging, so we may miss each other again, which would be awful. The doctors had a board on me the other day, and gave me six months sick-leave, they frightened me rather too. But they are only army doctors, & I shall get the best advice when I get home. Sun-stroke is a horrid thing, especially in my case, as I feel it more owing to the results of the concussion I had two years ago.

I would give 10 years of my life & more to find

you in London when I return. Missie I am so miserable, & want you with me so so much. You do love me as much as you used to, dont you darling? I am so glad to see in todays paper that Winston has escaped, and has left Delagoa Bay for Durban. I expect when you come out here you wont (or at least the *Maine*) wont be kept here permanently, but will be used to convey wounded from Natal to the Base Hospital here, in the same way as the Hospital Ship *Trojan* is used.

Well Good bye my darling little Missie I love you better than anything in the whole world, Please precious dont stay out here too long, I want you *so so* much,

                              ever your loving
                              George

write to me to Newlands Manor.

Jennie had learned of Winston's escape from the prisoner-of-war camp on 14 December, but it was only the day before she sailed that she heard of his safe arrival in Delagoa Bay. Though she must have felt mightily relieved, she set off in a glum mood about George. She wrote to Leonie on the 24th:

                              Hospital Ship *Maine*
                              Dec 24th, '99
                              Sunday

Dearest Snippy—Here we are off Dover—the Pilot will take this—There was such a fog we could not get out of the basin until this morning—It is awfully cold & wet on board—but I dare say we shall get all right —That fellow from Waring[4] altho' he was here days —left everything undone—no table (I am using my bridge table) no chair no glass—no hooks up—We are however settling everything before we get into rough water—You may imagine that I did not feel over lively last night—I had a cable from George saying that he was invalided home & was probably leaving immediately—You must promise to see him,

& write to me all he says—I am so devoted to him that it would be a terrible thing for me if I knew he blamed me for going—Heaven knows this is no pleasure—I *had to go*. Write to me fully—& look after George. The fog is so thick we have once more come to a standstill—We are rather glad, as it will give us a chance of unpacking. I will do my duty by the ship —but shall be back as soon as I can—Bless you darling & a Happy Xmas.

Jennie and George must have passed each other somewhere off Africa.

NOTES

1. Adela Grant, wife of the 7th Earl of Essex.
2. Mary Endicott, daughter of a former US Secretary of War. Chamberlain's third wife.
3. Elizabeth Mills Reid, wife of Whitelaw Reid, editor of the *New York Tribune,* and Ambassador to Britain 1905-12. Mrs Reid was on the board of the Nurses Training School at Bellevue, New York City, which provided the *Maine*'s nurses.
4. S. J. Waring & Sons Ltd, and Gillow Co., two leading house-furnishers, had just amalgamated to form the first of Waring & Gillow, Ltd.

12

THE MAINE

Jennie wrote about her expedition with the *Maine* no less than three times. First there was her official report to the *Maine* Committee in London. In it she described in detail the operation of the wards, the hours of duty, the method of issue of medicines and linen, the treatment of patients, and even the 'substantial' lunch with which they were provided on discharge—sandwiches, cheese, jam and lime-juice or Rosbach water. She also gave her report on the staff and crew: everyone was splendid, but she thought nursing sisters were probably a mistake on a hospital ship, in spite of the great comfort a woman could give a man in pain. The four on the *Maine* and their Superintending Sister had worked

well under trying circumstances. She went on to list all
the distinguished visitors they'd had, and to describe the
concerts on the poop deck. Eleanor Warrender, sister
of Hugh, had gone out with Jennie: she earned praise
for her management of the ship's library. (Her un-
mentioned activities as Jennie's right hand woman must
have been rather more arduous.) Religious observances
had been kept up; Jennie herself had played the organ
at Sunday services.

Jennie felt she had to explain why she had decided
to bring the ship home when she did. On arrival in
South Africa she discovered to her horror that the
authorities wanted the *Maine* to fill up with wounded
and take them straight back to England. This was not
at all what the Committee had had in mind: the *Maine*
was not a floating ambulance, it was a proper hospital,
with an operating theatre and surgeons. Jennie had to
fight hard against official pressure, but she knew everyone, of course, in South Africa as in England, and with
the help of Sir Walter Hely-Hutchinson, the Governor
of Natal, and Sir Redvers Buller, she was able three
times to frustrate efforts to send the *Maine* home. It
stayed in Durban, in fact, for two months, fulfilling its
original purpose. But after the relief of Ladysmith on 28
February 1900, there were a great number of sick and
wounded to be taken back to England, and Jennie
agreed to go. She was partly influenced by the desire to
gain the *éclat* of being the first hospital ship to return
with the heroes of Ladysmith, which had been besieged
for four months; also, the climate was beginning to tell.
Altogether 28 Officers and 326 Other Ranks had been
treated, and 12 Officers and 151 NCOs and men were
brought home. There had been only three deaths.

Jennie's report is efficient and business-like. Her
second version of the story, written at the same time,
but at much greater length, is more 'literary'. It is in
the form of a series of letters, which she published in
The Anglo-Saxon Review in June. Here she describes
in graphic detail the storms the *Maine* passed through
on its way to South Africa, the difficulty of trying to

play the piano on the high seas, and the charm of Las Palmas, where the *Maine* put in. Jennie thought it was like Monterey, in California, which she had visited on a much less happy voyage with Randolph. Soon they were at Cape Town, given a berth inside next to a collier. On shore, Jennie went to the telegraph office:

> Three little women came up, their anxious faces in marked contrast to their befeathered, bedraggled attire, and asked me to write a telegram for them. 'Come at once, hopeless', was the pathetic message.

Not too encouraging a start for someone on a mission of mercy, but undaunted, and after an inspection by Lord Roberts, the Field Marshal, the ship went on to Durban, passing through an astonishing storm with hailstones the size of small plums. At Cape Town Jennie had been joined by Jack: she makes no comment on her feelings on finding him there, though she had left him apparently safe behind in England.[1] He needed a passage to Durban, so he went on the *Maine*. Winston was waiting to greet them at Durban, and all three, with Miss Warrender, went to stay with Sir Walter Hely-Hutchinson at Pietermaritzburg. There Jack and Winston left for the war, while Jennie inspected hospitals and spoke to the wounded, before hurrying back to greet the first patients to arrive on board. Jennie was not, of course, a nurse, but she could write letters for the injured and illiterate:

> I was much amused by the letters which those unable to write dictated to me, generally beginning 'Dear Father and Mother, I hope this finds you as well as it leaves me'——then came a great scratching of heads and biting of fingers until I would suggest that a description of how they were wounded would start them off again——'Won't you send your love to anyone?' I asked. 'Not out of the family', with a reproving look, was my answer. One very gallant Tommy, who lay with a patch over his eye, an inflamed cheek, and a broken arm, asked me to add to his letter——'the sister

which is a writing of this is very nice.' The compliment was fully appreciated.

There were so many visitors to the ship, that Jennie had to limit them to specific hours, with great regret. She was against red-tape in all its forms, and that in military medicine was redder and tougher than most. She became very angry about wounded men's clothing:

On the subject of clothing it is astonishing how little the authorities have been able to cope with it; at the front many of the men were nearly naked, their khaki hanging on them in shreds, and what else could be expected, the uniform being made of such abominable stuff to wear and having to be worn for perhaps five or six months. But when one thinks of the thousands and thousands that have been spent on clothing for the hospitals, not only by the Government but by private individuals, it seems incredible that the sick and wounded should be allowed to leave a hospital to be drafted to another, or to a hospital ship, in the tattered garments they came with, brought in straight from the battlefield. I saw with my own eyes, among a party of wounded who were being transferred from a tug to the *Maine* and the *Nubia,* a man whose khaki trousers were conspicuous by their absence, both legs having been cut off, a pocket handkerchief being tied round one of his poor wounded legs. This man probably had been through several hospitals, and each time sent off again in his rags. Surely a reserve of uniforms or ordinary clothing might be kept for extreme cases such as this, and the principal medical officers allowed a little discretion in the matter. But when I discussed this point with one of the authorities, he said it would be an impossibility. 'You might as well have an office for recording the wishes and messages of the dying'. What a happy hunting-ground the red-tape fiend has in time of war! He sits and gloats on all occasions.

Jennie hoped that young people, unencumbered with ideas drawn from past and irrelevant wars, would improve things. She was an idealist.

Once the ship was operating properly, Jennie felt free to visit the front line. The necessary passes and permissions were granted, and Hely-Hutchinson lent his private railway carriage. Jennie was thrilled by every aspect of the expedition: on the way up, for instance, the train was searched for spies. She was flattered to find her reputation had gone before her. A gun had been named after her already, and at 5 a.m. she was woken by an officer in the Seaforth Highlanders who gave her a cup of coffee in the dawn, and poured out all his troubles. When the train passed the site of the ambush in which Winston had been captured, the guard rushed to point out the wreck of the armoured train. Jennie looked at the graves of those killed in the action, and thanked God Winston was not among them. Then they were at Chieveley, and the front:

General Barton and an A.D.C. met us at the station. We were taken all over the Camp—a wonderful sight. The weather-beaten and in many cases haggard-looking men, their soiled worn uniforms hanging on their spare figures; the horses, picketed in lines or singly, covered with canvas torn in strips to keep the flies off; the khaki-painted guns, the ambulance waggons with their train of mules, and above all the dull booming of 'Long Tom' made us realise that here was war! We sat down on the outskirts of the camp near a sham gun guarded over by a middy of the *Terrible*.[2] Here, too, was the gun which the bluejackets had named after me. Six miles off, through our glasses, we could see Colenso and the enemy's camp, the white tents being the ones they had taken from us. The whole panorama spread out, a grand sight. It was thrilling. I longed to be a man and take some part in the fighting, but then I remembered my red cross.

Breakfast was provided by the 7th Fusiliers—eggs, bacon, kidneys and strawberry jam. It might be South

Africa, it might be the front, but by God, a Fusilier likes his British breakfast. The flies were terrible, though. Afterwards, Jennie was installed in the General's tent, to write notes to Jack and Winston:

I looked round with curiosity and interest at the general's quarters—a camp bed, a washing basin, a box, nothing more. Sitting on a camp stool with my feet on a tin box I was scribbling away, when a rider galloped up, calling out with a cheery voice, 'General, are you there?' His look of blank astonishment when he caught sight of me was most amusing. A woman in the camp and in the general's tent! It was a novelty! I explained. After a few laughing remarks he rode off.

His day must have been made; but alas, he was to be killed the next week.

On her return journey, Jennie visited the remount depot, and saw 2000 horses, most of which had just arrived from South America:

What a fate to be penned up for days on a rolling ship, then crammed into an open truck in a blazing sun, to be taken out, stiff, sore and dazed, given two days' rest, and then sent up to the front only to be food for Boer bullets! Poor things. So understanding. Such good friends. The hardships they have to undergo, and the lingering death many have and will meet, is one of the most hideous features of the war.

Back on board the *Maine* Jennie put such thoughts from her. She pinned up a large map and stuck flags in it to show the patients how the war was going. Then she was entertained by Captain Percy Scott on board HMS *Terrible,* though not without a soaking first. 'I preferred getting wet up to my waist—being caught in a huge wave—to being hauled on board in a wicker basket like a bale of cotton,' Jennie said. It was there that she heard of the relief of Ladysmith.

As soon as they were told of it such a grand cheer went up from the men, and another equally hearty when their captain informed them that they were to have grog all round. Lights were flashed—messages heliographed from Captain Percy Scott's electric shutter—to all the ships in the harbour; the band played itself tired, and the men sang themselves hoarse; and at last, after a bouquet of fireworks, we went to bed.

Jennie was able to visit Ladysmith after the siege had been lifted. She went up there with Winston and Miss Warrender:

One must see it all to realise the stupendous difficulties, the harsh impossible ground to get over, how it had to be gained inch by inch, the smallest mistake costing hundreds of men. The masses of shell and bullets on either side of the line, the dead horses, and the newly made graves, testified to the fierceness of the struggle. At one point we crossed a small bridge built up with sandbags, over which our men had to run singly under a terrible fire from three kopjes; we lost sixty-six men here. After two hours we came to an open plain glistening with the discarded tins of the advancing army, and further on we went through Intombi Camp, broiling in the blazing sun, a place of desolation and misery, and so on into Ladysmith. Blinding dust up to your ankles, scorching sun, shut up empty houses, an expression of resigned martyrdom on everyone's face—such was my first impression of Ladysmith.

Things soon cheered up, though. After making 'a hasty and apologetic toilette', Jennie dined with Sir Redvers Buller in a tent overlooking the town. Jennie brought back a souvenir—a shellcase from the gun named after her, with an inscription telling her of the damage she'd done.

Then it was time to go home. The *Maine* filled up with wounded and set off, stopping at St Helena to water. Jennie was much impressed with the grimness of Napoleon's place of exile. She thought he must have found it torture. The ship put in again at Madeira, and arrived at Southampton on 23 April. It had been away exactly four months.

Jennie's final version of the story was written seven years later, for her *Reminiscences,* and is mainly a précis of the letters in *The Anglo-Saxon,* with one or two additions too forthright, perhaps, for 1900. The behaviour of some army reserve nurses whom the *Maine* had carried from Cape Town to Durban disgusted her, for instance. Some of them had actually brought *maids* with them. Jennie, who can never have gone anywhere before in her life without a maid, was superbly scornful. But it is what she did not put in any of her versions which is most interesting. She never mentioned, for instance, that Jack had been one of her wounded. From her brief diary we find that she heard about it on 12 February, and went on the 14th to Pietermaritzburg to meet him. He carried a letter from Winston:

Chieveley Camp,
Natal

My dearest Mamma,   13 February, 1900

It is a coincidence that one of the first patients on board the *Maine* should be your own son. Jack, who brings you this letter, will tell you all about the skirmish and the other action he took part in. He behaved very well and pluckily and the Adjutant, the Colonel and his squadron leader speak highly of his conduct. There was for ten minutes quite a hot fire. And we had about ten men hit. Jack's wound is slight though not officially classed as such. The doctors tell me that he will take a month to recover and I advise you not to allow him to go back before he is quite well. He is unhappy at being taken off the board so early in the game and of course it is a great nuisance, but you may be glad with me that he is out of harm's way for a month. There will be a great battle in a few days and his presence—though I would not lift a finger to prevent him—adds much to my anxiety when there is fighting. . . .

Poor Jack! It is hard being the younger brother of a genius. Winston had seen action all round the world, and been under fire more times than he could remember. Now Jack, who had wanted to go into the army, but had a bad eye, and anyway Jennie couldn't find the money —who had been made to go into the City, which he hated—who had jumped at the chance to come to war—Jack was wounded in his first skirmish, and Winston was glad he was out of the way, he was such a worry to him. He was something of a worry to Jennie, too, it seems. While Jennie was enjoying herself on the *Terrible* she sent a headmatronly signal: TELL MY SON HE IS UNDER MARTIAL LAW AND HAS GOT TO REMAIN IN BED. He stayed with the *Maine,* convalescing, till she sailed from Durban on her way home, when he returned to his regiment.

Another person who is not mentioned anywhere by Jennie is, of course, George. He felt rather jealous when he heard that Jack was one of Jennie's patients:

I was so fearfully sorry to get your cable yesterday morning announcing the fact that poor old Jack had been wounded. Thank Heavens it is not serious, still I hope he has been sent down to the base so that you can nurse him. I envy him darling being nursed by you. I wish it had been my lot. . . .

George was feeling sorry for himself. The sun-stroke had turned out to have very serious side-effects, and the situation at home was far from easy. He wrote Jennie a series of long plaintive letters, asking her to hurry home:

Newlands Manor,
Lymington, Hants
January 18th, 1900

Oh my precious little Missie, I am so miserable at your not being in England, but I know I am selfish, & I

suppose you had to go, as you had been more or less
the leading spirit in the organisation of the whole ship.
I shall never forget my feelings when I got your wire
at St Vincent and I am ashamed to say, I thought hard
things about you. That if you really cared for me, you
would have realized how being ill, I naturally leant all
the more to you, and wanted your tender love &
companionship; also that if you had wanted to see me
you could have gone by the mail steamer, and caught
up the *Maine* as I suggested to you in my last cable,
inasmuch as your services on the journey out, could
not have been required. But now that I have received
all your letters I realize that you couldn't very well
help yourself; and I am ashamed of ever having had
unkind thoughts about my little Missie. Of course
darling you know I will wait patiently till you return,
and then fly to your dear arms, I shall count the days
till the time arrives that I can press you to my heart,
and lift up your dear face to kiss your sweet lips. Oh
little Missie mine dont stay long out at the Cape I
implore you. When I get you again I shall stick fast
to you like a limpet. You can count on me to be
absolutely true & faithful to you in every act & thought
till you return.

I am better considerably than I was; but still not up
to much. I am sorry to say that the sun-stroke I had
has affected my heart, I had two attacks of 'Angina
Pectoris' on the ship coming home; my word doesn't
it hurt, I thought I was going to die once. I am going
up to London next week to see a good doctor. I
haven't told mother or any of my female relations, as
they get so easily alarmed, so dont say anything about
it to anyone, as it is certain to get back. There is no
cause for alarm Missie mine, as every day I get better
so *you* need not be frightened. I heard from Leonie
on my arrival, I shall go & see her when I am in
London. You poor darling what an awful tossing you
must have got; I never heard of such an experience,
'hove to for 48 hours' in 'the Bay' sounds too dreadful.
Poor little Patsy looks very C.D. her nerves seem

to have suffered in my absence. Naturally they are all
thankful to get me back, even in a somewhat debili-
tated condition. The Former (Patsy) goes off to Daisy
tomorrow.

We are anxiously expecting news of Bullers advance
in Natal, he ought to have fought a big engagement by
now, pray God it is a Victory.

Come back soon to me my precious Missie, I love
you so so dearly, and miss you more than you can
imagine, its hateful being in England without you.

> Your ever loving
> George

The tone did not alter:

> 50 Park Street,
> Grosvenor Square, W.
> February 2nd, 1900

Oh Missie darling if ever there was a man who wanted
the one creature on earth he loved to be with him I
am he.

I have just received your wire redirected from Mil-
ford-on-sea, saying you are going to remain at Durban
a month, your last wire said you were returning as
soon as possible, so I thought & hoped, that when once
you had arrived at Durban and got things started on
board the *Maine* you would think of returning, I felt
so much happier than I did before I thought I should
[see] my own darling little Missie by the end of
February at least, and had thought out all sorts of
plans. My doctor has ordered me to go abroad in
about 6 weeks time, and I thought how heavenly it
would have been to have gone with you somewhere if
you would have come. And now all my pleasant ideas
& plans are frustrated by your wire, if you leave
Durban say the beginning of March you won't be
home before the beginning of April, and may miss me
altogether as by that time I may be well enough to
rejoin my battalion. If you had been ill, and I had
been obliged to leave you I should not have wasted a

moment in flying back to you at the very first opportunity, but it seems you are different or have altered.

I love you Missie darling as I never have loved, or shall ever love another woman, I have given you all I had to give, and all that was best in me, and shall never regret it until the day of my death. I cant tell you what a trying time I am having at home, when my mother was there it was alright, but now she has gone to be with Daisy. I am alone with my Father who never loses an opportunity of dropping hints about financial difficulties and how easily they could be overcome if I married an heiress, he also takes a pleasure in abusing all your friends, though he knows he dare not mention your name thus to me. Then again I am so fearfully depressed at having to leave all my pals in the regiment up at the front, I feel so useless to them & the regt., not being able to stand a months hard work. And lastly and worst of all your not being here makes it fifty thousand times worse. I meant to write you an amusing letter this mail, but your wire has made [me] feel so wretched. Forgive me *darling,* PRECIOUS Missie mine, if you felt as ill and as depressed as I do you would understand. I only came up for the day to see the doctor, whose account of me was not very satisfactory, and to see H.R.H. who asked me searching questions which I refused to answer. Ah Missie come back to your George who loves you more than you were ever before loved, and who wants you so.

I feel so *selfish* but must write as I do,

George

The Prince of Wales was trying to find out whether absence had made either Jennie's or George's heart less fond. He not only saw and cross-questioned George, he wrote several times to Jennie in South Africa about what he woundingly referred to as her flirtation. On receiving telegrams from George like this, Jennie must have seriously thought of giving him up:

SEE NEWSPAPERS MAINE LEAVING IMMEDIATELY YET
YOU REMAINING DURBAN THIS IS YOUR EFFORT TO
RETURN

GEORGE

He quickly apologized. Life wasn't easy, he was ill and
irritable, and his only fun was making a golf-links in
the park to while away the time till her return.

On her way home to this importunate lover, Jennie
busied herself writing her report and her article for *The
Anglo-Saxon,* which had been carrying on perfectly well
without her. At Madeira she learned of the Committee's
plans for the *Maine.* She wrote to Winston, who was
supposed to pass the letter on to Jack:

The ship is coming out again within a week of arriving as we have plenty of money—I am much
worried as Leonie is going to have an infant the 1st
week of June & as she has not had one for 11 years
& is always rather bad—I hate being away—she is
counting on me—Yet I hate leaving the Ship—tho'
HRH. & everyone seems to take it for granted that I
am not going again & that I shall have done enough—
Bless you my darlings. . . .

She had asked Leonie to look after George while she
was away, and Leonie had done so to the extent of
enraging George's father:

I am aware that you have assisted Lady Randolph
Churchill in her insane infatuation for my son—because a telegram signed 'Melanie',[3] which I understand
is your name, fell into my hands in which you invited
him to meet the hospital ship *Maine* on its arrival at
Southampton.

I wish seriously to ask you if you consider a marriage which I am told is again talked of between Lady
Randolph and my son can possibly lead to the happiness of either? To begin with she is older than his
own mother. She will lose the name in which she is

best known to the world and its rank and position and she will find herself married to a young man of such an impressionable nature that only a few weeks ago he proposed marriage to a young and pretty girl who refused his attentions—notwithstanding his protestations of love and his repudiation of your sister. The life of a couple so ill-assorted is doomed, is painful to think of—and the marvel to me is that a woman as talented and experienced as your sister could coolly contemplate it as nothing out of the common.

I can only add that if this marriage takes place, it will estrange the whole of my family from my son and so I have told him.

Had George really proposed to someone else? It seems hard to believe. And telegrams do not usually 'fall into' people's hands—people pick them up deliberately. George was right to be wary of his family's snooping. At any rate, the row between him and his father may have been responsible for his failure to come, as promised, to meet Jennie at Southampton:

> Ruthin Castle,
> N. Wales.

My precious little Missie,   April 21st, 1900
I have written to you care of the harbour-master Southampton, to be given to you on your arrival. But in case you dont get it, I am sending this by Leonie to give you on seeing you. I could not allow you to set foot on English soil without receiving a message from me, as I shall not be there myself.
Oh my sweet little Missie the joy of seeing you again and clasping you to me, I *love you* darling I LOVE YOU. Do send me a wire care of Station Master Rugby, telling me of your arrival, & then I will come straight to you. My train arrives at 5.45. Please Missie Mine lets be quite alone the 1st evening can we do you think? I am counting every hour every minute till we meet. I am by way of beginning to do duty with the new 3rd battn. on May 1st. I put it off a week, as I want

you if possible to come away with me somewhere for that week Do! surely you deserve a holiday. If you cannot, I shall recommence duty at once, as it would not do to stop in London & not do so. Bless you my own, I kiss you a 1000 times.

> Your own devoted
> George

So Jennie was back, and nothing whatever had changed. The long separation—they had not seen each other for six months—had done none of the things devoutly wished by almost everyone except themselves. It seemed they really *must* get married now.

But Jennie still wavered and havered. She decided not to go back to South Africa with the *Maine,* however. Instead she resumed her old social round, dinners and operas and weekends in the country. She could not decide what to do. On 24 May she wrote to Winston:

[I] am more busy than I have ever been—preparing for the 3rd voyage of the *Maine*—finishing my 'Hospital Letters' which Longman is going to publish[4] & trying to cope with bills & bores!—The *Maine* ought to arrive today at Capetown—The Port Medical Officer has been asked to fill her up as quickly as possible—she is to return at once—& go out again—If this trip has not done well without me—I shall probably go out the 3rd voyage—But all my plans are vague—Sometimes I think I may marry G.W. I need not to you go over the old ground—but added to the reasons in favour of it is his extraordinary devotion to me through all these trying times & my absence—Also the fact that it is possible for him to help me in a money way in the future if not at present —There is no doubt that you will never settle down until you have a home of your own, & in the 4 years that I have had this house you have spent about 3 mths in all in it—I mention this to show you why I do not feel that I would be breaking up our home if I

do marry—But there are so many things against my
doing it that I doubt its ever coming off—At the same
time do not be astonished if I did—You know what
you are to me & how you can *now* & *always* count on
me—I am intensely fond of you, & apart from this—
my heart goes out to you & I understand you as no
other women ever will—Pamela is devoted to you &
if yr love has grown as hers—I have no doubt it is
only a question of time for you 2 to marry—What a
comfort it will be to you to settle down in comparative comfort—I am sure you are sick of the war & its
horrors—You will be able to make a decent living out
of your writings & your political career will lead you
to big things—Probably if you married an heiress you
would not work half so well—But you may have a
chance in America—tho I do not urge you to try—you
know I am not mercenary either for myself or you
boys—More's the pity! I long to see you & have a
good talk—My return home owing to the stupidity of
the Committee: was a fiasco—but people are gradually understanding the work I have done, & in any
case I have my own consciousness of something
accomplished.

That makes it clear that she was not thinking only of
herself, or only of her own marriage. Other people were
beginning to find the whole subject a bore. At Whitsun,
Jennie was supposed to go with George to stay with
Daisy Warwick, but she was summoned to Sandringham
instead, where she was reported to be 'just back from
her hospital ship which had been a boon in South
Africa, but fractiously insisting she is going to marry
George Cornwallis-West'. George, at Warwick Castle,
got more sympathy from a lady he took out in a launch,
who said they should simply consider themselves. He
asked Daisy if Jennie couldn't have got out of going to
Sandringham, and she thought she probably could have
done, but it was too late, of course.

If they were beginning to bore their friends, then
enough was enough. For Ascot, Jennie went to stay

with her old friend Consuelo Yznaga, now Duchess of Manchester: George came too. He hacked over to Pirbright each morning to attend parade, then returned for the racing in the afternoon. On the Thursday of that week, their engagement was announced in the *Daily Telegraph*. At once George received a peremptory order from his commanding officer to go to see him. If he married Jennie, he was told, he would have to leave the regiment. George saw red. Jennie was a friend of Colonel Hamilton's, everybody liked her, there was no rule against subalterns marrying: the ultimatum was an outrage. So he jumped into a hansom and went to see the Adjutant-General of the Army, Sir Evelyn Wood, whom he knew slightly. Wood was on his way to lunch, but let George explain the situation in the cab, and promised to help him. George, however, had gone to the wrong man, for the regimental commander regarded Wood as 'the enemy of the Brigade of Guards', and his intervention was bitterly resented. George was told his presence in the regiment was no longer desired.

He consulted with Jennie, who promptly wrote to Lord Lansdowne, the Secretary of State for War. Lansdowne said George should ignore his Colonel's threats, and as an old friend, wished her all possible happiness. The Commander-in-Chief of the Army, he told her, was entirely on her side. Civil as well as military authority was on Jennie's side by now, too. The Prince of Wales accepted that she was going to marry George, and helped in the crisis. Jennie managed to have a word with him:

Sunday, 8.20

My Precious Beloved, Your dear letter has just arrived, I love it, it was the next best thing to seeing you yourself, and went some way towards making my evening more cheery, although nothing will ever be able to make up for the actual person (your sweet self) not being wherever I am. I am glad H.R.H. is civil, I hope you will be able to have a talk with him this evening. If you do you might suggest I am very

anxious to have an interview with him on the subject.
But do not like to bother him. I see the Princess of
Wales H.S. arrived at Southampton yesterday. I
expect your *Maine* going to China will create any
amount of envy amongst 'Yeomanry Hosiptal' *chair-
men* & such like!! [5] Miss Warrender came and had a
chat with me, she seems nice, but does gabble so, I
cant understand half she says. Shelagh & my uncle
came but only stopped about 10 minutes. I was not
very sorry *entre nous* they are so frivolous.

The doctor does not think I shall be able to go out
tomorrow, my cough is very troublesome still. He told
me I might come down to the drawing-room so I
thought I might as well come down to the library
where it is warmer. Oh Missie darling I have been
thinking of you all day, & wanting you so, I long to
be married, & lay myself out to make the remainder of
your life as happy as it lies in my power to do. Bless
you my own Beloved Missie, I kiss you 1000 times
everywhere.

> Your own devoted
> George

I have been improving my mind by reading a history
of France.

Jennie saw to it that George got his interview. The
Prince went straight to the point. Did George intend to
make the army his profession for the rest of his life, or
not? If he did, he should sit tight. If not, there was no
point in making enemies of men who had been his
friends, he should go on half-pay for six months or a
year, and look round to see if there was something else
he would rather do. It was eminently sensible advice,
and George took it.

Not only was the Prince civil and sensible, his
brother, the Duke of Connaught, offered to put the
forthcoming marriage before Queen Victoria in its
proper light. Meanwhile Jennie had cabled to both
Jack and Winston, telling them the news. She followed

the cable to Jack with a letter—Winston was already on his way home.

35A, Great Cumberland Place, W.
June 23rd, 1900

My dearest Jack—I hope this will find you with yr face more or less turned towards home—I dined with Cassel last night—& he said he thought that now all danger was over—you had done yr duty by yr country, & that you ought to come home & attend to yr business—I pointed out to him that you might have to stay with the regt. until it disbanded—But perhaps this will shortly take place. It is rather hard on me never to hear one word from either of you boys. At the same time I understand how difficult it must be to find the time, & perhaps the material when one is on the move like you—My darling boy I wonder if you will have had the cable I sent you telling you that I was going to marry George? I also wrote a long letter to Winston on the subject telling him to forward it to you—I cant think what he is about—I hear he has not written to Pamela for 8 weeks—Now as regards my marriage I should like to tell you all my plans for you & myself—but it must be in a very concise form as time presses—& I have *such* a lot to do—*The Review* —my book—my marriage! I have much to write— Now listen darling boy—I have thought over everything & have come to the conclusion that for *many* reasons—it would be unwise for either you or Winston to live with us once we are married—Knowing how fond I am of you both you will believe that I have not come to this conclusion hastily—It seems hard—& it gives me a pang every time I think of it— but I *know* it is the wisest plan—I shd like you & Winston to have rooms together, which I would furnish for you, & arrange your life as far as material comfort goes to the best of my ability—I need hardly say how *more* than welcome you will always be here —you cld look upon it as yr home for everything but sleeping—George is helping me in every way possible

to make my income larger by putting my affairs
straight—As I wrote to Winston, I hope to be able to
make you both independent of me—by giving you a
certain amount of capital—Of course this wld have to
be worked out when you come of age next year—
Meanwhile if all goes well George and I propose getting married very quietly (but not at the Registry
Office) on the 28th of July—I have many things to
settle & arrange—We shall go to Paris—& then to
Aix—& after that here—God bless you—My *darling*
boy—You must stand by me—I have, & will, always
by you—

> Your loving Mother
> J.R.C.[6]

Jack felt rather abandoned in South Africa, and this
letter cannot have done much to raise the low spirits
in which he'd written on 2 June:

> I am beginning to feel like the prodigal son who is
> sent away to these horrible colonies with instructions
> never to be seen or heard of again. . . .

Winston had failed to forward letters as requested.
Jennie felt somewhat guilty about Jack, perhaps. She
wrote more regularly now. In her letter of 30 June she
said:

> Winston will be here in time for my wedding if all
> goes well—It will be very quiet—no breakfast—ex-
> cept for the family—but I won't do it in a 'hole &
> corner' fashion as tho' I was ashamed of it—I pray
> from the bottom of my heart that it won't make you
> unhappy— You know how dearly I love you both—
> & the thought that it may hurt you—is the one cloud
> on my happiness—But you won't grudge me the lat-
> ter?—Nothing could exceed George's goodness &
> devotion—& I think we shall be very happy—Every-
> thing I can do for you I will—Meanwhile my real
> friends are most kind—& have given me charming

presents—& they all like him so much that they are reconciled. . . . Leonie has had a boy—I do so *long* to hear from you & how you are—you must be rather short of clothing—Best love—

> Your loving Mother
> J.R.C.

When he got the news, Jack did not exactly put Jennie's mind at ease. He wrote at the end of a letter only 'Good best love to George'. What he thought, what he said to Winston, what Winston said to him—they neither of them put on paper.

On the morning of her wedding Jennie wrote to Jack once more:

> 35A, Great Cumberland Place, W.
> My darling Jack   July 28th, 1900

I am more than distressed to think that my letters with the exception of one have not reached you—You must know that your 'Mommer' would not forget you —I wired you & Winston that I was going to marry George—& here I am actually at the day—I would give much if you were here & I could give you a big fat kiss & could assure you with my own lips what you already know—& that is that I love you & Winston *dearly* & that *no one* can ever come in between us— I shall always remain your *best* friend & do everything in the world for you—You both can count on me—I am glad to think you know & like George—He has behaved like a brick—By next mail I will write & tell you all about the wedding—Sunny[7] is giving me away & I am well supported by the Churchill family. People have been most kind & given us heaps of presents— I want you to come home as soon as you decently can —Both Winston & I hate to have you away—I have all sorts of plans for you & want to make yr life as pleasant as possible. God bless you *my darling boy ever*.

> your loving Mother
> J.R.C.

The marriage took place at St Paul's, Knightsbridge. Winston was there, but none of the Cornwallis-Wests, to George's intense regret. For their honeymoon they went first to Broughton Castle, near Oxford, home of Lord Saye and Sele. From there George wrote to Winston on 30 July:

My dear Winston,

I would have written to you yesterday only there is only one post out, and that is at 8.45 a.m. so you can understand why you received no letter from me this morning.

This is an ideal place for any couple to come to, honey-moon or otherwise, we are most comfortable the best of food, drink and everything, besides a most delightful old rambling weather-beaten, stone-roofed house of the 14th century.

My dear Winston I cannot impress upon you how much I appreciate the line you have taken as regards my marriage to your mother. I have always liked and admired you, but I do so ten times more now. I only wish, as I wrote and told my father, that my family could have taken a leaf out of your book. Nothing could have exceeded the sympathy and kindness which you, and all the Churchills have shewn me. I hope always, as now, to be a real true friend to you, and never to come in between yourself and your mother. If I ever do, which God forbid, you can always refer me to this letter which is a record of the feelings I have in the bottom of my heart towards you and yours. We arrive tomorrow at 2.15 will you order lunch for 3 unless you have another coming. *A demain* my dear friend.

Always *your* sincere friend
George C-W

Winston reported on the wedding to Jack next day:

Mamma was married to George West on Saturday and everything went off very well. The whole of the

Churchill family from Sunny downwards was drawn in a solid phalanx and their approval ratified the business. The wedding was very pretty and George looked supremely happy in having at length obtained his heart's desire. As we already know each other's views on the subject, I need not pursue it.

After Broughton the newly-weds went to Paris and Belgium and Scotland: the honeymoon, in fact, lasted a couple of months. Staying, as she had so often in the past, at Guisachan, with the Tweedmouths, Jennie decided to leave George there for a few days, while she went and campaigned again for Winston at Oldham. She had been quarreling with John Lane, the publisher of *The Anglo-Saxon Review,* from early on, and the magazine's failure to make money was worrying: it needed her attention. But Winston begged her to come, so she went. He invited George, too, but no doubt Jennie thought she would be more effective on her own. George wrote to her on 29 September:

Guisachan,
Beauly, N.B.
Sept. 28th, 1900

My beloved little Wife

I was glad to hear from you today, that you are comfortable, & none the worse for your tiresome journey. Dont overdo it darling will you, for my sake.

I have read yesterdays *Daily Mail,* poor Winston, I can well understand his feelings, & how exasperated he must be.

My portmanteau has been found, and where do you think at Ballater, it was never put in there, I did not go stalking today but went fishing instead. I caught a salmon 8 lbs the first in my life, I was very excited, but it cant be compared to stalking.

I do implore of you really to make up your mind to get rid of Lane, this is a golden opportunity, which you must really take. You will never make the *Review* pay until you do.

Dearest little Missie you know well that anything

that I can do to make things easier, from a pecuniary point of view, is done more than willingly, & is nothing to what I would do for you. Bless you my own, come back safe & well to your loving

                                    Husband

As Winston said, George had obtained his heart's desire. He could call himself 'Husband', and give advice, and help with the bills. The only question was, how long would it be before his heart found some other object of desire? But no cloud marred Jennie's happiness that autumn. Winston was elected on 1 October. The Prince did not use his sanction, indeed he wrote to her as 'My dear Mrs Jennie Cornwallis-West! & *Chère Amie!*' All troubles behind her, Jennie was now ready to face the twentieth century.

NOTES

1. Though leaving later than Jennie, Jack travelled by the much faster mail steamer, and got to Cape Town first.
2. Captain Percy Scott of HMS *Terrible* was supposed to go on the expedition, but was too busy. It was from his ship that the gun named after Jennie came.
3. The Colonel seems to have become over-excited.
4. He did not, in fact, publish them, perhaps because they were not long enough to make a book.
5. The *Maine* did not go on a third voyage to South Africa, instead it went to China, where the European powers were busy suppressing the Boxer Rising.
6. Jennie was now signing herself Jennie Randolph Churchill.
7. Randolph's nephew, the 9th Duke of Marlborough.

13

MRS PAT

Jennie's new life was like her old. George was rather dazed by the splendour of it. As he wrote in his memoirs:

Those were wonderful days. Taxation and the cost of living were low; money was freely spent and wealth was everywhere in evidence. Moreover it was possessed largely by the nicest people, who entertained both in London and in the country. Dinners were Gargantuan affairs, far too long, but although there were innumerable courses, the foreign fashion of serving innumerable wines had disappeared. It was very seldom that sherry was even offered with the soup. Champagne, port and old brandy were the order of the day, or rather, night. One or two hostesses, notably Lady Hindlip, all the Rothschilds, and Mrs Ronnie Greville, had wonderful cooks, but on the whole the cooking was indifferent and meretricious, though the same could not be said of the wines. The champagne vintages from 'eighty to 'eighty-seven were infinitely superior to anything since produced. They were also considerably more potent.

Wealth was not quite as universal as George suggests. After paying many of Jennie's debts, he himself had only a small income to live on, and it did not begin to suffice for Jennie:

In money matters she was without any sense of proportion. The value of money meant nothing to

her: what counted with her were the things she got
for money, not the amount she had to pay for them.
If something of beauty attracted her, she just had to
have it; it never entered her head to stop and think
how she was going to pay for it. During all the years
we lived together the only serious misunderstandings
which ever took place between us were over money
matters. Her extravagance was her only fault, and,
with her nature, the most understandable, and therefore the most forgivable.

George resigned from the army, and sought the advice of Sir Ernest Cassel, who told him: 'There are
many young men of your class who should never go
east of Temple Bar. Perhaps you are one of them.'
George, he meant, was not for the City. More or less
the same advice came from the millionaire Mr Mc-
Ewen, father of the hostess with the wonderful cook,
Mrs Ronnie Greville. He looked at George and said:
'Some men are born to make money, it just comes
natural to them; others never will. Maybe ye're one
of the latter.' Both men were right. It was not in
George to make money. Cassel arranged for him to
become a director of the Potteries Electric Traction
Company, which he seems to have enjoyed, but four
years later he joined up with a northcountryman
named Wheater to found a small issuing house in the
City. He did not consult Cassel or any of his City
acquaintances before taking this step, which was to
prove disastrous. But in the beginning the new firm
prospered, making over £23,000 in its first year.
Even so, George was swindled by a crooked lawyer
in 1906 of £8000, and his brother-in-law the Duke
of Westminster had to come secretly to the rescue.

In 1905 Jennie and George moved from London to
a beautiful, moated, red-brick, Jacobean house near
St Albans, called Salisbury Hall. It was only seventeen
miles from Hyde Park Corner, but felt in the depths
of the country. There they gave week-end parties for
their many friends. The Salisbury Hall visitors' book

survives, and the names in it are a roll-call of the high and mighty: Connaught and Curzon, Manchester and Roxburghe, Marlborough, Harcourt, Lennox and Lytton. Frewens and Leslies were frequent visitors, of course, as were Jack and Winston and Winston's faithful secretary, Eddie Marsh. On 27 May 1906 the King came: the ground-floor rooms were rearranged for his convenience. With him that weekend were his current favourite, Mrs Alice Keppel, Mr and Mrs William James, the young American Duchess of Marlborough, Consuelo Vanderbilt, Prince Francis of Teck, and various others. It was Edwardian England at its most full-blown.

On more family occasions, two names stand out: Lady Gwendeline Bertie, always known as Goonie, and Clementine Hozier. Goonie was the daughter of the Earl of Abingdon, and it seems that Winston may have had thoughts of her for himself, but it was the quiet Jack whom she loved. Their engagement in the autumn of 1907 must have inspired Winston, for the following spring he fell in love with Clementine, daughter of Jennie's old friend from the 1880s, Lady Blanche Hozier. Both boys were married in the summer of 1908.

By then the prophets of doom had been proved right about Jennie's marriage to George. An undated note gives some indication of the strain it had undergone:

45 Devonshire Street,
Portland Place, W.

Darling old Puss-Cat

I have got back to bed as I am tired.

I'm awfully worried as I feel you thought I chasséd[1] you. You know I didn't & that I'd sooner see you than all the others.

Your loving
Husband

It hardly matters who 'all the others' were, but others there were. George's heart was weak in both senses. In

March 1906, only a couple of months before the royal visit to Salisbury Hall, two more notes show that Jennie and George were actually apart for a while:

> 50 Park Street,
> Grosvenor Square, W.
> March 8th, 1906

Darling old Puss-Cat

I didn't mean to be beastly last night. But you will admit the events of the last few days have been somewhat disturbing. Just off to hunt. Bless you

> yr loving
> Husband

> 50 Park Street,
> Grosvenor Square, W.
> March 9th, 1906

My Beloved,

I am not going down to the Guthries, who have put me off. So I have written proposing myself to Cassel. I will call & see you this evening about. 8.0. before dinner.

> Your loving
> Husband

The strain was apparent to everyone. George's sister, Daisy, Princess of Pless, wrote in her diary for 14 April 1907 that Jennie still loved George immensely, 'poor dear'. 'She is uncommonly nice and still very handsome, but of course the difference in age is a sad and terrible drawback (no babies possible).' It sounds as though George was beginning to make excuses. Jennie was unhappy, even bitter:

> Salisbury Hall,
> St Albans

Dearest Leonie   May 15th, 1907

I feel that I was cross & unreasonable the other day when I saw you—I am sorry—The fact is when I go to London—there are only 2 people I ever try to see, one is Winston the other you—Both are often sad disappointments—one on account of work—the other on account of pleasure. I go away feeling sore at heart —I snatch a few minutes of Winston's society, by driving him to the Colonial Office,[2] & the most you can offer me—are a few words uncomfortably (for me) at the telephone—But I have made up my mind —& shall not risk it any more—You know I love you & that when you want me I am to be found—I like to think that you are enjoying yrself & making up for all those dull years when as you say yrself—your greatest excitement was to see me dress for a ball—Make the most of it all while it amuses you—You looked very bright & happy last night Keep so—

> Yr loving
> Jennie

If ever a letter said 'Nobody loves me', this was it. But if Jennie showed Leonie her unhappiness, she had her own cure for it. She began to write her memoirs. She did not find it easy, particularly when Winston was scathing about her political chapters, but when *The Reminiscences of Lady Randolph Churchill* was published in England and America in 1908, it was quite a success, in spite of being extremely discreet. Jennie thought she might take a leaf out of Winston's book and do an American lecture tour. She consulted Henry James, the novelist, who sent her a most delightful reply:

Dear Mrs West   Reform Club,
                                       Pall Mall, S.W.
    Your letter overtakes me in town. I am much thrilled by your idea of possible Lectures in the U.S., & give you with pleasure the benefit of my very limited experience upwards of four years ago, I say very limited because that describes the real *accident* & the particularly circumscribed nature of my small per-

formance. I went to America (the 1st time for 24
years) with no such notion & nothing prepared; but
was almost immediately *asked*—promptly written to
by the Secretaries of those essentially American insti-
tutions known as Ladies' Clubs, & which swarm all
over the country. They earnestly proposed it—my
'addressing them on some literary or other subject',
& under competent advice I responded on trial, 1st to
Philadelphia. I had an old sketched lecture (a mere
beginning) on Balzac (planned & laid aside ten years
before:) this I sent out to England for, & 'worked up'
& finished & this I delivered to about twenty (*only*)
of the said Ladies' Clubs—& only in the big places.
It was a bad subject—nevertheless one had a degree
of success, & one saw thereby the place, the people
(the people oh *too* copiously!) the manners etc, as
perhaps one wouldn't have done otherwise. A 'personal' subject wd. have had of course much more
success—& if I had gone with a plan I should [have]
done differently. But I had nothing to do with any
bureau or agent or big organisation. *That* I could
never have stood—ruin, madness, illness, & perhaps
money, would have overwhelmed me on those lines. I
simply said Yes to the best & most important of the
Ladies Clubs that asked me & absolute no to the
others. That selection works best by the clue of fees.
When they inquired as to my Fee I said Fifty Pounds
& closed with those who wd. give that. (The smaller
clubs give less.) But twenty gave me the said $250 for
my hour—from New York to Los Angeles California.
And I delivered but the one poor literary Lecture—
warning them as to exactly what it would be. It was
interesting, amusing—& very fatiguing! The meeting
the number of *people* involved is the drawback—all
very pleasant & kind, but of a terrific monotony & in-
distinguishability! The being 'run' by a regular Agency
or 'Lyceum' must be awful & fatal—though, if done
on high terms, likely to be proportionally lucrative—
I mean as lucrative as dreadful! However, *you* can't
possibly fail, I am sure, to have a huge success &

vulgarly speaking, a big harvest. The only thing is to to be able to *stand* it—& to be confident of *being* able. Speak to them of your personal experiences & observations (could you have 'kept back' for the purpose part of the matter of your delightful book, *that* would have been the valuable note:) that is really all they want & to look at you for all they are worth. But don't *tie* yourself too much before getting there. Leave something—much—for the occasion.

> Your most truly
> Henry James

Oct. 5, 1908

Jennie abandoned the idea of a lecture tour, though one feels that Henry James was right, and she would have been a great success, even though she never enjoyed speaking in public. Instead, she wrote a play. It was called *His Borrowed Plumes,* and according to George, it was Jennie's own idea to get the celebrated actress and wit Mrs Patrick Campbell to produce it and play the leading role. That winter George and Jennie rented the Prime Minister, Mr Asquith's, house in Cavendish Square. Mrs Pat, as she was known, was a constant visitor, and agreed to do the play at a series of matinees the following summer. Later, Mrs Pat was to be scornful about the play and the great social flutter it caused, and even Jennie had early doubts. She wrote to Leonie in March saying 'Sometimes I feel despondent and doubtful of my being able to make it a really good play. I should hate mediocrity.' But when the play came to be rehearsed, she seems thoroughly to have enjoyed it:

> Polesden Lacey,[3]
> Dorking
> June 27th, '09

Darling Snippy—Yr good news was given to me by Mary[4]—I am *so* glad Norman[5] is improving—What a wretched time you have been having & we want you here so much. The Connaughts are coming to my play

on the 8th. I am rather surprised that they have not
invited me to tea, or to come & see me. But you know
I have always thought that they did not like me over
much—one in the family is enough—The rehearsals
are getting on & this week there are 2 be two daily—
Mrs. Pat. has really been an angel & the play wld not
exist without her—but we spar something of no consequence—I can't understand why I feel so calmly
about the play—Bernstein[6] tells me he is *dans les
trances*[7] weeks beforehand—Perhaps I do not know
the horrors before me!—I gave a supper party at the
Ritz last Friday—too successful for words. . . . We
kept it up till 2.30—even Gladys staying[8]—wild
dances—& fandangos—everyone taking the floor—

It was as well that the fandangos took place before
the play opened, for there were to be none after. *His
Borrowed Plumes* was not exactly a failure, but it was
not a success, either, and the fashionable audience and
its hats came in for as much appreciative comment as
the play itself. It was a comedy about two women
writers, one of whom tries to steal the other's husband.
Unfortunately, the events on stage were all too closely
paralleled by those off, and there was to be no happy
ending. As a result of the play, George went off with
Mrs Pat. They drove to Burnham Beeches and read
plays together. Though the marriage struggled on for a
few years, it was really over.

It must have been with very mixed feelings that
Jennie had heard of the death of Charles Kinsky's wife
earlier in 1909. The Kinsky's had been to stay at Salisbury Hall, so presumably Jennie was on friendly terms.
It is sad that the only letter of Charles's that Jennie kept
should have been this one:

Wien,
1, Freiung 4
23/IV. 09

Dearest Jennie,
    So many thanks for your kind letter.—Yes you are
right I feel it more &—deeper than I could say—but

I should feel small before her indeed & the memory
of all that quiet natural—honest pluck & courage with
which she died—if I was to give way.—The peace &
pluck thats left in me I owe to her—the best & last gift
of love that she left behind to me even in her sufferings
& her death.—& that is more much more than most
people could imagine. Its as real & honest as she has
been in life & even death.—

Your book I have found here on my return & I
shall read it as soon as I get a little rest of all the
tedious business that awaited me here on my sad
return & the hundreds & hundreds letters of condo-
lence that I have to answer now.—So many thanks
for it & above all for your letter & all the kind thoughts
of me.—from all my heart.

Yours ever
Charles

From all his heart, he said. What secret regrets there
must have been both in London and Austria.

II

The best cure for the blues, Jennie thought, was a visit
to the couturier Worth, but the next best was hard
work. Her experience in the theatre had not daunted her
—she wrote a second play, in fact, which was put on
briefly in Glasgow in 1913. If she could not make
money as a playwright herself, she could at least raise
if for other people. The National Theatre was then little
more than an idea, but Jennie sat on the Committee and
helped put on a successful Shakespearean ball at the
Royal Albert Hall in 1911. (She went as Olivia.) The
ball gave her the idea for a whole Shakespearean exhibition to be held at Earl's Court, with Elizabethan
shops and sideshows, and a special club called The
Mermaid Tavern. Jennie was not entirely altruistic
about it: she was to receive a percentage of the profits:

they might be very large: the exhibition might go to America and Canada.

Shapespeare's England, as it was called, was an excellent idea, which might today, with modern leisure and modern advertising, have been a great success with large crowds. Alas, in 1912 it wasn't. The reasons for its financial failure can be easily guessed from a study of the lavish programme for the Tournament which was to be the exhibition's climax. It was the first Tournament to be held since 1839, and it was highly spectacular, with real jousting by real dukes and earls, and a great parade of horsemen in splendid costume. All Jennie's friends and relations were made to take part, except Winston, who was now in the Cabinet, and perhaps felt he had enough tilting to be getting on with in the House of Commons. Jack Leslie and Hugh Warrender were among 'The Martiall's Men': Sunny Marlborough and Lords Ashby St Ledgers and Tweedmouth, all nephews of Randolph, were among the jousters: Eddie Marsh was a trumpeter. Claire Frewen, now married to Wilfred Sheridan, was one of the 'Wayting Ladyes' on the Queen of Beauty. Among others in the Queen's train were Muriel Wilson, Lady Diana Manners (later Cooper), and two girls to become notorious sixty years later for their stormy love-affair, Victoria Sackville-West and Violet Keppel. The Princess Errant was played by Daisy Pless: in her escort was Charles Kinsky. Jack Churchill led the parade of Knights: George brought up the rear.

It was all gorgeous and rich and colossally expensive, and the tickets were so dear that almost no one came. There were no profits from the exhibition or from the Mermaid Tavern. *Shakespeare's England* did not go to America, or Canada. Fortunately one of George's rich lady friends, Mrs Leeds, had stumped up a large sum, for which she got her reward in the shape of a husband: Prince Christopher of Greece, who had also been part of Daisy Pless's escort.

Jennie's own marriage, however, was nearing its end.

In August 1910 she had written to George's mother about it. Her draft, with its original erasures, survives:

My dear Patsy

Please don't apologize—I am only too glad that the house can be of use to you—I understand from Walden[9] that George returns tomorrow—It is tiresome for him that the City should require his presence so much—as fresh air and an active life would do so much for his health & incidentally his peace of mind —You know that our relations have become very strained ~~on my part~~ nearly to breaking point. As he is your son—your only son—& I am sure in your own way you love him—I implore ~~of~~ you to think out ~~for him~~ *without any consideration of me*—what is best for *him*—He can have his freedom if he wants it—free to marry Mrs Patrick Campbell or anyone else he thinks would make him happy—I have done my best & have failed—~~There is much that I could say but I will refrain.~~ In respect to money & extravagance ~~of~~ with which he has reproached me there is absolutely nothing to choose between us. In fact if our mutual finances were looked into I think mine would come out the best—I ~~make~~ seek no excuse for my own shortcomings—they are many—~~we are but human but in many ways I can claim to have done my best but~~ I have loved him more than anyone on earth & have *always* been true & loyal.

Yours affectly
Jennie C-W

By April 1911 things were so bad that Winston and Jack had to come to the rescue:

10 Talbot Square,
Hyde Park
April 4, 1911

Dear Mama—It was a shock to get your wire this afternoon. I went off to Winston who is much upset on your account—We tried to get hold of G., but he will not be back until tomorrow.

W will see him then, & have a clear understanding with him as to our opinion of affairs. What he can hope to gain by behaving like a blackguard I cannot understand.

Dont be too depressed—when all this is over—you will find yourself more settled & happier than you have been for some time, and you will come back again nearer to W & me whose love is always just the same.

Dont be pessimistic—The post is off, so goodbye —best love from both of us

I have sent £100 to Smith Bank—from both of us—50 is from Winston

                                        Jack

Winston found time from his duties to see George, and Clementine wrote a sympathetic letter:

                         Wednesday
My Darling B.M.[10]   33, Eccleston Square, S.W.

I am *so* grieved that you should be unhappy—This is just a line to bring you my love & sympathy—I can't bear that you should be sad. I have not seen Winston since he has seen G. but he telephoned to me & said G. seemed much upset—But of course he did not say much on the telephone.

Dearest try not to be too miserable—I am sure it will come right—after a little time—G must love you —You have been so much to each other. I don't know what has happened—Please don't think me indiscreet or impertinent to write to you about your private affairs, but you seem so far away abroad & I want to tell you how much we all love you & how sorry we are. I wish you were not away Darling B.M.

                         Your loving Bru
                         Clementine

Winston is at the House all the time this week. No dinner—no time for anything because of the Parliament Bill—He is in charge when the Prime Minister is not in the House.

Goonie wrote, too:

10 Talbot Square,
Hyde Park

My Sweet B.M.   7th April
    This is just a line to remind you that Jack and I are always there by you, ready to do anything and everything for you, that we love you & that you ask of us whatever you want or want us to do & it shall be done—dearest B.M. you must never forget that or hesitate a moment—Jacks is most frightfully unhappy about you, & he would give his blood for your happiness—you can trust him and rely upon him, he is the most devoted & loyal of sons—
    Bless you my dearest B.M. & I kiss you with my whole heart.

Your devoted
Goonie

Jennie could not ask for two nicer daughters-in-law.
    George must have asked to come back this time, for later that month Winston checked a draft of a letter Jennie wrote to him from their home in Norfolk Street, Mayfair:

2, Norfolk Street,
Park Lane,

My dear George   April 19th, '11
    Certainly come back to your own home—& with God's help we will start afresh—I see no reason why we should not be able to live in peace—I only want of you respect and *consideration* which is due to me as your wife And on my side I will always try & help you in every way possible—In respect to our financial arrangements—these can be discussed amicably later —I accept your statement in respect to the notices to servants writing to people, etc—I will only add that I

want you thoroughly to understand that you return at your own wish & without any pressure or coercion from me—I do not wish later on to be reproached for not having given you your freedom.

Meanwhile your room is ready for you when you choose to occupy it.

Yrs affectly
Jennie

Winston suggested cutting from 'reproached' to the end of the sentence. 'Freedom has more meanings than one,' he commented.

But if George returned, it was not for long. As his business slowly collapsed, he took to travelling. In 1910 he went to Mexico: in 1911 to America. On both occasions he was seriously ill. The end of the marriage came with the end of 1912. Jennie must have written to George that Christmas. He replied from Eaton Hall, the home of the Duke of Westminster:

Eaton,
Chester
Dearest Jennie   Dec 29th, 1912

I was glad to get your kind generous letter. I have put off answering it, as I honestly could not bring myself to write the other. However I am certain we neither of us wish to again go through the terrible ordeal of parting, and as after all that has happened we cannot go back,—I have written it—& enclose it. I can honestly say I have never done anything in my life that I so hated doing. I only pray I may not regret it as much. Even now I would not send it did I not feel that in the long run it may be best for both; & moreover if I did not think Dearest Jennie that we could be true friends after it is all over, I would tear it up now.—you are a splendid woman, & if I ever have done or are likely to do anything in the world, it has been & will be through your good influence. So far as the past is concerned it sounds silly to write this, as I have done nothing beyond trying to make an honest living, still I know some of my best endeavours, thoughts & ideals have emanated from you.

My future is in the 'Lap of the Gods' who alone know what fortune or misfortune is in store for me.

So far as you are concerned, it will always be my aim in life to provide for you according to your tastes & to the best of my ability. I am not waiting until the New Year to send the enclosed, as perhaps it will be better as we have made up our minds on the subject, to start afresh in 1913.

Bless you dearest Jennie, if you are ill communicate as I will with you.

always affectionately
George

Jennie kept a copy of her reply:

Coombe Abbey,[11]
Coventry
Dearest George   December 31st, 1912
I am glad that I was prepared for your letter—the blow falls hard enough as it is—But if the thing is to take place it can't be done too quickly now—& we shall both be happier when it is over—Thank God I have physical & mental strength & courage enough to fight my own battle in life—I only hope that you will have the same—It is not for me to preach but you will be a happier man if you set yourself a higher ideal of life than heretofore—I mean to—& altho' I know it is difficult—still one can but try. Of *course* we shall be friends—and it will not be my fault if we are not the best. My affection help & advice shall always be yours in the future as it has been in the past—When this & our financial difficulties are settled—a new & I hope prosperous life will be open to you—Make use of it in the best sense—& your happiness & prosperity will be my best reward for the sacrifice I am making in giving you up—No one knows better than you what

that sacrifice means to me—for I have loved you devotedly for 12 years—You have been ever in my thoughts & this love will only die—with me—Remember this in any dark hour which may come to you —God bless you & keep you from harm & prosper you is the prayer of

> yours ever affectionately
> Jennie

A few days later Jennie wrote again. George had taken rooms in Curzon Street, where he talked by the hour to his dog Beppo: 'Thanks for your nice letter', he wrote. 'I have been on the verge of ringing you up once or twice, but honestly I don't think I could bear to hear the sound of your dear old voice just now.'

Jennie's behaviour during the divorce proceedings the following year was dignified. George went to Brazil with his sister Daisy. Mrs. Patrick Campbell was ill, and when she recovered, busy with her mock-affair with Bernard Shaw. Jennie attracted wide sympathy. After an appearance in court, she received this from George's friend Rosamund Greaves, who had predicted the marriage would be such a success:

> Quenby Hall,
> Leicester
> Thursday, July 16th

One little line to tell you how much I have been thinking of you these last days. I know how brave and plucky you are & how deeply you feel. No woman was ever a better wife—& no one knows this better than poor George in his heart—you gave him *so much*. Poor George—

Now rest a bit if you can, you have such interests, so much intellect you will come up all brisk and fresh again. I cant tell you how much I admire you for not letting any bitter thoughts enter into yr *big heart*. Bless you—

If you want to be quiet come here any time after the 24th.

yr affecy R.

I filled up an Insurance paper & returned it.
How am I to address you?

Jennie changed her name back to Spencer-Churchill. Her friends were glad. Lord Curzon, for instance, wrote:

Hackwood,
Basingstoke
My dear Lady Randolph   Jan. 30, 1914

Good to get back to the old name or did we get in our old age to Jenny & George? I cant remember. Anyhow I am ready. This is to say why not come here for a Sat-Monday Feb 21–23? Do if you can.

Yours affec
C.

There was much wrangling between solicitors about bills, as there always is in a divorce case, but George and Jennie remained friendly. Jennie wrote to Leonie in October 1913, 'If you meet him don't be hard on him,' and on New Year's Eve George wrote to Jennie:

I hope you are well and happy. For me I have had a terrible year & shall not be sorry to see the last of 1913. I will drink a silent toast to you tonight dear Jennie for your health, happiness & welfare.

Jennie wrote back saying she was not unsympathetic about his business troubles and lack of money, *but*— To her lawyers she wrote suggesting a compromise. The decree was made absolute on 6 April 1914. George's sister Daisy sent telegrams urging Jennie not to let it go through, but Jennie knew what she wanted. On the 4th she wrote to George:

Ladies Athenaeum Club,
31 & 32 Dover Street, W.
My dear George   April 14th, 1914

Mr. Wheater brought me your message—The decree nisi will be made absolute on Monday—& I understand that you are going to be married on Tuesday—You need not fear what I may say—For I shall not willingly speak of you—and we are not likely ever to meet—This is the *real* parting of the ways But for the sake of some of the happy days we have had together—should you ever be in trouble & wanted to knock at my door it would not be shut to you—In returning to you my engagement & wedding rings—I say Goodbye—a long long Goodbye—

Jennie

George in fact married Mrs Pat a few hours after the divorce was made absolute. Jennie was showered with sympathetic messages:

JENNIE DEAREST YOU DID YOUR BEST ITS AWFUL AND HE WILL REGRET JUST READ IN PAPER AM MISERABLE HOPE SEE YOU SOON MUCH LOVE—DAISY

George's other sister Shelagh wrote a letter:

Rome
Dear Jennie   April 15th

I must write you a little line as I feel so much for you during this last year and especially by the announcement of last week. George must have been absolutely driven or out of a sense of honour to you and us he would never have acted with the indecent haste he did. Believe me Jenny I knew all the time what you were going through; and I admired what you did for him more than I can say. . . .

From Ireland, Leonie wrote three times:

Monday
Glaslough,
Co. Monaghan

Darling, I sent you a wire because Moreton wrote that
the Decree N. wd be today—and I know what you feel
now that George has his liberty—Dearest—you have
done *all* you could—and we can only *deplore* the
folly, if he commits it, of marrying Mrs P.C.—I know
how generous & noble you have been—and how you
made the sacrifice, hoping it wd be for his good—It
is not yr fault if he follows his own foolish way—
Poor man—what a hash he has made of the whole
thing. We, who look on, can only rejoice however,
that you are free from him—You wd have been in
your grave if that strain of life in Norfolk Street had
continued—

I am glad Easter is coming, & you will get away
from London again. Leonora[12] is a kind being—and
you will feel better at Overstrand—Write to me
Darling—I will tear up yr. letter—and it will do you
good to give vent to yr feelings—

Politics—& art and *joie de vivre*—how much we
have to fill our lives—

Yr devoted & loving
Leonie

Two days later it was:

Darling—You take it in the right way—You are very
fine—courageous—and human—I did not know it
was a *fait accompli* when I wired Monday—just a
kind of telepathy made me do so, knowing the Decree
was that day—I must say I felt very hateful & revenge-
ful—and looking forward to the stony stare I cld give
them—& the 'serve you right' to Daisy & Sheelagh. But
yours is the right spirit—no animosity—no bitterness
—just—*Fini*—The only tiresome part, is she is always
in the papers with her acting—& one may be occasionally reminded of them—Jack very disgusted. . . .

Three days later:

I won't refer to that beastly marriage—but I must just
say this once—that I think it was disgraceful of G. to
put such an indignity on you—and that I never want
to see either of those two, or speak to them—*Ce n'est
pas permis* to be such a weak fool—and to show such
ingratitude to you—I resent it for you—altho' you
are big & noble enough to forget it—He should never
have come in to yr life—And as for Her—Well there
is nothing too bad to describe my feelings about her—
the only consolation, is that *she* will have a pretty bad
time of it, if she cares for him—& serve her right—
there. . . .

Mrs Pat *was* served right. Her marriage to George
lasted even less time than Jennie's, though there was
never a divorce. George and Jennie kept in touch. Winston provided him with a job at the beginning of the
war, and George wrote to thank Jennie for having
'seconded the appointment'. When George's mother was
involved in an unsavoury scandal about a young soldier,
Jennie wrote him a brief note:

> 8 Westbourne Street,
> Hyde Park
> My dear George   Jan. 5th, '17
>   I feel I must write to you a few words of sympathy
> in, what I know is to you a very great trial—Please
> believe that I feel most deeply for you—But remember
> that a son should always seek & find extenuating cir-
> cumstances for his Mother—
>   Apart from this sorrow, I hope life is treating you
> gently
>
> Your affecty
> Jennie R.C.

This does not seem to be a copy, and perhaps she
had second thoughts and decided not to send it. In
1919 she wrote to him again. By that time his marriage
was virtually over.

8, Westbourne Street,
Hyde Park

My dear George   17.6.19

I heard all about you from Claire therefore was not surprised at your letter—I am glad you wrote—& in your heart of hearts, you must know that I never could have any but kindly feelings towards you—I never think of you but to remember all the happy days we spent together—I have forgotten everything else— I do wish you all that is best—Peace is an essential of life—& if you have that, you are on the fair way to happiness—Life is frightfully hard. One's only chance is within oneself—I shall hope to see you again soon. Bless you—

Always your best friend
Jennie R.C.

Though George and Mrs Pat had separated for ever, she refused to give him a divorce, and he was not able to marry again till after her death in 1940. His third marriage was announced on the day of Mrs. Pat's memorial service. He had filled in the years shooting, fishing and writing. His plays were not usually performed, but a novel was published with some success, as well as a biography, two volumes of memoirs and a book called *Us Dogs*. In old age he suffered from depression and then Parkinson's Disease. In April 1951 he shot himself. He was seventy-six.

Thirty years earlier, when Jennie died, he wrote to Winston:

May I be allowed to write & tell you how grieved I am to read of the death of your mother.

I find it difficult to say all I feel: perhaps you would not believe me. But I can truly say I never had anything in my heart for her but affection & admiration. I realize that, from my point of view, the greatest mistake I ever made in my life was in allowing myself to be persuaded into a separation from her. I can assure you that I have lived & am living to bitterly regret it. It is a joy to think that I saw her not much more than 18 months ago, & learnt from her own lips that she bore me no ill will for the hurt I had done her. Thank God I could never have harmed her, her position was far too secure. I wonder how you & Clemmy & Jack & Goonie are? I so often think about you all, & the old days.

Yours ever
G. C-W.

NOTES

1. Sent you away.
2. Winston became Under-Secretary of State for the Colonies in December 1905.
3. Home of Mrs Ronnie Greville.
4. Probably Leonie's sister-in-law, Mary Crawshay.
5. Leonie's second son.
6. Henry Bernstein, popular French playwright.
7. Shivering in his shoes.
8. Probably de Grey, now Marchioness of Ripon.
9. Jennie's long-serving butler.
10. Both daughters-in-law called Jennie B.M., short for *belle mère*.
11. Home of William George Robert, 4th Earl of Craven. He was married to Cornelia Bradley Martin, a New Yorker, whose parents once gave so flamboyantly expensive a fancy-dress party there were popular riots.
12. Leonora Speyer, wife of Sir Edgar Speyer, the banker. Jennie went to stay with the Speyers at Overstrand in Norfolk that week. Their house was called 'Seamarge'.

14

ARMAGEDDON

Jennie hated growing old, and sometimes she could not help saying so. She wrote to Jack from Monte Carlo in the spring of 1914, about the sordid details of her financial arrangements with George. She was sixty and felt low:

... apart from Goonie & perhaps little Johnnie,[1] who cares if I return or not? Not that I do not know that you and Winston love me, & are very good to me—but you lead busy lives, & have your own families to be absorbed in. What am I? Only an old 5th wheel—I am not complaining, only stating facts. ...

Love to Goonie & keep some for yourself tho' you don't send me any! I suppose I'm a sentimental old goose & don't deserve any for all the ennuis I cause you. My letter seems peevish but I am really not so.

No? She took things out on Leonie, too:

I wish we could see more of each other. Life is so short and we are both so down the wrong side of the ladder! The fact is that we are 'Marthas' instead of 'Marys' and allow things which do not really count to take up our time and to keep us apart. We pander to the world which is callous and it only wants you if you can smile and be hypocritical. One is for ever throwing away substance for shadows. To live for others sounds all right—you do, darling!—but what is the result? You are a very unhappy woman all round!

As for me every effort I make to get out of my natural selfishness meets with a rebuff. My sons love me from afar and give me no companionship even when it comes their way. The fault is undoubtedly with me. Every day I become more solitary and prone to introspection, which is fatal.

Leonie indignantly denied that she was unhappy, and the idea of Jennie as a self-sacrificing Martha must have caused some mirth in the Leslie family. But Jennie did not always feel so low. Not, for instance, when she went to Rome for the wedding of her nephew Hugh Frewen to the daughter of an Italian Duke. Hugh had been in the Colonial Service, and among his friends at the wedding was a small, neat, prematurely white-haired man who had served with him in Nigeria. His name was Montagu Porch. He was thirty-seven, three years younger than Winston, but found Jennie very attractive and on his way back to Nigeria wrote to her:

R.M.S. *Mendi*
Dear Lady Randolph,   16 May 1914
You said I might write to you so here goes!

We are now well on our way to Nigeria for tomorrow all being well we shall reach Sierra Leone. I say 'we' for I am taking out a young soldier servant & a puppy of the Great Dane breed.

In my choice of both I have been lucky the former is a cheerful looking fellow & a keen sportsman. The latter a handsome darling creature black as a nigger already considers herself our protector & tries to bark off all intruders.

We are bound for Kaduna the new capital of the federated Nigerias—There, we aspire to great deeds, that our names may be inscribed with glory in the annals of our country & that I may win your approval, dear friend.

I am greatly looking forward to my sojourn for the prospect is very pleasing.

The weather is glorious—The sun shines from out

an azure sky on to an azure sea—a light cool breeze
steals in under the awning where stretched on deck
chairs we are lazing away the noontide. My thoughts
turn towards my loved ones & I think with regret of
all the disciplines often self-imposed & the pleasures
that I let escape me.

Then I remember you dear kind friend, all the nice
things you said of me & I would they were true or at
least that you believed what you said.

Have you so soon forgotten that I want your photograph—will you send it to me please—one that can
live in my lettercase. The likeness of a dear friend I
couldn't bear to expose to the rude gaze of the vulgar.

Your essay, too, on Friendship am I not to have
it. I would like it very much & a kind word straight
from you would buck me up enormously.

I've heard nothing from my Italian friends save
from Paolina Marchesa Rusconi who posted me fare-
well in the form of a little gold cross & from Card:
Merry del Val [2] who sent me an excellent photograph
of himself with his very virile autograph—inscription.
Of all my Roman friends only Cardinal Merry del Val
remembered me.

Tomorrow we stop at Sierra Leone. The Governor
Sir Edward Mereweather & his Dame I know, so I
shall go ashore & pay them my respects.

Goodbye, dear Lady Randolph—I want your
friendship & I mean to get & keep it. *Nil difficile
volenti.*

Don't think me conceited will you I am only finding
expression.

                                                Montie

Porch's literary expression was rather quaint, but no
doubt Jennie was amused and delighted by his presumption. At any rate, she wrote back. She was doing a lot
of writing—a series of essays for a magazine, later
published as a little book called *Small Talks on Big
Subjects.* The essay on Friendships contains the passage
already quoted about Pearl Craigie turning a ploughed

field into one enamelled with flowers. Jennie was writing to make a little money, for as usual her finances were precarious. Jack felt obliged to read her a little lecture on the subject:

> . . . you have over £2000 a year. . . We have begged you so often to live within your income—which is not a very severe demand. Your income is larger than mine in most years and you have nothing whatever to keep up. Unless you are able to do so and if you start running up bills again—there is nothing that can save you from a crash & bankruptcy.

'Lots of others whom you know', he added, 'are in much worse positions than you.' The Edwardian world was cracking up. Quite soon, and no one seemed to know why or how, the first world war was destroying everything Jennie had known. Winston, at the Admiralty, was right at the heart of events, and kept Jennie informed. Jack, in the City, was appalled at the panic of late July:

> The world has gone mad—the whole financial system has completely broken down. . . . Be careful with what you have got—Gold will soon be unobtainable. . . .

Jennie hastened to pass this news to Leonie, with other rumours:

> 72 Brook Street, W.
> Aug. 1st
>
> Darling Sniffy
> Only a line to tell you that W. tells me Poincarré[3] has written an impassioned letter to the King imploring his aid—The fleet (British) will be mobilized today probably—Germany is holding up English vessels—& has mobilized & massed troops on the French Frontier—Money is fearfully tight here & one cannot get a cheque cashed—& the Banks will give no gold —But W. says the financial situation will be easier

as they are going to issue at once paper pound notes
—Paris is in an awful state risings in the streets—
The whole world seems to have gone mad. I am
depressed beyond words—Ireland seems to have sunk
out of sight—for the moment—The Volunteers of
both parties are sure to be commandeered. Just off to
Ramsey Abbey till Tuesday—

> Love
> Jennie

War was declared on 4 August. Jennie plunged at
once into hospital work again. Clementine and Goonie
were staying with their children at Overstrand, and
Jennie seems to have complained that they weren't
sending her enough news in these exciting times:

                                    Beehive Cottage,
My darling B.M.   Overstrand
    Of course I love you and if I have not written to
say so, it is because I have been worried and sad
about ourselves—Jack & I & the children—as you
may have realized we have not a 'bob' left in the
world and I do not know what the future holds in
store for us—however this is not the moment to la-
ment about ones own private affairs—It is splendid
of you to get this hospital scheme going & I am sure
it will be an engrossing & congenial work for you—
& you will do it with great skill and energy—Jack
has gone off to join his Yeomanry, & is at Banbury
at this present moment. I am very glad for his sake
that he is occupied & busy, for it would have been
intolerable for him to have had leisure to brood over
the situation—It is very exciting here being on the
Coast & in the zone of 'danger'—There is no reason
why the Germans should not come along & shell
Overstrand—Clemmie & I may qualify for a war
medal afterwards! She, Clemmie, is very flourishing
& we lead a healthy & quiet life with our children,
on the beach—I play a little bad tennis at the Speyers
& we go & look at the troops who are now quartered

at Cromer & such like innocent pastimes. Father [4] &
brother Jimmy [5] are staying with me and are consol-
ing me for Jack's absence—my Jacko—I wish he
had not to go, but I am proud that he is serving his
Country! It was very dear of you to find time to
write to me & I appreciated it very much indeed—
Could I get another letter from you? We hear all the
news here, as Clemmie gets on the telephone daily to
the Admiralty, but your news I would like to get
sometimes—

> Your loving bru
> Goonie

X from Johnnie
X from Peregrine—and Father sends his love.

When she got back to London, Goonie went to
dinner with Jennie, who had a great gift for buying
houses, doing them up, and selling them again. It was
one of her few really profitable ventures. Goonie's account to Jack not only describes Jennie's latest house, it
gives a very good idea of the gloom with which people
were approaching the war:

> 41 Cromwell Road
> Darling— Sept 1st, 1914

On my arrival in London I went to lunch at the
Admiralty & Winston told me that Lord Kitchener
said that the Yeomanry will train for three or four
months at Churn & then go on active service as Divi-
sional Cavalry—I am not happy as you may imagine,
as that means you will come face to face with those
swines of Germans, who by that time will be more
savage & desperate than ever—Everybody, or at least
every woman is going to be unhappy this year, so
I am no exception, but it is cruel that this is to be so
—I want to be with you all the time now till you go—
In three or four months lots of things might have
happened & there is always a glimmer of hope that
you will not be called upon to expose your self to
be slaughtered by the Germans—Write to me darling
and console me—I do try to be brave—Would you

have preferred to have gone to Egypt? Winston did not know who they were going to send to Egypt—Some Territorials I think—Commodore Keyes [6] was at Lunch, just back from Heligoland—He was not very voluble & *he* looked like if he had gone through a tremendous strain—It appears most of the German sailors desert their ships too soon—& in consequence get shot at in the water by their officers—Winston said he might go down to Churn to see you today—but he would not take me, as he said it was all men & I would be in the way in fact? When can I come & where could I stay? . . . who is close?—I dined with B.M. last night at 72 Brook Street—Needless to say we had a seven course dinner beautifully served, Platters of luscious fruits etc. all in a lovely diningroom the walls of which were decorated with lovely pictures—We afterwards sat in a 'pickled' oak room, beautifully lighted in the cornices by invisible electric Lights, & filled with lovely bibelots, furniture, rugs, flowers, in fact it looked very rich & opulent, comfortable & luxurious—I did not go up the thick pile carpeted staircase to the drawing [room] but I hear its quite beautiful, green painted & tapestries & wonderful lighting—Then further up there is a silver bedroom, a white bathroom and a blue dressingroom—but this I have not seen either—Downstairs alone I espied several new pieces of furniture—writing tables, chairs, tables, etc—but perhaps she has exchanged it for some of her old furniture—

The children are well & very pleased to get back to their old nurseries—I am trying to get the House clean and I have a charwoman hard at work scrubbing & washing—We shall get straight I hope soon—What is your telegraph address—The post office says there is no office at Churn—so I have been sending telegrammes to Didcot—Have you received them alright? Love from

yr loving wife
Goonie

Jennie was meanwhile keeping Leonie in touch:

72, Brook Street, W.
Aug 16th, '14

Darling Sniffy—

I telephoned to Marjorie [7] yesterday early to ask for news of you but she knew nothing! My 'poor child' I am sure you are going through bad moments, but we are more or less in the same boat. . . . I saw W. in the afternoon—No fresh news the 2 Armies are not likely to meet for a few days—& until then we shall hear nothing. I am hoping against hope that my Jack won't have to go but W. thinks he will probably volunteer—He is at present at Bury St Edmunds or somewhere near with the Oxfordshire Yeomanry —I have written to Goonie to offer to take her & the children for the winter—or in fact till Jack returns —It will be a squeeze but I think I can manage it— as I write I hear the tramp of the troops going off— The Reveille sounds at 5.30 but I was so tired this morning I heard nothing—Our American War Fund is progressing—but Minnie Paget is a great care— however if anything goes wrong I propose to stick to the Hospital. . . . I wish I had some news to give you —Rest a little & get fit for the strain to come—Let me know if there is anything I can do about yr house.

Fond love
Jennie

Love to Jack

The strain to come was indeed appalling, and an individual's happiness or otherwise seems irrelevant when compared to the general horror of the First World War. But the death of a loved one always counts more than the death of a whole army of strangers. Jennie was to lose many friends and relations in the war: her nephew, Norman Leslie, was killed before the year was out, and Wilfred Sheridan died in 1915. Her own son Jack went all through the war, in France and Gallipoli and France again; Winston, too, served in the trenches after he was forced to resign in 1915, following the failure of the Gallipoli expedition. Jennie defended him tigerishly, and could never forgive Asquith for what she regarded as his disloyalty. As for herself—she did the things she was good at: she organized concerts and matinees for military charities, she took in Goonie and her children for a while, and paid for Johnnie's schooling, she edited a book on *Women's War Work,* she visited the bereaved, and, never forgetting the country of her birth, she worked at American hospitals in Paignton and London. Sometimes she did things she wasn't so good at: she knitted a scarf for Hugh Warrender, who was in the trenches, which was so big that he used it as a blanket instead. In war, she wrote, 'To be dressed in the latest fashion is not to be in the right note.' And: 'the more virile a nation becomes the more she seeks for, and asks for, simplicity and truth. All the shallow, stupid, snobbish habits which were beginning to blot out our horizon are vanishing like mists before the sun.' Doing her bit to help the process, she gave up her footmen, and substituted footmaids in the men's cut-down uniforms. And she let herself go. Her hair became white, and the figure which had once been so slim, and carefully kept to look so, took on its actual ample proportions. She wrote to the troops, too. She kept up a regular correspondence with Hugh Warrender, and with his sister Eleanor, busy nursing the wounded. She had toyed with the idea of marrying Hugh, who was still devoted: things went so far that Jack asked what they wanted for a wedding-present. But that was before the war, and before Jennie met Montagu Porch. She was writing to him in Nigeria and he was writing back:

> Tati river, E. of Takum,
> Nr Anglo German Boundary,
> Muri Province, Nigeria
> 5 Oct. 1914

How sensational—your dear letter written on the eve of 'Armageddon' finds your humble friend at the front beating back the attacks of the covetous Huns.

At the outbreak of hostilities I was sworn in a soldier transferred from Zaria to this Province & shortly afterwards appointed Intelligence Officer to this column.

Takum was attacked on 19th ult when the Germans got more than they bargained for. Their O.C. killed 1 European seriously wounded & a lot of native soldiers killed & wounded—our casualties were a bruised thumb; so cunningly were our block houses arranged.

I send you a relic of the fray the legend explains itself—who was the wounded man one wonders & where is he now?

Many died of wounds in their flight back to Kamerun—a week later I held 2 of their skulls in my hand, chalk-white like museum-exhibits, so well had the vultures done their work.

I will write to you again dear Lady Randolph. Two of my spies have just come in & I am anxious to hear their news.

We are a very happy family here—20 Europeans in the column—I feel v. responsible for these dear souls—our native troops are playing up v. well.

Goodbye, dear friend, I will write again & you must write to me for I am lonely too.

Montie

There was more to Porch than met the eye. He seemed quiet, dapper, nothing very much, but he proved a good soldier in awful conditions:

The Residency,
Zaria, Nigeria
2 October 1915

Forgive you, of course & with all my heart. Your dear letter has touched me deeply. How kind & like you, thank you.

Ohimé this horrible sickening war, will it ever end. Almost all the men one has ever heard of seem to be either killed or wounded. Poor Lady Leslie, I heard of her loss. All my men kith & kin are in the trenches save brother-in-law Gillmore who is with his regiment in India.

It is well for you that you have lots to do, dear friend, you will then have less time for grief and heartache. I am indeed glad you are running the American hospital. History repeats itself. Jan: 15 years ago I, a trooper coming of age on my way to the front, passed a gorgeously equipped American hospital ship run by one of the most brilliant & beautiful women in England. Now you are again taking your part in this bigger & more frightful war.

I too have played my small part all they would let me do. Aug. 8th '14 I was transferred from peaceful Zaria to our Front the Nigerian-Kamerun Border where I was attached as Intelligence Officer to the Nigerian Regt West African Frontier Force. Our column was a very small one & had to run up & down 200 miles of border & shoo off the Huns whenever they appeared.

Lots of scraping we had & I lost some gallant comrades. As yet our campaign has received little recognition—Far greater dangers than trench work have been endured by our men who winter and summer have braved swamp and jungle, fever and bush ambuscades, heavy marches & fighting in terrible heat. Tormented by insects, stung by all the creatures of the bush, scorched by unshaded sun in the fiercest heat of an African summer—such has been our lot.

In January I was recalled from the column to resume my duties as Resident in charge of this Province. In May and August I had to take patrols into my Pagan Districts who had revolted against the Native Administration & didn't want to pay their taxes after having heard that the white men of consequence had all gone off to the Great War. However I went & saw —one of the tribes put up a little fight, got well wopped, came to their senses & promised never to do it again.

I am 5 months overdue for leave and sail on October 26th. I shall go straight to Kewstoke Somerset, where a patient old housekeeper & a man await me in a roomy cottage poised on a spur of Mendip which dips into the Bristol Channel. I dread the first few days in Somt. Relations to be visited & tenants seen. Duty done I shall hie me to town. I shall live at the United Empire Club quite near you but won't be a nuisance. I'll only come when I'm called.

Edgarley Lodge my little place near Glastonbury has just been let on a seven years' lease!—Thank goodness.

Think I shall have seven months leave, what *shall* I do—I would go Dardanelles—if Bonar Law [8] will accept my resignation—If I can't get to the front I shall make shells or be guided into doing something else useful.

Au revoir dear Lady Randolph,

> Your devoted friend
> M.P.

Montie Porch must have been visiting London, and Jennie, when an extraordinary telegram appeared in the papers, addressed to His Majesty The German Emperor, Berlin, from New York.

The name of Napoleon fades before the prowess of your mighty deeds, Sir. May 1916 bring to the world that peace which for years we have had the high honour of hearing Your Majesty insist upon and may God guide and bless you, Sir.

> Katherine and Jordan Mott,
> Ritz Hotel.

Kitty Mott was Jennie's cousin, through her mother, and the three Jerome sisters were outraged. Leonie wrote at once to Jennie:

> Thursday
> Glaslough,
> Co. Monaghan.

Darling—

Moreton has just sent me this extraordinary cable of Kitty's to the Emperor—No use asking her to deny it! One recognises her style—Poor Devil, I suppose she thought if she mollified the Emperor with flattery he wd listen to the *Peace* suggestions—Pretty mean of him to publish it, knowing it wd be resented—

I am *really* sorry for Kitty—she is such a d—— fool about the war—She adores England & English, does not want ever to see Germany again, but she is persuaded if she could see the Emperor for ½ hour she could get him to make Peace—

She doesn't understand that it is *up to* the Allies to decide when Peace is to be & NOT to the Emperor —Claire is *terribly* upset!—& is returning the little cheque Kitty sent her for Xmas.—

Do write, we've no news.

Aff. **L.**

Jennie wrote sharply to her cousin:

72, Brook Street, W.
Dear Kitty,   Jan. 10th '16

The enclosed appeared in the *Pall Mall* a few days ago—Needless to ask if you wrote it—The style is too peculiarly yr own—With the views you hold— I don't suppose you care if England is shut to you for ever—for I tell you frankly you can never return here—When I think of the glorious deaths of Norman Leslie and Wilfred Sheridan.—of Hugh Frewen in a hospital, of Oswald at sea [9]—of Jack in Gallipoli & Winston in the trenches in Flanders—When I think of all the horror of this war, conducted by the Kaiser with the most awful cruelty & barbarism ever known since the world began—which a stroke of his pen could have stopped—I feel I cannot write one more word to you. . . .

To Kitty's husband, Jennie wrote:

72 Brook Street, W.
My dear Jordan   Jan. 10th, '16

I can hardly believe that you were a party to Kitty's telegram to the Kaiser—It was intercepted by wireless & published here—I cannot tell you how deeply

the family is ashamed of it—If it was done without
your knowledge or sanction & your name wrongly
used—I should be glad if you would write & deny it.

Yrs ever
J.R.C.

Jennie might have been born in America, but her
loyalties were entirely English now. Later that year she
wrote to Shane Leslie in America:

. . . How truly magnificent is this country—We promised 160,000 men, & we have given 5 millions, besides
keeping the seas & financing every ally—England will
be the greatest nation in the world when the war is
over—Yes not excepting America—for she missed
her chance of coming out as a nation—not that I
really blame the U.S. for keeping out of the war—
but the consequences will not tend to glorify the
States. . . .

From New York Shane reported the result of the infamous telegram:

You are wrong about Kitty Mott! She will simply
have to live in London, because nobody will speak to
her over here. They have begun to insult and avoid
her. How one can suffer for one moment of madness!

He added in a P.S.: 'There is a window in Broadway
entirely devoted to a "Lady Churchill" cigar with an
imaginative portrait of you.' Jennie's fame had long
been transatlantic.

How much Jennie actually saw of Montagu Porch
that winter is unclear. He was very discreet, doubtless,
and so was she. He had brought her a present from
Nigeria which she doesn't seem to have appreciated:

The Residency,
Zaria, Nigeria
22 June 1916

Dear Lady Randolph
I have just got here & have taken over charge of
the Province. That is I am the Resident in charge of

Zaria Province which from its central position brings one much under the limelight. Three Railways in my Province & Kaduna the future *capital of Nigeria.* Hurray. This childs work.

Do please send me a word to inspire me to further effort—I am so lonely.

If you wont wear the Crown Birds crests yourself please burn 'em. That no one else may wear 'em— that would be the most unkindest cut of all.

> Very sincerely yours,
> M.P.

Jennie had another admirer, at a distance of another sort:

My dearest Lady Randolph,

You will perhaps think my presumption amazing, but not if you knew my feelings. I have felt drawn towards you since the time you came to England, even when you were a bonnie bride, you are indeed sweeter to me than at that time, I have always called you my Jennie, I have followed your career, your sweet personality has always been uppermost in my life and foremost in my thoughts. I have always felt that you have a very warm temperament, only fitted to be mated with such a one as mine.

Dearest I have kept pure for you alone, and never until the last few days have I ever thought of letting you know this, it has always been my life's secret, sacred to myself, but love is stronger than, shall I say commonsense and here I stand convicted self confessed, of loving the sweetest woman in the world, my Jennie always my Jennie, I am yours body & soul, to do with me what you will, when I am thinking of you dearest my physical senses make me feel a superman, *your man,* Jennie darling, do you want me, if so, I am yours, one cur I would like to thrash, the one who humiliated my darling.[10] I felt at the time if only I were a friend, God help him, dearest if you can respond will you please answer through *Daily*

Telegraph personal column, or *Times,* under the name
of Jennie, but if you treat it with contempt, let my
great love for the sweetest, on God's earth, be my
only excuse.

Yours for ever & ever.
Jack

It seems that Jennie did not reply in the manner requested:

My dearest Lady Randolph   13/12/16
    I greet you sweet one. After much longing, I saw
a personal ad in *Times* Dec 2nd and thought it might
be yours, but after reflection wondered if you would
condescend to acknowledge my poor epistle, even
after writing I half relented having done so, my
presumption (in cool moments) I considered to be
amazing. I am much afraid that at times the heart
overrides the brain, but dearest, one thing stands out,
every word was the hearts truth, call it folly or what
you will, although, I feel that you have sympathy if
nothing more, for one who just craves one single
thought from the one whom he worships night & day,
from the one always in his thoughts, the sweetest
woman in creation, my one wish is for your happiness, if only I could be the one to make you so, that
would be my gladness, dearest *do forgive* but I want
to be yours your very own, yours only for always.
I long for you and you alone, my own sweet Jennie,
darling I always think of you as Jennie Jerome, my
own sweet love, please do not spurn this, it is life to
me, and dearest I am longing to know if you really
answered, will it be asking too much, if it was so, to
repeat in *Times* on Wednesday next 20 inst, if you
will please, indicate as J.J. also if I may write again,
then I will write you more fully and disclose my
identity. Goodnight my own sweet love fondest wishes
from yours most lovingly

Jack

Goodnight my own in thought always.

Jennie's spirits went up and down, but perhaps all this attention cheered her up, for she clashed with the rationing authorities about disclosing her age. She obviously felt younger than her 64 years in January 1918, and she was damned if she could see why any red tape should make her admit to them:

> *Local Food Control Committee,*
> *St Marylebone*
>
> 6 Holles Street,
> Oxford Street, W. 1.
> 18th January, 1918
>
> Dear Madam,
> Adverting to your letter of the 14th December last enclosed with declaration forms in the envelope which you handed to your Retailers, I am directed by the Ministry of Food to inform you that the particulars of date of birth asked for under the Sugar Distribution Scheme are required for two reasons:—
> 1. In case of dispute to afford individuals a simple and more expeditious method of proving their identity than would otherwise be possible.
> 2. In order that the particulars of age given may be taken into account in connection with any general scheme of rationing which may hereafter be established for the purpose of determining the appropriate rate of allowance in each case.
> I am to ask you to be so kind as to fill in the particulars on your declaration form which I am returning for the purpose.
>
> Yours faithfully,
> R. A. V. Morris
> Executive Officer

Jennie seems to have lost that battle. She doesn't seem to have got very far with another, either. The sculptor Jacob Epstein asked her to try to use her influence to get him out of the ranks and into propaganda work where his talents might be more useful. Jennie appealed to Lord Beaverbrook, then Minister of Information.

Jennie was conducting that particular campaign from Castle Leslie, in Ireland, where she was staying with Leonie. With her was Montagu Porch, on leave again. As well as eating legs of lamb—unknown in wartime England—they decided to get married. The wedding took place on 1 June, at Harrow Road Register Office. Jennie told the novelist George Moore: 'He has a future and I have a past so we should be all right.' What the family thought is not recorded. It took everyone by complete surprise. Montie wrote to Winston on the morning of his wedding:

Connaught Hotel
1/6/18

Dear Winston,

I am very glad you are able to come to our Wedding. It seems almost incredible that today, when the world is in anguish, I should be allowed so much happiness.

I would now assure you that this, the most important step in my life, is not taken in the dark. I have carefully considered the position from every point of view—your Mother's financial affairs are understood.

I love your Mother, I can make her happy. Her difficulties & obligations from henceforth will be shared by me—so willingly.

I thank you for your kindness & consideration. We shall be good friends.

Your very truly
M.P.

Winston went over to France a few days later, and saw Jack. They'd heard the story about Jennie's obligations being undertaken before, of course. Jack's reaction on hearing the news was:

General Headquarters,
British Armies in France
25/5/18

Dear Mamma,

What a surprise! Your letter has just been forwarded to me. Whenever I go to war you do these things! I feel sure that you have thought it all out carefully, and that you are certain that you are acting wisely. I know the last few years must have been lonely for you. With both of us married it was inevitable that you should be alone. I do not remember hearing you talk of him and I have never met him. If he makes you happy we shall soon be friends. I wish I could get over for the day—but it is impossible as I am just taking on a new post and I shall probably be moving on the 1st June.

Now, my dear, you know that no one can make any change in our love for one another, and it will be something to know that you are no longer alone. And so I send you my best love and wishes, and pray that all will be well. . . .

It sounds as though the brothers may have been secretly rather relieved that Jennie was off their hands again. Winston was a witness, as was Jack Leslie. Clara and Goonie and Clementine all signed, too. The family was loyal. Even Lady Sarah Wilson, Randolph's youngest sister, was there. As her past was loyal to her, so was Jennie loyal to her past. She was Mrs Porch in law, but she continued to be known as Lady Randolph Churchill till her death.

NOTES

1. Jennie's eldest grandson, John Spencer-Churchill.

2. Cardinal Rafael Merry del Val had a Spanish father and an English mother, and was born and partly educated in England. A swimmer and mountaineer, he became Secretary of State to Pope Pius X, and a Cardinal, in 1903. 'Physically he was the most artistic sight in the basilica of which he became archpriest, St Peters's.' (Shane Leslie, in *The Catholic Encyclopedia*.)

3. Raymond Poincaré, 1860-1934, French President.

4. The Earl of Abingdon.

5. The Hon. James Willoughby Bertie, 1901-66.

6. Commodore Roger Keyes, who had commanded the British submarines at the Battle of Heligoland Bight on August 28th.

7. Wife of Leonie's eldest son Shane.

8. Andrew Bonar Law had become Colonial Secretary in the Coalition Government formed by Asquith in May 1915.

9. Both sons of Clara.

10. Presumably a reference to George.

15

BLESS YOU AND
AU REVOIR

Jennie was very happy with Montie Porch, and after the war was over resumed a busy social life. She danced, she took to flying in aeroplanes, she organized parties in France for rich Americans, she kept up with everything and everyone. Montie did his best about her extravagance, but no one ever succeeded in curbing it for long, so in 1921 he decided he'd better go back to Africa and make some money. He went to Coomassie in the Gold Coast (now Kumasi in Ghana), where he had very high hopes of making a quick fortune. Jennie planned to go out and join him, as soon as he'd got a house properly organized. When he set off in March, Jennie wrote him a little note:

My darling,   March 8, 1921
  Bless you and au revoir and I love you better than anything in the world and shall try and do all those things you want me to in your absence.
                          Your loving wife,
                              J.
P.S. Love me and think of me.

Montie found it in the pocket of his coat as he went on board his ship.
  While he was away, Jennie went back to Rome, where she had met him, and stayed, as she had stayed that time, too, with Vittoria, Duchess of Sermoneta.

She had a lovely time, as she wrote to Leonie from Florence on 20 April:

> I shall come home as good and sweet-tempered as a cherubim. How wonderful is this place! and what fun I am having! It seems positively selfish to be having such a good time and you in Ireland. Winston, Clemmie and I stayed with the Laverys [1] at Cap d'Ail and he painted some delightful pictures. Vittoria met me in her car and I found Rome very gay, races, dances, *antiquaires*. Her palazzo charming but not grand like the Colonna palace where I lunched. Such magnificence! They all play bridge *madly* and for very high stakes. I had to stop, you know how badly I play and the Romans are rapacious to a degree!

Jennie thought of taking a big country place and having the whole family to stay with her. She ordered a great many very expensive antiques. She also bought a pair of shoes. Eddie Marsh said she was the sort of woman for whom life did not begin on a basis of less than forty pairs of shoes. Back in England she went to stay with her friend Lady Horner, at Mells, in Somerset. One of those forty pairs of shoes—perhaps the new one—betrayed her. She slipped on the stairs and broke her ankle.

Communications between Coomassie and England were not good, and it was a few days before Montie heard the news. His letters, for the same reason, were written over several days, there being only a few posts. He was so upset when he heard that he put May for June:

> S. Cyprian's House,
> Coomassie,
> The Gold Coast
> 8 May, 1921

My own Darling—I am so terribly distressed, I can hardly pull myself together to write to you some words of comfort & sympathy. Your poor darling little foot—the cable telling me you had broken it met me this morning on my way to the town early. I am terribly upset. My sweet love you will never be able to dance again—you may be crippled. But I shall love you very very much to make up for all the pain & anguish you have suffered.

Thank God, you are at home in your comfortable house with the good tempered & loyal Etienne to look after you—You have your sons near you your sisters & your many friends around you for all this I am v. thankful.

Darling, I am ready to come to you any day—this I have cabled to you. But my business would suffer v. much—my business that has turned out an amazing success.

10th Friday
The Bishop of Accra arrived this evening, as usual I sent my Agent & car to meet him—I should have met him myself but for my business He understands that so well.

The good man was so sympathetic when I told him of my great trouble.

Sunday 12th
Today has been a repetition of last Bishop's Sunday here. Mass at 8.30 & back in time to hear the Bishop's sermon at S. Cyprian's Church.

On the 13th, before closing his letter, he heard news that distressed him terribly. Jennie's ankle had become gangrenous, and her leg had to be amputated above the knee.

13th
My sweet precious Darling only now that you are maimed & tortured I know how much I love you— You poor Darling are in pain—Terrible suffering you must be going through while I am here powerless to help & comfort you. My head aches, my eyes pain me,

my throat is swollen with passion & despair—I am ill.

The Bishop has had a steadying effect on me—I showed him Winston's cable I could not tell him about it. I have managed to pull myself together—somehow.

Saturday night I could not sleep—perfectly well & no worries save the anxiety about your poor little foot—I only got to sleep at Dawn—the time I'm usually awake—I told the Bishop what a wretched night I had—I put it down to telepathy from you to me.

Jennie Darling I will help you to bear all this. How can I ever love you enough—I will be very good to you, considerate & faithful—I could never be disloyal to you now.

Bless you sweet Darling—I send you all my love & kisses & more kisses for the poor little place where the stitches are.

> Your devoted husband M.

Jennie made a good recovery at first. Winston was able to cable on 23 June that the danger was over. Montie Porch was deeply relieved, but still, naturally, very worried:

> S. Cyprian's House,
> Coomassie, The Gold Coast
> 25 June 1921

My own Darling, I love you very much & I am suffering agonies of anxiety. Winston's last cable that 'Danger was definitely over' was re-assuring—still I am often frantic with apprehension & fear. I have no one in the world but You that is no one I love, as I love you. Darling, I implore you for my sake to take care of yourself. You must never attempt to move without assistance. Another fall might kill you. Do be careful sweetheart. I long to be with you—it will be such a joy to look after you. I don't mind what I do or how hard I work to help get the comfort you need & deserve.

Thank goodness I have established this wonderful

business—it was an inspiration, before long the railway from Accra the capital of the Gold Coast will reach Coomassie. Trade here will then be doubled (v. map).

I have made S. Cyprian's House so nice for you—I shouldn't have spent so much money on myself. And now perhaps you will never come—I can't bear the thought.

Business in general is bad, mine in particular is doing well.

I am picking up the Ashanti language & am getting the Ashanti custom.

The Bank Manager came to my office yesterday—he thinks I am doing amazingly.

I still need a little capital & have written to Terrington to arrange a mortgage of £2000 on 8 Westbourne St. He will then be able to pay Williams the £1000 the other £1000 he will put to my credit at Parrs Bank, Weston S. Mare.

27th

I have arranged with the Inland Revenue Authorities to pay our 1920–1921 tax by instalments the last instalment in Jan 1921. You will therefore have your own little income—entire.

Strachey's *Queen Victoria* has arrived I know I shall enjoy it v. much. The lavender water & toothpaste has reached me too: thank you ever so much, Darling.

A mail arrived yesterday. I got a v. nice letter from my Mother—she is so happy about me & my business venture. But Darling there was no letter from You—but I'm not angry with you for not writing—I shall never be angry with you again.

Mail closes this afternoon so I'll close this in good time. And I'll just say again what you say I can never tell you too often that I love you & will devote my life to you.

Your loving husband M.

He enclosed a map, showing how the railway would run and make his fortune. Jennie knew how worried he must be, and wrote out a cable on the 28th of June saying she'd got his letters and was much comforted and she was all right and was sending him things. The following morning, she suddenly told her nurse that her hot-water bottle must have burst. The nurse pulled back the bed-clothes to see. Jennie saw, too. It was a haemorrhage. She died almost at once.

Years later Montie Porch wrote to Seymour Leslie, sending that last precious note he'd found in his pocket. 'Our married life was a perfect union of temperament & culture where spirituality had its place,' he said. At the time, of all the hundreds of letters which came to Jack and Winston, one from Violet Bonham Carter said everything: 'Your mother was the most intensely living being I have ever known.' Winston himself wrote to Lloyd-George: 'My mother had the gift of eternal youth of spirit.' But perhaps another great Edwardian beauty, Daisy Warwick, should have the last word: 'Do you remember all the fun we had together in the old days, dear Jennie?' she once wrote. 'But I never *regret* anything, do you? We have both *lived* our lives.'

Jennie had indeed lived her life. Now she lay in the little churchyard at Bladon, near Blenheim, next to Randolph. And there, in 1965, she was joined by her famous son.

---

1. Sir John and Lady Lavery. Winston had taken up painting during the war, and Sir John encouraged him. Sir John was an A.R.A. He was knighted in 1918.

REFERENCES

The following abbreviations are used:

AL = *Jennie,* by Anita Leslie, 1969.

ASR = *The Anglo-Saxon Review*.

B = Marquess of Blandford, later 8th Duke of Marlborough.

Blenheim = Blenheim archives.

CJ = Mrs Jerome.

FM = Frances, wife of 7th Duke of Marlborough.

G = George Cornwallis-West.

J = Jennie.

Jk = Jack.

L = Leonie Leslie.

LJ = Leonard Jerome.

LRC = *Lord Randolph Churchill,* by Winston S.
Churchill, 1906.

M = 7th Duke of Marlborough.

MP = Montagu Porch.

ND = undated.

PSC = MSS in possession of Peregrine S. Churchill.

R = Randolph.

Rems = *The Reminiscences of Lady Randolph
Churchill,* 1907.

W = Winston.

WSC = *Winston S. Churchill,* by Randolph S. Churchill and Martin Gilbert, Vols I–III, and Companion
Vols, 1966–72.

Chartwell Trust papers are referred to by their file
numbers, beginning 28.

Conjectural dates are in brackets.

CHAPTER ONE

The basis for all accounts of Jennie and Randolph's courtship is a typed document in the Blenheim archives (A IV/11) called *Early Recollections,* which Jennie seems to have written for Winston's benefit when he was writing LRC. There are, however, discrepancies between it, LRC and the account given by Randolph to his father. Jennie says that she invited Randolph back to dinner after the ball on the *Ariadne,* which took place on a Tuesday afternoon, and that Randolph asked her to marry him on the third evening of their acquaintance, i.e. Thursday. Randolph told his father he had proposed on the Friday evening. LRC says that Randolph was invited for the Wednesday evening, and proposed on the Thursday.

page

4. R to J (16/8/73), 28/2.
5. J to R (17/8/73), 28/92.
    R to J (18/8/73), 28/2.
6. R to J (19/8/73), 28/2.
7. Dod's *Parliamentary Companion,* 1873.
8. LRC, I, passim.
    R to M 20/8/73, LRC, I, 40–3.
11. LRC, I, 35.
    R to J (21/8/73), 28/2.
13. B to R 25/8/73, Blenheim A IV/21.
16. R to J (30/8/73), 28/2.
17. J to R (1/9/73), 2/92.
18. M to R 31/8/73, WSC I, Comp I, 12.
19. R to J, 4/9/73, 28/2.
20. R to J, 7/9/73, 28/2.
22. R to J, 10/9/73, 28/2.
    CJ to R, 9/9/73, 28/103.
23. B to R, 7/9/73, Blenheim A IV/21.
27, 28. Francis Knollys to R, 12 & 19/9/73, Blenheim A/IV23.
28. R to J, (17/9/73), 28/2.

CHAPTER TWO

32. J to R, 16/9/73, 28/92.
34. *The Court Journal,* 13 & 20/9/73.
35. R to J, 18/9/73, 28/2.
38. J to R, 18/9/73, 28/92.
    fn. 4 Elizabeth Eliot, *They All Married Well,*
    153ff.
39. R to J, 19/9/73, 28/2.
43. R to J, 20/9/73, 28/2.
45. J to R, (19/9/73), 28/92.
46. R to J, 22/9/73, 28/2.
49. J to R, 22/9/73, 28/92.
50. R to J, 23/9/73, 28/2.
54. J to R, 26/9/73, 28/92.
55. LJ to J, (8/9/73) & 11/9/73, 28/1.
56. CJ to R, 29/9/73, 28/103.
57. R to CJ, 30/9/73, WSC I, Comp I, 15.
    J to R, 29/9/73, 28/92.
59. R to CJ, ND, WSC I, Comp I, 17.
    J to R, (3/10/73), 28/92.
60. LJ to J, 7/10/73, 28/1.
    J to R, 24/10/73, 28/92.
61. FM to J, 7/1/74, 28/42.
62. J to R, (28/3/74), 28/94.
    R to J, 30/3/74, 28/4.

CHAPTER THREE

67. Rems, 57ff.
68. FM to CJ, 30/11/74, WSC I, 2.
    R to CJ, 30/11/74, WSCI, 1.
70. FM to CJ, 3/12/74, WSC I, Comp I, 4.
70.–72. R to B, 31/10/75, B to FM, (2/11/75), M
    to R, 4/11/75, and R to M, 4/11/75, are all
    Blenheim A IV/27.
72.–73. J to FM, (5/11/75), and FM to J, 5/11/75,
    both 28/42.
75. B to R, (5/11/75), Blenheim A IV/27.
76. R to J, 16/1/76, 28/6.

77. R to J, 17/1/76, 28/5.
    J to R, 18/1/76, 28/95.
79. Hawkins to R, 22/12/75, Blenheim L IV/17.

CHAPTER FOUR

82. Philip Magnus, *Edward VII*, 132ff.
83. *Society in London, By a Foreign Resident*
    (1885), quoted in Anita Leslie, *Edwardians in
    Love,* 120ff.
85. The Aylesford affair can be followed in detail in
    WSC I, Comp I, 23–77. Occasional corrections
    to the printed text have been made from MSS.
87. J to R, 19/4/76, 28/97.
88. J to R, 20/4/76, 28/102.
89. R to J, 20/4/76, 28/5.
90. J to R, 21/4/76, 28/102.
91. WSC I, 33–4.
93. J to R, (30/6/76), 28/97.
94. R to J, 30/6/76, 28/5.
95. J to R, (2/7/76), 28/97.
96. R to J, 2/7/76, 28/5.
    R to J, 4/7/76, 28/5.
    R to J, 5/7/76, 28/5.
97. J to R, 6/7/76, 28/102.
101. *W, My Early Life,* 18–19.
     J to R, 28/96 passim.

CHAPTER FIVE

104. Rems, 91.
105. R to J (1/5/77?), 28/6.
106. J to R, ND, 28/96.
     R to J, 15/8/81, 28/7.
107. J's Diary, 28/43.
     fn 2. Anita Leslie, *The Fabulous Leonard Je-
     rome,* 254–5.
108. J to CJ, ND, Anita Leslie, *The Fabulous Leonard
     Jerome,* 220.
109. J to R, 10/1/83, 28/98.
110. J to R, 17/12/82, 28/98.

111. J to R, 19/12/82, 28/98.
     J to R, 29/12/82, 28/98.
112. R to J, 1/1/83, 28/7.
115. J to R, 3/1/83, 28/98.
116. R to J, 5/1/83, 28/7.
118. fn. 21 Anita Leslie, *The Fabulous Leonard Jerome,* 16, 254 & 284.
     J to R, 8/1/83, 28/98.
     R to J, 11/1/83, 28/7.
120. J to R, 11 & 12/1/83, 28/93.
     J to R, 16/1/83, 28/98.
122. R to J, 16/1/83, 28/7.
     R to J, 17/1/83, 28/7.

CHAPTER SIX

125. W to R, 5/12/84, 28/99.
126. J to R, 5/12/84, 28/99.
127. Miss Thomson to J, 17/12/84, 28/99.
128. J to R, 19/12/84, 28/99.
     R to J, 9 & 24/1/85, 28/7.
129. Mr Thomas to FM, 15/1/85, 28/7.
130. J to R, 13/2/85, 28/99.
     J to R, 20/3/85, 28/98.
132. Rems, 124–7.
134. Sir Henry James to J, Rems, 127.
     Francis Knollys to Sir Henry James, 15/3/84, WSC I, Comp I, 77.
     Roose to R, 20/6/85, Blenheim N IV/I(a).
137. Winston's illness may be followed in detail in WSC I, Comp I, 116–22.
     Roose to R, 31/3/86, Blenheim N IV/I(a).
138. R to J, 20/4/86, 28/7.
139. R to J, 10/7/86, 28/7.
     R to J, 13/7/86, 28/7. In LRC, II, 123, this and the preceding letter are run together.
140. Roose to R, 23/7/86, Blenheim N IV/I(a).
141. LRC, II, 125–7.
142. CJ to J, 5/8/86, 28/1.

CHAPTER SEVEN

144. FM to J, 8/9/86, 28/42.
146. FM to J, 10/9/86, 28/42.
147. R to J (13 /9/86), 28/7.
148. FM to J (13/9/86), 28/42.
    Lord George Hamilton, *Parliamentary Reminiscences,* II, 38–40.
149. R to J, 25/9/86, 28/7.
150. FM to J, 26/9/86, 28/42.
152. FM to J 3/10/86, 28/42.
153. R to J, 6/10/86, 28/7.
154. R to J, 8/10/86, 28/7.
155. R to J, 12/10/86, 28/7.
156. LRC, II, 171–2.
    R to J, 18/10/86, 28/7.
    FM to J, 24/10/86, 28/42.
157. R to J, 1/11/86, 28/7.
158. FM to J, 19/11/86, 28/42.
    The Letters of Queen Victoria, Third Series, I, 223–5.
159. FM to J, 29/11/86, 28/42.
    Lady Gwendolen Cecil, *Life of Robert Marquis of Salisbury,* III, 327.
    Rems, 141.
160. Brisbane to J, 14/1/87, Blenheim K IV/23.
161. R to Brisbane, 14/1/87, Blenheim K IV/54.
    Brisbane to R, 14/1/87, Blenheim K IV/55.
163. J to R, 6/2/87, 28/100.
165. J to R, 15/2/87, 28/100.
    R to J, 21/2/87, 28/8.
    J to R, 21/2/87, 28/100.
167. J to L, ND, AL, 122.
    J to R, 5/3/87, 28/100.

CHAPTER EIGHT

170. R to Edward Hamilton, 20/8/94, PSC.
    J to R, 29/4/91, 3/9/91, 7/12/91 & 2/10/91, all in Blenheim H IV/27, 28 & 29.
172. WSC I, Comp I, passim.

173. J to L, 4/8/94, 28/115.
174. J to C, 18/11/94, WSC, Comp I, 535–6.
    Jk to R, 30/11/94, 28/30.
175. J to L, December 1894, Anita Leslie MSS.
176. J to L, 3/1/95, WSC I, Comp I, 545.
    J to Jk, 14/1/95, PSC.

CHAPTER NINE

179. W to J, 24/2/95, WSC I, Comp I, 559.
180. Rems, 278.
    For George Cornwallis-West's family and back-
    ground, see the highly enjoyable biography *Per-
    fect Darling,* by Eileen Quelch.
181. *Edwardian Hey-Days,* 101–2.
182. G to J, 3/7/98, 28/34.
    G to J, ND ,28/34.
183. G to J, 13/7/98, 28/34.
184. G to J, 19/7/98, 28/38.
    G to J, 25/7/98, 28/34.
185. G to J, 29/7/98, 28/34.
    G to J, ND, 28/38.
    G to J, 1/8/98, 28/34.
186. G to J, 5/8/98, 28/34.
    G to J, 23/8/98, 28/34.
187. G to J, 25/8/98 & 2/9/98, 28/34.
    Edwardian Hey-Days, 38–9.
    Curzon to J, 7/9/98, WSC I, Comp II, 975.
188. G to J, 12/9/98, 28/34.
    J to Jk, 20/9/98, PSC.
    AL, 223.
    G to J, 7/10/98, 16/10/98 & 2/11/98, 28/34.
189. G to J, 3/11/98 & 9/11/98, 28/34.

CHAPTER TEN

191–2. Rems, 285, & J, *Small Talks on Big Subjects,*
    31–2.
193. Oscar Wilde to J, ND, Rems, 217.
    Rems, 279ff & 285.
    W to J, 1/1/99, WSC I, Comp II, 997.
194. W to J, 2/3/99, WSC I, Comp II, 1012.

195. J to Jk, 24/2/99, PSC.
     G to J, 6/3/99, 28/35.
196. G to J, 10/4/99, 28/35.
     J to Jk, 24/2/99, PSC.
     G to J, 7/6/99, 28/35.
197. *Oldham Daily Standard*, 27 & 28/6/99.
     G to J, 11/7/99, 28/35.
198. G to J, 15/7/99, 28/35.
     Edwardian Hey-Days, 118.
     Confessions of the Marquis de Castellane, 225.
199. G to J, 11/8/99, 28/35.
     G to J, 12/8/99, 28/35.
     G to J, 14/8/99, 28/35.
200. G to J, 19/8/99, 28/35.
     G to J, 20/8/99, 28/35.
201. G to J, 22/8/99, 28/35.
     G to J, 23/8/99, 28/35.
     Lady Curzon to J, 3/11/99, 28/66.
     G to J, 24/8/99, 28/35.
202. G to J, 12/9/99, 28/35.
     G to J, 14/9/99, 28/35.
203. G to J, 16/9/99, 28/35.

CHAPTER ELEVEN

205. G to J, 6/10/99, 28/35.
206. Prince of Wales to G, 15/10/99, *Edwardian Hey-Days*, 105.
     Edwardian Hey-Days, 105–6.
207. G to J, 21/10/99, 28/35.
     Edwardian Hey-Days, 107.
208. WSC I, Comp II, 1052.
     W to J, 3/9/99, WSC I, Comp II, 1046.
208. For details of the *Maine, see The American Hospital Ship 'Maine' Fund: Reports, List of Subscriptions, Donations, Etc.* N.D.
209. For Fanny Ronalds, see Anita Leslie, *The Fabulous Leonard Jerome.*
     Clara Frewen to L, ND, Seymour Leslie MSS.
     Rems, 316.

210. Patsy Cornwallis-West and Kinsky to J, ND, 28/69.
     Rosebery to J, ND, 28/67.
     G to J, 3/12/99, 28/35.
212. *Edwardian Hey-Days,* 114.
     Rems, 322.
     G to J, 23/12/99, 28/35.
     Edwardian Hey-Days, 116.
213. G to J, 23/12/99, 28/35.
214. J to L, 24/12/99, Anita Leslie MSS.

CHAPTER TWELVE

216. *Maine* Reports, passim.
217. ASR, V, 218–37.
222. Rems, 329–30.
223. W to J, 13/2/1900, WSC I, Comp II, 1149–50.
224. J to Jk, ND, PSC.
     G to J, 16/2/00, 28/36.
     G to J, 18/1/00, 28/36.
226. G to J, 2/2/00, 28/36.
227. G to J, 6/2/00, 28/36.
228. J to W, ND, PSC.
     Colonel Cornwallis-West to L, ND, Seymour Leslie, *The Jerome Connexion,* 54–5.
229. G to J, 21/4/00, 28/36.
230. J to W, 24/5/00, PSC.
231. Lord Knutsford, quoted in Anita Leslie, *Edwardians in Love,* 226.
     Edwardian Hey-Days, 120.
232. Lansdowne to J, 20/6/00, WSC I, Comp II, 1181.
     G to J, ND, 28/36.
233. *Edwardian Hey-Days,* 121.
     J to Jk, 23/6/00, PSC.
235. Jk to J, 2/6/00, 28/32.
     J to Jk, 30/6/00, PSC.
     Jk to J, 5/7/00, 28/32.
236. J to Jk, 28/7/00, PSC.
     G to W, 30/7/00, WSC I, Comp II, 1187.

237. W to Jk, 31/7/00, WSC I, Comp II, 1188.
238. G to J, 28/9/00, 28/36.

CHAPTER THIRTEEN

240. *Edwardian Hey-Days,* 119–22, 128 & 137.
241. WSC II, Comp I, 591–2.
    Eileen Quelch, *Perfect Darling,* passim.
242–3. G to J, ND, 8/3/06, & 9/3/06, 28/38.
243. *From My Private Diary,* by Daisy, Princess of Pless, 206.
    J to L, 15/5/07, Anita Leslie MSS.
244. Henry James to J, 5/10/08, 28/78.
246. J to L, 23/4/09, Seymour Leslie, *The Jerome Connexion,* 56.
    J to L, 27/6/09, Anita Leslie MSS.
247. Kinsky to J, 23/4/09, 28/78.
249. See the programme for the Tournament: *The Triumph holden at Shakespeare's England on the eleventh day of July in the third year of the reign of King George the Fifth.*
250. J to Mrs. Cornwallis-West, 14/8/10, PSC.
    Jk to J, 4/4/11, PSC.
251. Clementine Churchill to J, ND, 28/80.
252. Gwendeline Churchill to J, 7/4/11, 28/135.
    J to G, 19/4/11, 28/28.
253. G to J, 29/12/12, 28/39.
254. J to G, 31/12/12, 28/39.
255. G to J, 7/1/13, 28/39.
    fn. 11 Elizabeth Eliot, *They All Married Well,* 269.
256. Lady Henry Grosvenor to J, 16/7/13, 28/38.
    Curzon to J, 30/1/14, 28/84.
    J to L, 7/10/13, Anita Leslie MSS.
    G to J, 31/12/13, 28/39.
    J to G, 5/1/14, 28/39.
    Daisy, Princess of Pless to J, 4/4/14, 28/39.
257. J to G, 4/4/14, 28/39.
    Daisy, Princess of Pless to J, 7/4/14, 28/39.
    Shelagh, Duchess of Westminster to J, 15/4/14, 28/39.

258. L to J (6/4/14), 28/136.
     L to J (8/4/14), 28/136.
259. L to J (11/4/14), 28/136.
     G to J, 5/11/14, 28/39.
     J to G, 5/1/17, 28/129.
260. J to G, 17/6/19, Anita Leslie MSS.
     G to W, ND, Chartwell Trust MSS, 1/143.

CHAPTER FOURTEEN

262. J to Jk, 4/3/14, 28/152.
     J to L, 24/7/14, Seymour Leslie, *The Jerome Connexion,* 57.
263. MP to J, 16/5/14, 28/84.
264. fn. 2 Shane Leslie, article on Cardinal Merry del Val in *The Catholic Encyclopaedia,* Supplement II (1951).
265. Jk to J, 14/2/14, 28/33.
     Jk to J, 31/7/14, 28/33.
     J to L, 1/8/14, Anita Leslie MSS.
266. Gwendeline Churchill to J, ND, 28/135.
267. Gwendeline Churchill to Jk, 1/9/14, PSC.
269. J to L, 16/8/14, Anita Leslie MSS.
270. J, *Small Talks on Big Subjects,* 109–11.
     Jk to J, 14/2/14, 28/33.
271. MP to J, 5/10/14, 28/84.
     MP to J, 2/10/15, 28/122.
273. Katherine Mott to the Kaiser, 28/127.
     L to J, ND, 28/136.
274. J to Katherine Mott, 10/1/16, 28/127.
     J to Jordan Mott, 10/1/16, 28/127.
275. J to Shane Leslie, 3/9/16, Anita Leslie MSS.
     Shane Leslie to J, 30/1/16, 28/127.
276. MP to J, 22/6/16, 28/127.
     Anon to J, ND, 28/127.
277. Anon to J, 13/12/16, 28/127.
278. Local Food Control Committee to J, 18/1/18, 28/130.
279. Letters about Epstein in 28/130.
     MP to W, 1/6/18, Chartwell Trust MSS, 1/129.
261. Jk to J, 25/5/18, 28/121.

CHAPTER FIFTEEN
282. J to MP, 8/3/21, AL, 350.
283. J. to L, 20/4/21, Seymour Leslie, *The Jerome Connexion*, 88.
     Edward Marsh, *A Number of People,* 154.
     MP to J, 8/6/21, 28/133.
285. MP to J, 25/6/21, 28/133.
287. MP to Seymour Leslie, Seymour Leslie MSS.
     Violet Bonham-Carter to W, 28/138.
     W to Lloyd-George, 28/138.
     Daisy Warwick to J, ND, 28/136.

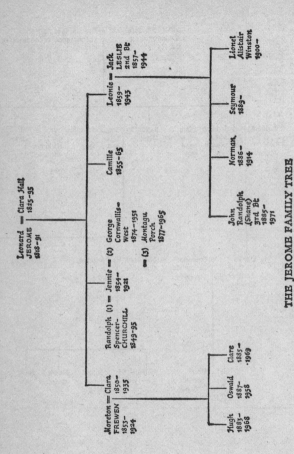

THE JEROME FAMILY TREE

303

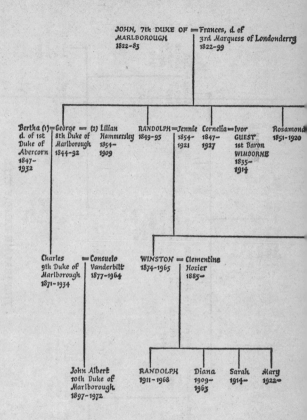

JOHN, 7th DUKE OF = Frances, d. of
MARLBOROUGH   3rd Marquess of Londonderry
1822–83   1822–99

Bertha (1) = George = (2) Lilian
d. of 1st   8th Duke of   Hammersley
Duke of   Marlborough   1854–
Abercorn   1844–92   1909
1847–
1932

RANDOLPH = Jennie
1849–95   1854–
           1921

Cornelia = Ivor
1847–   GUEST
1927   1st Baron
           WIMBORNE
           1835–
           1914

Rosamond
1851–1920

Charles   = Consuelo
9th Duke of   Vanderbilt
Marlborough   1877–1964
1871–1934

WINSTON = Clementine
1874–1965   Hozier
            1885–

John Albert
10th Duke of
Marlborough
1897–1972

RANDOLPH
1911–1968

Diana
1909–
1963

Sarah
1914–

Mary
1922–

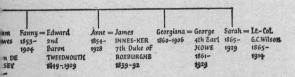

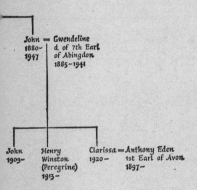

INDEX

309

☆ HOLLYWOOD ☆

When the twenties roared and the thirties sizzled

ANITA LOOS

the fabulous, talented brunette who gave the world
GENTLEMEN PREFER BLONDES,
and now wickedly remembers and delectably recounts
the scandals, gossip and glorious intimacies
of the golden age of Hollywood!

☆ A GIRL LIKE I ☆

INCLUDES 32 PAGES OF PHOTOGRAPHS

AND

☆ KISS ☆ HOLLYWOOD GOOD-BY

INCLUDES
16 PAGES OF
PHOTOGRAPHS

▼ **Both available at your local bookstore or mail the coupon below** ▼

BB BALLANTINE CASH SALES
P.O. Box 505, Westminster, Maryland 21157

Please send me the following book bargains:

QUANTITY	NO.	TITLE	AMOUNT
....	24653	A Girl Like I $1.75	_____
....	24447	Kiss Hollywood Good-By $1.50	_____

Allow four weeks for delivery.   Mailing and handling ____ .50
Please enclose check or money order
We are not responsible for orders containing cash.   **TOTAL**_____

(PLEASE PRINT CLEARLY)

NAME..

ADDRESS...

CITY........................ STATE..................... ZIP............

BB 73/75

The Brown Derby...champagne hangovers...long-stemmed ladies...
fake palm trees—this was Hollywood as he remembers!

RAY MILLAND
WIDE-EYED IN BABYLON

An Autobiography
WITH
16 PAGES OF PHOTOGRAPHS

"A BAWDY DELIGHT..."
—Publishers Weekly

$1.75

▼ **Available at your local bookstore or mail the coupon below** ▼

ⓑ BALLANTINE CASH SALES
P.O. Box 505, Westminster, Maryland 21157

Please send me the following book bargains:

QUANTITY	NO.	TITLE	AMOUNT
....	24609	Wide-Eyed in Babylon $1.75	_____

Allow four weeks for delivery.   Mailing and handling ___ .50
Please enclose check or money order
We are not responsible for orders containing cash.   **TOTAL**_____

(PLEASE PRINT CLEARLY)

NAME...

ADDRESS..

CITY....................STATE....................ZIP..............

BB 68/75

AH~ONE, AH~TWO!
LIFE WITH MY MUSICAL FAMILY

LAWRENCE WELK
with BERNICE McGEEHAN

"A WORTHY SUCCESSOR TO THE BEST-SELLING *WUNNERFUL, WUNNERFUL...* TO WARM ALL OUR HEARTS!" —*Philadelphia News*

"A book filled with the stuff of which the American dream is made!" —*The New York Times*

"All the drama, humor and excitement that have made Lawrence Welk and his Musical Family household words!" —*Vallejo Times-Herald*

With unforgettable personal photos of Welk and all his Musical Family!

$1.75

▼ Available at your local bookstore or mail the coupon below ▼

BB BALLANTINE CASH SALES
P.O. Box 505, Westminster, Maryland 21157

Please send me the following book bargains:

QUANTITY	NO.	TITLE	AMOUNT
....	24576	AH-ONE, AH-TWO, Life With My Musical Family $1.75	_____

Allow four weeks for delivery. Mailing and handling ___ .50
Please enclose check or money order
We are not responsible for orders containing cash. TOTAL_____

(PLEASE PRINT CLEARLY)

NAME..

ADDRESS...

CITY.....................STATE...................ZIP...........

BB 69/75